W9-BGS-790

Washington's Southern Tour

1791

WASHINGTON'S SOUTHERN TOUR

1791

By

ARCHIBALD HENDERSON

WITH ILLUSTRATIONS

BOSTON AND NEW YORK
HOUGHTON MIFFLIN COMPANY
The Riverside Press Cambridge
1923

The Riverside Press
CAMBRIDGE · MASSACHUSETTS
PRINTED IN THE U.S.A.

TO

JOHN HUSTON FINLEY

TOURIST

OF

WORLD AND MIND

PREFATORY NOTE

THROUGHOUT the present volume, references to Washington's Diary indicate the following work: "The Diary of George Washington, from 1789 to 1791; embracing the Opening of the First Congress, and his Tours through New England, Long Island, and the Southern States, together with his Journal of a Tour to the Ohio, in 1753. Edited by Benson J. Lossing (Charles B. Richardson & Co., New York, MDCCCLX)." Identical sheets, bound up, with a similar title, were issued by the Virginia Historical Society (Richmond, 1861). In 1920 a volume was published at Summerfield, North Carolina, by Joseph A. Hoskins, entitled: "President Washington's Diaries, 1791 to 1799." Much of this material had never thitherto been published. In Lossing's volume, the last entry in the diary of 1791 was June 1st, whereas the diary runs continuously to July 4th of that year.

Throughout the present volume, any footnotes copied from the Lossing volume first mentioned will be followed by the designation: (B. J. L.)

Of the original journals, eleven are in the Government archives at Washington, Library of Congress, two others are known to be extant, and there is probably a third. These journals, as described by Theodore F. Dwight ("The Journals of Washington," in *Magazine of American History*, VI, 2) are "thin, oblong in form, bound in half sheep, measuring seven by four and seven eighths inches, and are numbered respectively 1 to 11. The entries are continuous from January 1, 1785, to February 2, 1789. Two of the series, numbered 13 and 14, it is understood, were presented to a friend by Judge Bushrod Washington. . . . There are among the archives thirteen leaves, evidently of sheets of letter paper, folded, cut, and pinned together, continuing the account of his Southern tour from June 2 to July 4, 1791. . . ." Mr. John C. Fitzpatrick, Assistant Chief, Manuscript Division, Library of Congress, Washington, D.C., states that, according to a memorandum, the Washington Diary covering the first five months of 1791 were some years ago in the possession of Mr. Bushrod Washington Adams, of Philadelphia.

The extent of the investigations made in preparing this volume, the number of people supplying information, the number of libraries, historical societies, and other institutions which have been consulted, make a formidable total. While certain scholars have been particularly helpful and generous in supplying special information, in this place no distinction will be made in the acknowledgment, which takes the form of a simple catalogue of names, arranged alphabetically. For assistance rendered me in the preparation of the present volume I am indebted to the following individuals and institutions:

American Antiquarian Society; Dr. Joseph S. Ames, Baltimore, Maryland; A. B. Andrews, Raleigh, North Carolina; Atlanta, Georgia, Carnegie Library; P. H. Baskervill, Richmond, Virginia; P. B. Beard, Salisbury, North Carolina; Rev. Allen A. Beman, Fairfield, Connecticut; Boston Athenæum; John Carter Brown Library, Providence, Rhode Island; Miss Fannie B. Brownfield, Summerville, South Carolina; Dr. Philip Alexander Bruce, University, Virginia; James A. Bryan, New Berne, North Carolina; Mrs. Henry Buist, Charleston, South Carolina; Langdon Cheves, Charleston, South Carolina; D. M. Clark, Greenville, North Carolina; Corcoran Art Gallery; John Crerar Library, Chicago, Illinois; Professor W. F. Dunaway, State College, Pennsylvania; Mrs. Emma Henderson Dunn, New Berne, North Carolina; James Dunn, Petersburg, Virginia; Herman Le Roy Edgar, New York City; Thomas Fell, formerly President St. John's College, Annapolis, Maryland; William H. Fleming, Augusta, Georgia; Miss Helen Frick, New York City; Miss Adelaide L. Fries, Winston-Salem, North Carolina; W. H. Gibbs, Columbia, South Carolina; Professor Alexander Graham, Charlotte, North Carolina; Miss Ida Hamilton, Asheville, North Carolina; William Harden, Savannah, Georgia; Harvard University; Walter Hazard and Miss Minnie Tamplet Hazard, Georgetown, South Carolina; Joseph Jackson, Philadelphia, Pennsylvania; H. K. Jenkins, Charleston, South Carolina; Theodore Jervey, Charleston, South Carolina; Charles Edgeworth Jones, Augusta, Georgia; Lucien Lamar Knight, Atlanta, Georgia; Casenove G. Lee, Jr., Washington, D.C.; Mrs. Harriet K. Leiding, Charleston, South Carolina; John F. Lewis, Philadelphia, Pennsylvania; Miss Sarah Martin, Winston-Salem, North Carolina; David Maydole Matteson, Cambridge, Massachusetts; Albert Matthews, Boston, Massachusetts; H. R. McIlwaine, Richmond, Virginia; W. B. McKoy, Wilmington, North Carolina; Fitzhugh McMaster, Columbia, South Carolina; Miss Fannie McNeely, Salisbury, North Carolina; Mrs. Lewis H. Meader, Providence, Rhode Island; John M. Morehead, Charlotte, North Carolina; W. D. Morgan, Georgetown, South Carolina; New York Public Library; North Carolina Historical Commission, Raleigh, North Carolina; North Carolina University Library, Chapel Hill, North Carolina; R. A. Nunn, New Berne, North Carolina; Pennsylvania Historical Society, Philadelphia, Pennsylvania; Mrs. W. H. Perry, Charleston, South Carolina; Walter G. Peter, Washington, D.C.; Miss C. W. Phifer, Charlotte, North Carolina; Robert P. Phifer, New York City; Miss Louisa B. Poppenheim, Charleston, South Carolina; Miss Lida T. Rodman, Washington, North Carolina; Archibald Rutledge, Mercersburg, Pennsylvania; A. S. Salley, Jr., Columbia, South Carolina; Miss Ruth Savord, New York City; Miss Maud G. Sites, Washington, D.C.; D. E. Huger Smith, Charleston, South Carolina; Henry A. M. Smith, Charleston, South Carolina; Henry Louis Smith, Lexington, Virginia; Yates Snowden, Columbia, South Carolina; Dr. F. A. Sondley, Asheville, North Carolina; Miss Florence P. Spofford, Washington, D.C.; Dandridge Spotswood, Nashville, Tennessee; William G. Stanard, Richmond, Virginia; Paul C. Standley, Washington, D.C.; Franklin Stearns, Alexandria, Virginia; G. N. Phelps Stokes, New York City; Earl G. Swem, Williamsburg, Virginia; Benjamin F. Taylor, Savannah, Georgia; George

C. Taylor, Columbia, South Carolina; Lyon G. Tyler, Holdcroft, Virginia; United States Navy Department, Washington, D.C.; Edward V. Valentine, Richmond, Virginia; Valentine Museum, Richmond, Virginia; Virginia State Library, Richmond, Virginia; Mrs. Gabrielle de Rosset Waddell, Wilmington, North Carolina; Zebulon V. Walzer, Lexington, North Carolina; Rev. William Way, Charleston, South Carolina; Miss Mabel L. Webber, Charleston, South Carolina; David R. Williams, Camden, South Carolina; Wisconsin Historical Society, Madison, Wisconsin; Mrs. Bayard Wootten, New Berne, North Carolina; Miss Eleanor P. Wragg, Stony Creek, Connecticut; Yale University.

CONTENTS

ILLUSTRATIONS

Illustrations

Illustrations

Illustrations

Illustrations

Illustrations

INTRODUCTION

Washington and the American People

IN Washington's tours of Northern, Eastern, and Southern States in 1789, 1790, and 1791, "swinging around the circle" for the first time entered American history. It is singular, indeed almost inexplicable, that the biographers of Washington have passed over, with but casual observation, these tours of the country by the first President.[1] For the story of these tours, as preserved in the literature, press, and correspondence of the time, is a fruitful instrumentality for discovering and disclosing to us the character of Washington — his attitude toward the people, his modes of thinking, his "reactions" to externals, his principles and theories, and even his vanities and prejudices. The picture which unrolls before us in bright pageantry is — if you please — American Democracy on the Grand Tour.

The central figure in this unfolding panorama is Washington. The background, scarcely secondary to him in interest, is the American People. The Southern tour, with which we are here concerned, gave Washington — and gives us — a clear view of the South of that day, its agricultural, political, social, and cultural condition. An extraordinarily keen observer, trained as surveyor, farmer, and soldier, Washington noted in his deliberately imper-

[1] Neither Woodrow Wilson nor Henry Cabot Lodge even so much as makes mention of the Southern tour.

sonal diaries the features of the country which came under his immediate observation, and interpreted them with skill and sagacity. Through his eyes we see the South of 1791 — its fields and streams, mountains and plains — not as mere beauties of nature, but as the instruments of farmer and planter, of manufacturer and trader. As in an open book he read the story of the Republic — the place and the people.

Fortunate, indeed, was Washington in enjoying his legend in his own lifetime. Few are they who are witnesses of their own immortality. The decision to tour the country was a mark of true wisdom. Intoxicated with the heady draught of the Revolution, the American people proudly rejoiced in the conscious belief that the President of the United States, as a dramatic and conspicuous figure, was unrivalled by any sovereign of Europe. With almost naïve pride and authentic hero worship, the people adored the very name of Washington, and revelled in every opportunity afforded them to pay him the sincere and lavish tributes of affection and gratitude. "There was everywhere" — on this Southern tour as on Washington's journey to his first inauguration — "a running together from all the country roundabout of people who bore themselves not as mere sight-seers, but as if they had come out of love for the man they were to see pass by. It was not their numbers but their manner that struck their hero with a new sense of responsibility. . . . He was . . . their guarantee of the new government's good faith, of its respect for law and its devotion to liberty; and they made him know . . . their confidence in the very tone of their greeting. There was the manifest touch of love in the reception everywhere prepared for him." [1]

There need be no cause for wonder that the people looked up to Washington as a hero. For he was indeed a knightly figure. Washington was the very embodiment of the popular idea of a hero. Six feet four inches tall, balancing the scales at two hundred, he was distinguished in figure, majestic in mien, benignant in expression. As surveyor, fox-hunter, continental courier, wilderness ambassador, soldier and military commander, he had lived a strenuous life in the great open spaces; and was known as the most graceful horseman of his age. A man of intense passions held under rigorous control, he had mild gray eyes which on occasion could flash lightning and pale cheeks which could mantle with the flush of anger. Diffident in manner, aloof in spirit, he knew how to unbend, to charm with the graciousness of his smile, the friendliness of his disposition. The firm forehead, Roman nose, deep-set eyes, and powerful lower jaw united to form the very facial image of a man born to command. The gravity of his mien was accentuated by the conviction that in this way he could impress the people with the dignity of the office of President of the United States.

The clever, vitriolic Bache held up to scorn Washington's "stately journeyings through the American continent in search of personal incense." And the unspeakable Callender ranted of "the vileness of the adulation" paid

[1] Woodrow Wilson: *George Washington.*

to Washington, in atrabiliar mood asserting that "the extravagant popularity possessed by this citizen reflects the utmost ridicule on the discernment of America." And even Jefferson, in none too gracious a mood, frankly admits that "such is the popularity of the President that the people will support him in whatever he will do or will not do, without appealing to their own reason or to anything but their feelings toward him." Far from going on tour "in search of personal incense," Washington was actuated by the desire to win the good-will, the support, of the people for the General Government. This he hoped best to accomplish through his own presence; and through his addresses in which he made constant appeal for the support of the Federal Government. "Its policy," as embodied in himself, "must make the States a nation, must stir the people out of their pettiness as colonists and provincials, and give them a national character and spirit." The following words from his first inaugural address might almost serve as the epitome of his policy as President, of which his tours of the country were but a single expression: "The propitious smiles of Heaven can never be expected on a nation that disregards the eternal laws of order and right, which Heaven itself has ordained; and the preservation of the sacred fire of liberty, and the destiny of the republican model of government, are justly considered as *deeply*, perhaps as *finally* staked, on the experiment intrusted to the hands of the American people." This ideal he could forward by touring the country. For he was past-master in the art of social correctness — to which John Adams attributed much of his celebrity. And, as we have seen, his head was aureoled with the halo of heroism. "The personal appearance of the President, representing the whole people, would serve to bring home to the public mind the existence and reality of a central government, which to many if not to most persons in the outlying States seemed shadowy and distant. But General Washington was neither shadowy nor distant to any one. Every man, woman, and child had heard of and loved the leader of the Revolution. To his countrymen everywhere, his name meant political freedom and victory in battle; and when he came among them as the head of a new government, the government took on in some measure the character of its chief. His journey was a well-calculated appeal for his cause, to the warm human interest which a man readily excites, but which only gathers slowly around constitutions and forms of government."[1]

The story of Washington's journey through the Southern States is fully worthy of narration — if for one reason only. On this tour, we see Washington the man rather than Washington the statesman. Once again he lives the life he loved best — the life of the free air and the open road. The cultured and discerning gentleman who was his constant companion and aide upon the tour gives us this arresting picture of Washington: "Enriched by Nature with her choicest gifts — she had with equal liberality, bestowed upon him the greatest advantages of external form, and the highest degree of intellectual endow-

[1] H. C. Lodge: *George Washington.*

ment. To the noble port of a lofty stature, were united uncommon grace, strength, and symmetry of person. And, to the commanding aspect of manly beauty, was given the benignant smile, which, inspiring confidence, created affection." Upon this tour the whole armory of Washington's qualities and gifts — personal, political, social — were tested to the full. Even affairs of state could not be wholly set aside — for documents and letters continued to pursue him, if with somewhat laggard pace. For the most part, however, Washington's business was pleasure — in a word to prove himself a "good mixer," to justify the veneration amounting to adoration entertained for him by the people, irrespective of rank, class, age, or sex. Many incidents of this tour give color, life, and animation to a figure commonly regarded as frigid and remote. The stilted chromo which was the *eidolon* bequeathed to posterity by the earlier biographers of Washington is giving place to a lovable figure of genuine human interest.

Although it be the fashion of British historians to speak of Washington as an English country gentleman, certain it is that he was a native of Virginia. By the American people of his day, Washington was regarded as the supreme embodiment of the genius, wisdom, and leadership of the South. It is true that Washington was a citizen of the world, as well as head of the whole country — a country which, in the course of his military campaigns in the French and Indian War and the Revolution, he had come to know intimately and deeply to love. Yet we should not lose sight of the fact that Washington was a typical Virginian of his day. When Washington visited New York, New England, or Pennsylvania, he was travelling off his native heath. When he journeyed through Virginia, the Carolinas, and Georgia, he was travelling around at home. . . .

In supreme degree, Washington exhibited the distinctive attributes of Virginia and the South. "Something in her air or her life," says Woodrow Wilson in speaking of the Virginia of that period, "had given her in these latter years an extraordinary breed of public men — men liberated from local prejudice, possessed of a vision and an efficacy in affairs worthy of the best traditions of statesmanship among the English race from which they were sprung, capable of taking the long view, of seeing the permanent lines of leadership upon great questions, and shaping ordinary views to meet extraordinary ends." [1] The great Virginians, as Garrott Brown has pointed out — Washington and Henry and Jefferson, Mason and Marshall and Madison, the Lees and the Randolphs — "were anything but gay cavaliers": they were "deliberate and stately, slow of thought and full resolved in action." [2] Deficient in the debonair light-heartedness all too glibly attributed to the Southern cavalier, Washington was endowed with all the social graces of the old Virginia aristocracy. About him was an air of benignant gravity, of high seriousness, which comported well with the temper of the age. "In battle, calm and collected; in council, dignified

[1] *George Washington* (1897).
[2] "George Washington, Southerner," *The Independent*, vol. 56.

and serene; in society, gracious and condescending." By no means deficient in the sense of humor, he held as firm a rein over his risibility as over his temper. His personal relationships and friendships were numerous and cordial. His was that rare quality — the gift of at once winning friendship and inspiring reverence. Toward men he was friendly without intimacy, cordial without familiarity; toward women he was genial and winning, his manner touched with something of ardency and sentiment.

In the eyes of the people, Washington was the ideal leader — confident, self-contained, imperturbable. The unbreakable tenacity of his purpose, the wisdom of his decisions, the unselfishness of his nature, the purity of his character — these qualities blended in a well-nigh perfect whole. "The acknowledgement of his transcendent merits," says his inseparable companion upon the Southern tour, "was the delightful theme of every class and condition. Infancy was taught to lisp his praise — youth and manhood poured forth the effusions of their gratitude — and the blessings of age were expressed with the fervor of feeling and the solemnity of religion."

Washington's Southern Tour

1791

WASHINGTON'S SOUTHERN TOUR

∴

CHAPTER I

THE SOUTHERN TOUR

Plans and Preliminaries

AMONG the important decisions concerning the duties of his high office which Washington gravely reached shortly after becoming first President of the American Confederation was to visit every part of the United States during the course of his administration of the government. As early as May, 1789, he had given definite expression to the idea of making a tour of all the States "in order to become better acquainted with their principal characters and internal circumstances, as well as to be more accessible to numbers of well-informed persons, who might give him useful information and advice on political subjects." During the recess of Congress, in anticipation of making a tour of the Eastern States, he discussed the matter with Alexander Hamilton (October 5, 1789), who thought it a very desirable plan and advised him to carry it out. The purpose of the trip, as Washington explained, was "to acquire knowledge of the face of the country, the growth and agriculture thereof — and the temper and disposition of the inhabitants towards the new government." Being eventually convinced of the propriety of making such a tour, Washington visited the Eastern States, being away from New York for the interval October 15 to November 13, 1789. During nearly the whole distance he was attended "by military escorts, which were prepared to receive him at different points on the route. In all the principal towns, also, he was greeted with public addresses, the ringing of bells, entertainments, and every demonstration of joy from the whole body of the people." [1]

At the time of making this tour Rhode Island had not yet become a part of the Union. In consequence, Washington did not pass through that State on his tour of the Eastern States. Following the ratification of the Constitution by Rhode Island on May 29th, Washington visited that State in August, 1790, being absent from the 14th until the 24th. A secondary reason for both these trips was to escape for a time from the cares of office, the confining duties of the Presidency, and to secure the beneficial effects of exercise in the open air. This was especially true in the case of the Rhode Island visit, which followed a serious illness in the May preceding. He returned from this trip, on which he was "everywhere cordially welcomed by the inhabitants," much improved in health — the sea air, as well as the exercise and change of scene having proved beneficial.

As early as October 7, 1789, the question of a tour of the

[1] Sparks: *Writings of Washington*, vol. x, footnote pp. 46–47.

Southern States was broached. When Washington on this day consulted John Jay as to the propriety of his "intended tour into the Eastern States, he (Jay) highly approved it," says Washington in his diary, "but observed, a similar visit will be expected by those of the Southern." There was little choice between East and South — for each section exhibited the spectacle of a single State still holding out against the Constitution; the East with Rhode Island and the South with North Carolina. With characteristic courtesy, Washington made his first visit to the East — for the South was his own place. But after North Carolina ratified the Constitution on November 13, 1790, there was no longer any reason why he should not go on a tour of the Southern States — and "make it unanimous." This he was doubtless eager to do — because already a "spirit of jealousy" toward the Eastern States was fast growing in the South, especially in Virginia.[1]

To let the people see him and come in contact with him in a democratic way, to ingratiate himself in the favor of the masses, to awake their sympathies and evoke their support for the general government through attachment to his own person — surely these were guiding motives in making this tour, no less than those already cited which Washington gave out to the public. If at times, as Chauncey Ford somewhat hypercritically suggests, Washington appeared "to have been too anxious to test the popular feeling, and to place too high a value upon opinion as

[1] Consult letter to Washington from Dr. David Stuart (Abingdon, Virginia, March 15, 1790).

expressed to him by those who stood well with the people," surely his tour of the Southern States exhibits a thoroughly laudable human trait — the desire to discern the true trend of public opinion, the true complexion of the popular mind, for his guidance in the proper conduct of the affairs of government. It is not to be a demagogue to inform one's self regarding the consensus of opinion in a democracy.

In a letter written to Washington at New York from Charleston, South Carolina, December 14, 1789, Governor Charles Pinckney said: "From your late tour we are flattered with the hope of your one day visiting this country — whenever you so far honour us I am sure that every thing in our power will be done to render your Visit pleasing and agreeable to you." To this letter, Washington made the following reply (New York, January 11, 1790):

> My late tour through the eastern States has been of salutary consequence in confirming my health. I have likewise had an opportunity of seeing how far the country is recovered from the ravages of war, and how well the inhabitants are disposed to support the general government.
>
> Not being master of my own time, nor accustomed to make personal engagements, which from contingency might become impracticable, I can only say in regard to the last paragraph of your letter, that nothing would give me more pleasure than to visit all the Southern States.

The news that Washington contemplated making this tour gradually spread through the Southern States. It eventually reached Governor Alexander Martin, of North Carolina, a great admirer of Washington, with whom he had been thrown in close relations during the Revolution.

ALEXANDER MARTIN

Plans and Preliminaries

On August 7, 1790, Washington appointed William Blount,[1] of North Carolina, Governor of the "Territory South of the Ohio River." [2] Blount had commended himself to Washington by his active efforts in behalf of the adoption of the Constitution by North Carolina at the convention in Fayetteville, in November, 1789. Of titled ancestry, courtly in manner, of commanding presence, a man of the world, Blount was certainly the choice of the western inhabitants as well as of the State of North Carolina. Upon receiving notice of his appointment, Blount set out for Mount Vernon to consult the President upon his new appointment. The letter which follows, hitherto unpublished, is here printed in full, because of the intimate picture it

[1] William Blount, son of Jacob Blount and Barbara Gray, his first wife, was born in Bertie County, North Carolina, March 26, 1749. Pursued preparatory studies in New Berne, North Carolina. Paymaster of Continental troops, North Carolina line, 1778; member North Carolina House of Commons, 1780–84; sat in the Continental Congress in 1782, 1783, 1786, and 1787. He was delegate to the convention that framed the Federal Constitution in 1787; and it was here at Philadelphia that Washington made his acquaintance. He was a member of the North Carolina State Senate, 1788–90; and represented Pitt County in the State Convention of 1789 which adopted the Federal Constitution. After serving as Governor of the "Territory South of the Ohio River" and Superintendent of Indian Affairs, 1790–96, he was elected to the United States Senate. He held office from August 2, 1796, until he was found guilty "of a high misdemeanor, entirely inconsistent with his public trust and duty as a Senator," and was expelled July 8, 1797. It was charged that he was active in a plan to incite the Creeks and Cherokees to aid the British in conquering the Spanish territory of West Florida. During the trial he was elected to the State Senate of Tennessee and chosen its president at the opening of the session, December 3, 1797. He died in Knoxville, Tennessee, March 21, 1800.

[2] After the efforts of the pioneers of what is now Tennessee to establish the independent State of Frankland had proved abortive, North Carolina ceded these lands to the United States, which were accepted by Congress, April 21, 1790. The ceded area was erected into "The Territory South of the Ohio River." Consult Archibald Henderson: *Pioneers of the Old Southwest.* (Century Co., New York, 1920.)

presents of the life of the Washington family at Mount Vernon, as well as for its reference at this early date to Washington's plans, already well matured, for visiting the Southern States following the conclusion of the approaching session of Congress:

John Gray Blount Esquire,
Washington, North Carolina.

I arrived here on Friday; visited the President at Mount Vernon on Saturday, stayed all night and returned yesterday. He has referred me to the Attorney General Mr. Randolph, at Philadelphia. And I shall proceed to him to-morrow morning at 3 o'clock in the Stage and if I do not lose a Stage I shall be here again on this day week at 12 o'clock. From this I shall proceed to the ceded Territory without delay.

I have been much pleased with my visit to Mount Vernon, the President appears great and amiable, indeed admirable. Mrs. Washington is certainly one of the most agreeable ladies of the whole world. Major Washington, his nephew, is a handsome, genteel, attentive man, his lady, Mrs. Washington's niece, is handsome and elegant, and the little grandchildren of Mrs. Washington, the children of Mr. Custis are very promising. Except that the President is too awful, I verily believe he is as awful (awe inspiring) as a God, Mount Vernon is the most agreeable place I ever saw. The house is not elegant having originally been begun on too small a scale, but it is now very roomy and commodious and the dining room is very large and elegant. It stands about 200 paces from the brink of the hill which overlooks the Potomac, the height of the bank is from 80 to 100 feet above the bed of the River. Mount Vernon is highly improved with a number of necessary buildings, good gardens, and if I am a judge fine and elegant ones. Delightful walks, straight, circular and serpentine handsomely and tastily shaded with the best chosen trees. Among them the Lombardy poplar, or the poplar of the Po of which Ovid sang many hundred years ago is found and much admired.

The style and manner of his living surpasses what I have before seen particularly in dignity; and I suppose I saw him living on his own funds, not those of the United States in fact Major Jackson so informed me.

At the request of Governor Martin, I asked him if it was true as we had heard to the Southward that he intended this autumn to visit the Southern States, he answered that he wished to do so but had not time as his presence at Philadelphia would be necessary some days previous to the meeting of Congress. Then the subject was dropped and afterwards he renewed it by saying that he supposed the approaching session of Congress would not be a long one and that the new Congress would not hold a Spring Session and in that case he should make a Tour to the South as far as Savannah and Augusta in the months of March, April and May. That he should proceed by the lower road and return by the upper, or the reverse, and from what fell in the course of conversation on the subject I think he will proceed via Norfolk, Edenton, Washington, New Bern, Wilmington, Charleston, Savannah then up to Augusta and return by way of Columbia, Campden, Charlotte, Salisbury thence the most direct Road to Richmond leaving Petersburg to the right.

I have given this information to Gov. Martin so that you may shortly expect to hear of pompous orders for equiping and training the Cavalry. And perhaps it may induce the Overseers of Roads and Ferry-Keepers to *mend their ways* and repair, or rebuild new boats. If the very greatest attention and respect is not paid to him, he will be greatly disappointed and mortified for to the North the contention has been who should pay him the most.

Major Jackson says from Boston to the line of New Hampshire he was attended by 400 Cavalry and was there met by Governor Sullavan [?] at the head of 700. Give Sam Simpson notice that he may have his company in complete order.

I want Mollie and my children to see him for certainly such another Man will not appear again in these days. I would not like the contents of this letter to get into the press yet I would wish it generally known to such as would be induced to prepare for his Reception in any way whatever. His object in coming I suppose is more to be seen and to gratify the Southern people in seeing him than to see himself, tho' his ostensible object is to see the Southern States.

Yours — &c

WM. BLOUNT.[1]

In the midst of the trying duties of the Presidency, Washington looked forward with eagerness to the thought of the Southern tour. As the spirit of the dust-begrimed traveller eagerly looks to the green and cool oasis, so the heart of Washington turned toward the South. Reminders of his project reached him from time to time, in the shape of letters of invitation, notably one from his kinsman, Colonel William Washington, who lived in Charleston, with a country place, "Sandy Hill," some fifteen miles distant. In his reply, written from Philadelphia (January 8, 1791), Washington gave voice to that cautious and tactful purpose which, characteristically enough, he had thus early formulated concerning the question of entertainment on the contemplated tour.

It is my intention to visit the Southern States next spring, provided the Congress should not meet immediately on the rising of the present, which will be on the 3d of March. If it should not be in my power to leave this place by the middle of next month I must give up my tour for this reason, as set-

[1] This letter was courteously supplied me by Miss Lida T. Rodman, of Washington, North Carolina, a descendant of the Blount family. She is the author of a biography of William Blount soon to appear. John Gray Blount, brother to William, was a pioneer as a youth with Daniel Boone in Kentucky; and became a man of great prominence, wealth, and influence in Beaufort County, North Carolina. The "Mollie" of the letter refers to William Blount's wife, Mary, daughter of Colonel Caleb Grainger, prominent in the Revolution. Cf. *Life and Services of William Blount*, by M. J. Wright. (Washington, 1884.)

WILLIAM BLOUNT

EDWARD RUTLEDGE

ting out at a later period would bring me into the Southern States in the warm and sickly months, a circumstance which I would wish by all means to avoid. But, Sir, you will permit me to decline the acceptance of your polite invitation; for I cannot comply with it without involving myself in an inconsistency; as I have determined to pursue the same plan in my southern as I did in my eastern visit, which was, not to incommode any private families by taking up my quarters with them during my journey. I am persuaded you will readily see the necessity of the resolution, both as it respects myself and others. It leaves me unembarrased by engagements, and by a uniform adherence to it I shall avoid giving umbrage to any, by declining all such invitations.

In this same letter Washington states that the trip—full of hardships of a sort, over many a bad road, and requiring the not infrequent interruption of the habitual routine of sleep and rest—would prove too severe a tax upon Mrs. Washington, who would, therefore, not accompany him.

Another letter of invitation, from a very warm friend, Edward Rutledge,[1] of South Carolina — the third friend

[1] Edward Rutledge, born in Charleston, 1749; died there, 1800. Student of law at the Temple, London. Attended courts of law and Houses of Parliament for four years. Married Harriet, daughter of Henry Middleton, soon after his return to Charleston. Practiced law successfully. In 1774 he was sent to the Continental Congress. Signer of the Declaration of Independence. Remained Member of Congress until 1777. As captain in the Charleston Artillery, of which he afterwards became lieutenant-colonel, he assisted in dislodging British regulars from Port Royal in 1779. Captured in 1780, he was confined at St. Augustine for a year. Member of State Constitutional Convention in 1790. Declined office of Associate Justice, United States Supreme Court, in 1791. Elected Governor of South Carolina in 1798, but did not live to complete his term. In an obituary in the *Charleston City Gazette and Daily Advertiser* (January 25, 1800) occur these words: "His eloquence, which shone forth in the Senate, and at the Bar, was brilliant and impressive; it pleased the ear and went home to the heart. Rich in ideas and happy in his manner of expressing them, he was accustomed to command attention, to delight as well as to persuade his audience."

to write him from Charleston extending invitations to him to visit that place and personally offering hospitality — deserves quotation in full, as does Washington's reply. It is believed that neither letter has hitherto appeared in print. The affectionate, even lovable tone of the letters is to be noted. It was said of Rutledge as a lawyer by Dr. Ramsay, the historian of South Carolina: "To advance his personal interest was a secondary object; to do good, to promote peace, to heal breaches, to advance justice, was a primary one." Follows Rutledge's letter to Washington:

CHARLESTON *Nov^r^* 11th 1790

MY DEAR SIR,

I have lately received Letters, from some of my Friends in Congress, which give me Reason to hope that, the time is not far distant, when we shall have the Happiness of seeing you in this State; and there is no Citizen in this Country, who feels a stronger attachment to you than I do, or would be more rejoiced at your coming, I hope you will permit me to request that, you would make my House your Head Quarters, whilst you remain in this City. I know there are many Persons who would prize the Honor which I seek, as justly as they ought; but the great, & never failing Regard that I have cherished towards you, from the first moments of my Political Life, thro' all the Chances of War, & the Turns of Fortune, gives me I should hope at least an equal, if not a superior Claim to you; & entitles me, to lodge under my own Roof, the President, in the Friend. As another Inducement, I must assure you my dear Sir, that we have not, one Public House, in the whole State, which is fit for your Reception; and that to be accomodated with even a moderate Degree of Convenience, you must receive it in a private House. If therefore you will not take up your Residence in mine, I must provide you with one from among some of my particular Friends who may be in the Country. It is your only alternative; and as I know full well, how your own Inclination would direct you,

I hope that no Consideration may intervene to prevent it. Excuse me my dear Sir if I shew too much Solicitude on this occasion, & attribute it to its true Cause, — the real attachment with which I ever am, your very affectionate Friend
and obliged Hble Servt

ED: RUTLEDGE[1]

Washington replied in the following letter:

PHILADELPHIA, 16 *January*, 1791.

MY DEAR SIR,

I can but love and thank you, and I do it sincerely, for your polite and friendly letter of the 11th of November, which came to my hands the day before yesterday *only*. The sentiments contained in it are such as have uniformly flowed from your pen, and they are not less flattering than pleasing to me.

The present Congress can sit no longer than the 4th of March, and should it not be found expedient to convene the new one immediately upon the rising of it — and should not the old one, by Acts of the present session, cut out work for the Executive, which may render my absence from the seat of government (soon after the adjournment) incompatible with my public duties; I shall most assuredly indulge myself in a tour thro' the Southern States in the Spring — But it will readily be perceived that this event must depend upon the time I shall be able to *commence* the journey, for I do not hesitate to acknowledge, that I am not inclined to be in the southernmost States after the month of May; and my journey must, on many accounts be made slow and easy.

It was among my first determinations when I entered upon the duties of my present station to visit every part of the United States in the Course of my administration of the government, provided my health and other circumstances would admit of it — and this determination was accompanied with another: viz. — not, by making my head quarters in private families, to become troublesome to them in any of these tours — The first I have accomplished in part only, without departing in a single instance from the second, although

[1] In Letters to Washington, the Washington MSS., Library of Congress.

pressed to it by the most civil and cordial invitations—After having made this communication you will readily perceive, my dear Sir, that it is not in my power (however it might comport with my inclinations,) to change my plan, without exposing myself to the charge of inconsistency, if not something more exceptionable — especially too, as it is not more than ten days since I declined a very kind and friendly invitation from my namesake and kinsman Colonel W. Washington of your State to lodge at his house when I should visit Charleston —

With affectionate esteem and regard
I am, my dear Sir,
Your most obedient Servant,
G. WASHINGTON.[1]

Despite the unsettled state of the Northwest due to the recalcitrancy of the Indians, the country on the whole was in a stable and prosperous condition. Washington felt that he could now undertake the tour of the Southern States with a carefree spirit. To his warm friend and admirer, Colonel David Humphreys,[2] our minister to Portugal, he

[1] Washington MSS., Library of Congress.

[2] David Humphreys, born at Derby, Connecticut, July, 1754. After his graduation from Yale College in 1771, he entered the army at the opening of the Revolution with the rank of captain. In 1778 he was attached to the staff of General Putnam, whose biography he afterwards wrote. In 1780 he was appointed aide-de-camp to Washington, which place he retained until the close of hostilities. At the siege of Yorktown he was particularly distinguished, and for his gallantry was voted an elegant sword by Congress. Following the conclusion of hostilities, he accompanied Washington to Mount Vernon, remaining there for nearly a year. In 1784, through Washington's influence, he was appointed secretary of legation to Benjamin Franklin, John Adams, and Thomas Jefferson, who were sent abroad to negotiate treaties of commerce and amity with European Powers. At Washington's invitation, he again took up his residence at Mount Vernon in 1790. In that year he was appointed the first United States Minister to Portugal. After seven years of residence at Lisbon, he was appointed Minister to Spain and resided at Madrid until he was succeeded by Charles C. Pinckney in 1802. He won distinction as poet and man of letters, receiving the

could write (Philadelphia, March 16, 1791): "Peace and tranquility pervade the territory of the United States, except on the northwest side of the Ohio. . . . Our public credit is restored, our resources are increasing, and the general appearance of things at least equals the most sanguine expectation, that was formed of the effects of the present government." Washington mentions that he is setting off "to-morrow or next day on a tour through the Southern States," and that he is under the necessity of commencing his journey with very bad roads, in order to "take such advantage of the season as to leave the southern extremity before the travelling shall be rendered disagreeable and perhaps dangerous by the heat." Washington's satisfaction with the general condition throughout the country is voiced in similar strain in a letter to Lafayette (March 19, 1791): "Our country, my dear Sir (and it is truly *yours*) is fast advancing in its political importance and social happiness. . . . The laws of the United States, adapted to the public exigencies, are framed with wisdom and moderation, and acquiesced in with cheerfulness. The administration of them, aided by the affectionate partiality of my countrymen, is attended with no unnecessary inconvenience, and every circumstance is auspicious to the felicity of your fellow citizens in this section of the globe."

LL.D. degree from Brown (1802) and Dartmouth (1804), and being elected a fellow of the Royal Society of London. He died at New Haven, Connecticut, February 21, 1818.

CHAPTER II

THE START

Philadelphia to Mount Vernon

IN devising plans for the Southern tour, Washington — the most methodical and provident of men — anticipated every need for making such a journey. The three important questions to be decided were those of a secretary, a route, and a coach and retinue. A subsidiary question, on which Washington's mind was already made up, was that of entertainment — which he either accepted at the expense of the municipality or paid for himself. In a few cases — due to personal association or exigencies of the road — he accepted private hospitality; but these were specific exceptions which he made to his general rule.

When Washington as President went to Philadelphia to take up his official residence, he appointed two men as his secretaries, Tobias Lear, Esq., and Major William Jackson. With a reputation as a soldier and a diplomat, Jackson had earlier so won the approbation of Washington as to be selected Secretary of the Constitutional Convention.[1] Jackson here played an important rôle, making daily notes of the secret sessions; and these notes, which Jackson promised Washington should not be published during the latter's lifetime, have never yet, it appears, seen the light of day. Jackson accompanied Washington on his

[1] Relying on the endorsement of such men as Laurens and Lincoln, Washington pronounced in favor of Jackson, although Franklin is said to have made strong pleas for the selection of his grandson, who was not so well fitted by ability and training for the post.

tour of the Eastern States; and proved so efficient in that capacity that Washington found him indispensable for the Southern tour. Jackson was a facile speaker and gifted writer; and his oration before the Society of the Cincinnati (July 4, 1786) and his eulogy on the character of Washington (February 22, 1800) have been highly praised. All of the replies to the numerous addresses made to Washington on his Southern tour were drafted by Jackson and merely signed by Washington. These compositions are not of sufficient literary merit to invite discussion regarding their authorship; but doubtless Washington ordinarily blocked out the essential features of his reply in talk with Jackson, and afterwards carefully revised the draft submitted to him. When Washington received an address, it was his custom — as he was wholly lacking in the readiness and volubility of the orator — to transmit to the body presenting the address a formal written reply at a later time. Although printed simultaneously, it was seldom that address and reply were delivered in immediate succession. This happened when a definite hour was set for the public address, and Major Jackson was supplied in advance with a copy of the address to be delivered. Major Jackson was an ideal secretary — and spared Washington all possible drudgery and detail. Washington could never quite escape the cares of office, however — for official letters pursued him and lay in wait for him at different stages of his journey.[1]

[1] William Jackson was born in Cumberland, England, March 9, 1759 — his mother being of Scotch descent. Removing to Charleston before he

The various routes for the journey were studied — and both tables of distances and maps of the highways passed beneath Washington's eye before his departure. He carefully considered the relative merits of the two routes from Petersburg, Virginia, to New Berne, North Carolina, one by Halifax, the other by Edenton. "A wide ferry, and its being a little further," we read in a Charleston newspaper, "deterred him from going by Edenton, as his time is precious." Before his departure, Washington carefully drew up in his own handwriting an exact itinerary giving dates and distances, of date March 10, 1791, and labelled "Route & Stages of G. Washington in the yr. 1791 which he performed at the time." [1] So precise was Washington in

was seventeen, he quickly obtained a commission as Lieutenant in the First South Carolina Infantry, of which his guardian, Owen Roberts, was Major. During the Revolution he served with ability, was commissioned Captain with rank of Major in October, 1779, and was captured at the surrender of Charleston in May, 1880. Soon exchanged, he became secretary to Colonel Laurens, whom he accompanied to France, whither Laurens went as special envoy in 1781. As the result of his successful diplomatic negotiations with Franklin, which smoothed the way for the successful expedition of the French fleets and army to the United States, he won the commendation and good-will of John Adams. After a few years he settled down to the practice of law in Philadelphia, where he was admitted to practice in 1788. In 1795 he was married to Elizabeth Willing, second daughter of Thomas Willing, President of the Bank of North America, one of Philadelphia's greatest merchants of the period. From 1796 to 1802 he was Surveyor of the Port of Philadelphia; and after his removal, on political grounds, by Jefferson, he edited the Federalist organ, *The Political and Commercial Register*. Dying December 17, 1828, he was buried in the burial ground of Christ Church, Philadelphia, near the grave of Franklin.

[1] This large sheet is headed: "If the President of the United States should be able to commence his tour through the Southern States on the 10th of March it will be regulated as follows." Other routes memoranda, mainly in Washington's handwriting and found in volume 249 of the Washington Papers, Library of Congress, are as follows: Table of distances endorsed "Road from Phila. to Charleston" (the date is 1781, but this is a palpable mistake for 1791); Table headed "Distances giving miles by

WILLIAM JACKSON

his arrangements that he actually supplied his Cabinet officers in advance of the tour with a complete itinerary and time schedule.

Long in advance of the trip Washington had his "Charriot," [1] as he called it, thoroughly overhauled by the firm of

stage between Petersburg & New Berne by 2 routes"; Map showing the above routes (large double folio page), partly in ink, partly in pencil — one route by Halifax, the other by Edenton; Route from Richmond to Edenton; Memorandum "for Maj. Jackson concerning the Road through N. & S. Carolina," three and a half pages in length; Route from Petersburg to Charleston via Edenton and via Halifax; Route from Savannah to Augusta.

[1] Lossing's sketch of Washington's coach, in his book on Mount Vernon, is incorrect in several particulars — although it is a true replica of the coach in shape. He shows the crest on the doors, not enclosed in ovals; the four seasons on the quarter panels, and Venetian blinds in the front of the coach with apparently no glass. The coach was a duplicate in shape of the Powel coach displayed at the Centennial Exposition in Philadelphia in 1876; and was, it is supposed, ordered from England at the same time as the Powel coach. The bill submitted Washington by Messrs. Clark, printed below, is very informing. It should be read in connection with certain letters in the Washington Correspondence, Library of Congress, Washington to Lear, September 5, 1790; Daniel and Francis Clark to Washington, September 13, 1790; Washington to Daniel and Francis Clark, September 17, 1790; Tobias Lear to Washington, October 24, 1790. Compare also Custis: *Recollections*, p. 424; Scharf and Westcott: *History of Philadelphia*, p. 473; and *The Washington Coachee and Powel Coach*, by Mrs. Mary Stevens Beall for Robert L. Brownfield (Washington, 1908). Follows the bill, in the Washington Correspondence, of Daniel and Francis Clark:

Taking out the Creans and Reasing higher & a pair of new Shafts		£7.10.0
A new iron Coach box Sett		3.15.0
A new Ruff Leather & new Conish		4.12.6
linning the Boady with 11½ yards of Superfine Cloath at 37-6 pr yard	21.11.3	
Leaces Glass string &c' a	8.14.0	38.5.3
making and putting in Do	8.10.0	
A new fulle trimed hamer Cloath		12.0.0
repairs wanted to the boady & 2 pair of new hinges		2.0.0
A pair of new double inside foulding Steps		5.10.0
4 new bands to the hoobs of the wheels		0.10.0
Painting the Boady and high Varnishing		5.10.0
Boarder rond all the pannels from £8. to £115		
Ornaments & Coats of Arms		4.10.0
Guilding the frame work Solid		6.00.0
Painting Carraige and wheels		2.10.0

carriage-makers, Daniel and Francis Clark, of Philadelphia. This was his "old coach," which means, I take it, that it was not his newest one. In color the chariot was white; there were beautiful designs of the four seasons by Cypriani painted on the doors and front and back; the Washington coat of arms within ovals was painted on the four quarter panels; there were four Venetian blinds on the side in the shape of quarter-ellipses, and four (two each) on front and back of rectangular shape; and there were glass windows in the front of the coach; the whole framework and the springs were gilded; there were plated door handles, plated brass buckles, plated mouldings round the roof, and a pair of double inside folding steps. "In this tour," says Washington in his diary, "I was accompanied by Major Jackson, my equipage & attendance consisted of a Charriot & four horses drove in hand — a light baggage waggon and two horses — four saddle horses beside a led one for myself and five — to wit — my Valet de Chambre, two footmen, Coachman & postilion." The outriders in their bright livery of red and white gave a touch of gallantry and distinction to the equipage and cavalcade. Writing to Lafayette on March 19th, Washington says: "The tender concern, which you

Picking in Do	1.10.0
8 Vinison blinds	22.10.0
Gilding the Springs	2. 5.0
A sett of Silke festoon Curtains with fringes and tosals to all the insid of the Ruff	8. 0.0

In the *Gazette of the United States* (Philadelphia, March 23, 1791) the coach is described as a "new charriot," "built by Mr. Clark of this city, and may be pronounced a superior specimen of mechanical perfection in that time." It appears that it was neither "new" nor "built" by Mr. Clark.

express on my last illness, awakens emotions, which words will not explain, and to which your own sensibility can best do justice. My health is now quite restored, and I flatter myself with the hope of a long exemption from sickness. On Monday next I shall enter on the practice of your friendly prescription of exercise, intending at that time to begin a journey to the southward, during which I propose visiting all the Southern States."

On Monday morning, March 21st, a small crowd gathered in front of 190 High Street, the large double house occupied by the Washington family, to witness the departure of the President on his Southern tour. On the boot of the white chariot was John Fagan, the Hessian coachman;[1] and attending the President were the Honorable Thomas Jefferson, the Secretary of State, General Henry Knox, Secretary of War, and the President's Secretary, Major Jackson. At eleven o'clock, in the language of a contemporary, "the coachman gave a rustling flourish with his lash, which produced a plunging motion in the leading horses, reined in by the postilions, and striking

[1] Fagan drove for the President throughout his whole tour of the Southern States. "On the president's return," says G. W. P. Custis, "Clarke was in attendance to learn the success of [the coach in withstanding the hardships of the journey]. No sooner had the horses stopped at the door of the presidential mansion than the anxious coach maker was under the body of the white chariot, examining everything with a careful and critical eye, till Fagan shouted from the box, 'All right, Mr. Clarke, all right, sir, not a bolt or screw started in a long journey and over the devil's own roads.'" So delighted was the coach-maker that he held a jollification at his shop over the splendid showing of the coach which he had so excellently repaired. If the story is true, it is highly probable that Fagan was "spoofing" Mr. Clark about the bolts and screws. Compare G. W. P. Custis, *Recollections and Private Memoirs of Washington* (New York, 1860), pp. 424–25.

flakes of fire between their heels and the pebbles beneath — when

> Crack went the whip, round went the wheels,
> As though the High Street were mad."

Washington was accompanied as far as Delaware by Mr. Jefferson and General Knox. The events of the next few days — in particular a certain dangerous and alarming experience — are fully described by Washington in his diary as follows:

Monday.

Left Philadelphia about 11 o'clock to make a tour through the Southern States. — Reached Chester about 3 o'clock — dined & lodged at Mr. Wythes — Roads exceedingly deep, heavy & cut in places by the Carriages which used them.

In this tour I was accompanied by Majr. Jackson . . .

Tuesday, 22nd.

At half past 6 o'clock we left Chester, & breakfasted at Wilmington. — Finding the Roads very heavy — and receiving unfavourable Accts. of those between this place and Baltimore, I determined to cross the Bay by the way of Rockhall — and crossing Christiana Creek proceeded through Newcastle & by the Red Lyon to the Buck tavern 13 miles from Newcastle and 19 from Wilmington where we dined and lodged. — At the Red Lyon we gave the horses a bite of Hay — during their eating of which I discovered that one of those wch. drew the Baggage waggon was lame and apprd. otherwise much indisposed — had him bled and afterwards led to the Buck-tavern.

This is a better house than the appearances indicate.

Wednesday, 23d.

Set off at 6 o'clock — breakfasted at Warwick — bated with hay 9 miles farther — and dined and lodged at the House of one Worrell's in Chester; from whence — I sent an Express to Rock Hall to have Boats ready for me by 9 o'clock to-morrow morning — after doing which Captn. Nicholson obligingly set out for that place to see that every thing should [be] prepared agai^{n}st my arrival.

The lame horse was brought on, and while on the Road apprd. to move tolerably well, but as soon as he stopped, discovered a stiffness in all his limbs, which indicated some painful disorder — I fear a Chest founder — My riding horse also appeard to be very unwell, his appetite had entirely failed him.

The Winter grain along the Road appeared promising and abundant.

Thursday, 24th.

Left Chestertown about 6 o'clock — before nine I arrived at Rock-Hall where we breakfasted and immediately: after which we began to embark — The doing of which employed us (for want of contrivance) until near 3 o'clock — and then one of my Servants (Paris) & two horses were left, notwithstanding two Boats in aid of the two Ferry Boats were procured. — Unluckily, embarking on board of a borrowed Boat because she was the largest, I was in imminent danger, from the unskillfulness of the hands, and the dulness of her sailing, added to the darkness and storminess of the night — for two hours after we hoisted sail the wind was light and ahead — the next hour was a stark calm — after which the wind sprung up at So. Et. and increased until it blew a gale — about which time, and after 8 o'clock P.M. we made the Mouth of Severn River (leading up to Annapolis) but the ignorance of the People on board, with respect to the navigation of it run us a ground first on Greenbury point from whence with much exertion and difficulty we got off; & then, having no knowledge of the Channel and the night being immensely dark with heavy and variable squals of wind — constant lightning & tremendous thunder — we soon got aground again on what is called Horne's point — where finding all efforts in vain, & not knowing where we were we remained, not knowing what might happen, till morning.

Friday, 25th.

Having lain all night in my Great Coat & Boots, in a birth not long enough for me by the head, & much cramped; we found ourselves in the morning within about one mile of Annapolis, & still fast aground. — Whilst we were preparing our small Boat in order to land in it, a sailing Boat came of to our assistance in wch. with the Baggage I had on Board I landed, & requested Mr. Man at whose Inn I intended lodging, to send off a Boat to take off two of my Horses & Chariot which I had left on board and with it my Coachman to see that it was properly done — but by mistake the latter not having notice of this order & attempting to get on board afterwards in a small sailing Boat was overset and narrowly escaped drowning.

Was informed upon my arrival (when 15 Guns were fired) that all my other horses arrived safe that embarked at the same time I did, about 8 o'clock last night.

In the *Maryland Journal and Baltimore Advertiser* (April 5, 1791) appeared an account of the delayed embarcation at Rock-Hall quite characteristic of the sentimental style of the day, referring to Washington amusingly enough — though doubtless all readers accepted it with unbroken solemnity — as the "chief treasure of America." Says this account: "The vessel, which contained the chief treasure of America did not enter the river Severn until ten o'clock in a dark tempestuous night. She struck on a bar, or point, within about a mile of the city; and although she made a signal of distress, it was impossible, before daylight, to go to her relief. The guardian-angel of America was still watchful; and we are happy in assuring our countrymen that the health of their dearest friend has not been at all affected by an accident far more distressing, to those who were apprized or rather apprehensive of his situation than to himself."

As soon as the Governor, John Eager Howard,[1] heard on Thursday evening that Washington was on his way to Annapolis from Rock-Hall, he in company with several gentlemen set sail in a boat to meet the President — "but turned back when it grew dark and squally." On Friday morning he called upon Washington at Mann's Tavern, and extended to him two invitations: to attend a public dinner that day to be given at Mann's Tavern by the citizens of Annapolis, and to dine with him the next day, both of which the President accepted. After breakfast, attended by the Governor and a "number of respectable citizens," he went for a walk about the city. Crowded with fateful recollections — though the "historic sense" seems strangely in abeyance in Washington if we judge by the diary alone — must have been his visit to the State House "which seems to be much out of repairs." Here in December, 1783, the Continental Congress assembled to receive his resignation as Commander-in-Chief; and here

[1] John Eager Howard, son of Cornelius and Ruth (Eager) Howard, was born on his father's estate, on the Reisterstown Road, Baltimore County, Maryland, near the site of present Garrison Forest Church, on property now owned by Howard Sills, Esq., June 4, 1752, and educated by private tutors. He served throughout the Revolutionary War; was in the battle of White Plains, October 28, 1776, and at the battle of Germantown, October 4, 1777. In June, 1779, he was promoted Lieutenant-Colonel. He was present at the battle of Camden, and was the hero of the battle of Cowpens, turning defeat into victory for the Americans.

Howard was a member of the Continental Congress in 1787 and 1788, and Governor of Maryland 1788–91. He served in the United States Senate, 1796–1803. In 1795 he was offered the portfolio of war by Washington, but declined it. He was a prominent Federalist. He died at Belvedere, October 12, 1827.

he stood as the memorable reply of Congress, written by Jefferson, was pronounced, concluding with these words: "Having defended the standard of liberty in this new world; having taught a lesson to those who inflict, and to those who feel oppression, you retire from the great theatre of action with the blessings of your fellow-citizens; but the glory of your virtues will not terminate with your military command, it will continue to animate remotest ages."

At ten o'clock the party reached the College of St. John, at which, records Washington, "there are about 80 students of every description." One immortal in patriotic verse, Francis Scott Key, entering November 11, 1789, was graduated here in 1796. This college has a history connected with the earliest efforts to establish a college in Maryland (1671) and had its foundation in King William's School, provided for in a legislative act of 1696. The charter of St. John's College, however, was not actually granted until nearly a century later (1784). The college was formally opened, with solemn ceremonies, on November 11, 1789.[1] Washington had close affiliations with the college — among the students during the early period of St. John's College being George Washington Parke Custis, a stepson, and Fairfax and Lawrence Washington, nephews of the President. During his visit at this time Washington "ex-

[1] The brick school-house of King William's School was completed in 1701. The man chiefly instrumental in obtaining the passage of the act resulting in the establishment of this school was the Reverend Doctor Thomas Bray, who had been appointed Commissioner of Maryland by the Bishop of London, and who is credited with being the originator of the Society for the Propagation of the Gospel. Consult Philip R. Voorhees: *St. John's College.*

SAINT JOHN'S COLLEGE, ANNAPOLIS, MARYLAND

pressed much satisfaction at the appearance of this rising seminary." On the day following Washington's visit, the faculty of the college drew up an address to the President which is here given in full:

To the President of the United States.

Sir,

We, the Faculty of St. John's College beg leave to express the sincere joy which the honour of your presence in our infant seminary afforded us. In common with all those who superintend the education of youth, we must feel a lively gratitude to the defender of liberty, the guardian of his country, and consequently the great patron of literature. But as this seminary was begun since the united voice of free America called you to preside over its most important interest, and ensured to them the continuance of those blessings which your calm foresight and steady fortitude had been the happy means of procuring, it seems in a peculiar manner to look up to you with filial respect. That it dates its birth from this grand aera, which has placed you at the head of fifteen distinct sovereign states united into one mighty republic, is regarded by its friends as an auspicious circumstance and flattering assurance of its future eminence and usefulness. To the friend of virtue and his country, the rise of colleges where the youth of generations yet unborn, may be taught to admire and emulate the great and good, must give a heartfelt delight, as they promise perpetuity to the labours and renown of the patriot and hero.

Our earnest prayers, that a kind Providence may constantly watch over you, and preserve a life, long indeed, already, if measured by deeds of worth and fulness of honours but too short as yet for your country.

Signed in behalf, and at the request of the Faculty,

John M. Dowell, Pr.

March 26, 1791.

To which the President made the following reply:

To the Faculty of St. John's College.

Gentlemen,

The satisfaction which I have derived from my visit to your infant seminary, is expressed with real pleasure, and my wishes for its progress to perfection are preferred with sincere regard.

The very promising appearance of its infancy must flatter all its friends (among them I intreat you to class me) with the hope of an early, and at the same time, a mature manhood.

You will do justice to the sentiments, which your kind regard towards myself inspires, by believing that I reciprocate the good wishes contained in your address, and I sincerely hope the excellence of your seminary will be manifested in the morals and science of the youth who are favoured with your care.

G. Washington

After accompanying Mrs. Howard (whom Washington calls Mrs. "Howell") to the Governor's home, the President dined at Mann's Tavern with "a numerous company of inhabitants." The following toasts were proposed at the conclusion of the dinner each of which was announced by the discharge of cannon:

1. The People of the United States of America.
2. The Congress.
3. The dearest Friend of his Country.
4. The State of Maryland.
5. Wisdom, Justice and Harmony, in all our Public Councils.
6. Agriculture, Manufactures, Commerce, and Learning, may they all flourish with virtue and true Religion.
7. The king of the French.
8. The National Assembly of France.
9. The Sieur la Fayette, and generous Friends to America in the Day of her Distress.

10. The memory of all those who have fallen in the Cause of America.
11. The Patriots of all Nations and Ages.
12. The powers of Europe friendly to America.
13. May all inhabitants of the Earth be taught to consider each other as Fellow-Citizens.
14. The virtuous Daughters of America.
15. The perpetual Union of distinct Sovereign States under an efficient Federal Head.

Symptomatic of an unsophisticated society was the next to the last toast with its superfluous adjective; while the last is significant of the slowly maturing faith in the Union.

Saturday, 26th, was a day full of happenings — although there is nothing of note to record. In the forenoon, the President remained in his room — preparing papers and documents in anticipation of the coming meeting at George Town on the following Monday, concerning laying out the district for the federal seat. The President dined at Governor Howard's with a large company; and in the evening until half past ten o'clock he attended a ball, "at which was exhibited everything, which this little city contains of beauty and elegance." The pleasure of the entire community in the visit of the President manifested itself through the columns of a Baltimore newspaper in which we read: "It is no exaggeration to declare that, during two days, all care seemed suspended; and the inhabitants of a whole town were made happy in contemplating him whom they consider as their safest friend, as well as the most exalted of their fellow-citizens and the first of men." At nine o'clock on Sunday morning the President left the city "under a discharge of Artillery," being accompanied by "many of the Gentlemen of Annapolis (among whom was the Chancellor of the State)" as far as the ferry over South River. On his journey to Georgetown he was accompanied by the Governor, a Mr. Kilty of the Council, and Mr. Charles Stuart. Records the President: "Bated at Queen Ann, 13 miles distant and lodged at Bladensburgh."

The location of the federal district was a matter of national interest. The negotiations which had to be carried on and the numerous difficulties which had to be encountered were tests of Washington's patience, wisdom, and diplomacy which he amply met. The decision as to the location of the federal district was made on January 24, 1791, on which date the President sent a message to Congress regarding the matter, suggesting amendatory legislation for extending the limits of the federal district. The suggestions of Washington were incorporated by Congress on March 3d in an amendatory law; and the commissioners appointed by Washington were Thomas Johnson [1] and

[1] Thomas Johnson, son of Thomas and Dorcas (Sedgewick) Johnson, Maryland's first State Governor, was born at St. Leonard's on November 4, 1732. He studied law in Annapolis; was a leader in the pre-Revolutionary agitation in Maryland; became a prominent member of the first Continental Congress, being reëlected in 1776. On October 2, 1774, when a resolution was passed by Congress that an address to the Crown should be prepared, Mr. Johnson was selected, with R. H. Lee, John Adams, and Patrick Henry, to write it; he was a member of the provincial committee of correspondents, and a member of the Council of Safety. It was he who on June 15, 1775, nominated George Washington for Commander-in-Chief of the Continental forces. He was Governor of Maryland 1777–79. He was returned to the Provincial Congress in 1780 and became a member of the House of Delegates in the same year. From 1781 to 1787 he sat in the Continental Congress, became a supporter of the Constitution, and was a member of the Maryland Convention which ratified that instrument in 1789.

THOMAS JOHNSON

DANIEL CARROLL

Daniel Carroll,[1] of Maryland, and David Stuart,[2] of Virginia.

Certain of the property-holders within the district interposed many obstacles, notably the man who has gone down in the annals of the city as "the obstinate Mr. Burns." More than a month prior to the time the commissioners first took up their work, the President appointed Andrew Ellicott [3] to survey the bounds of the district and Pierre

On April 20, 1790, he was appointed Chief Judge of the General Court of Maryland, surrendering the office November 7, 1791, that he might assume the duties of Associate Justice of the Supreme Court of the United States.

When Edmund Randolph resigned the portfolio of State in 1795, President Washington wrote to Mr. Johnson as follows: "The office of Secretary of State is vacant, occasioned by the resignation of Mr. Randolph. Will you accept it? You know my wishes of old to bring you into the administration. Where, then, is the necessity of repeating them? . . . No time more than the present ever required the aid of your abilities." Mr. Johnson's letter declining the office reveals the extreme modesty which worked such havoc with his fame.

Mr. Johnson was a member of the commission which laid out the city of Washington. He died at Rose Hill, Frederick, October 26, 1819.

[1] Daniel Carroll was born in Prince George's County, Maryland, in 1756. He received a classical education and lived on his estate, afterwards part of the City of Washington, D.C. From 1780 to 1784 he was delegate from Maryland to the Continental Congress. He was also a delegate to the Convention that framed the Federal Constitution. In 1788 he was elected Representative from Maryland to the first United States Congress, serving from March 4, 1789, to March 3, 1791. He was active in securing the establishment of a seat of government, and in 1791 was appointed by President Washington a commissioner to locate the District of Columbia and the capital city. He died at "Duddington," his home near Washington, in 1829.

[2] David Stuart, son of the Reverend William Stuart, was born in King George County, Virginia, August 3, 1753, educated at William and Mary College, and studied medicine at Edinburgh and Paris. He served in the Virginia Legislature. He later removed to Alexandria, where he practiced his profession of medicine with great success. He was a Federalist and a strong friend of Washington. He married Eleanor Calvert Custis, the widow of John Parke Custis, son of Martha Washington by her first marriage. He was father of Charles Calvert Stuart, of Chantilly, Fairfax County, Virginia.

[3] Andrew Ellicott, an American civil engineer, was born in Bucks

Charles L'Enfant [1] to prepare a plan of the city. By the middle of March both were well under way in their work — Ellicott to make a survey and map, L'Enfant to make "drawings of the particular grounds most likely to be offered for the site of the federal town and buildings." Writing to his agents for negotiating with the somewhat recalcitrant property-holders, Washington shrewdly suggests that the spectacle of L'Enfant making a survey solely of the lands on the Eastern Branch might cause the property-holders to prove more amenable. This was the situation just prior to Washington's arrival at George Town. The President's diary for the next three days is full and instructive:

Monday, 28*th*.

Left Bladensburgh at half after six, & breakfasted at George Town about 8; where, having appointed the Com-

County, Pennsylvania, in 1754. In 1789 he was appointed by Washington to survey the lands in western Pennsylvania and New York, near Lake Erie, and in the same year made the first accurate measurements of Niagara Falls and River. In 1790 he was engaged in surveying and laying out the new city of Washington, and in 1792 was appointed Surveyor-General of the United States. From 1801 to 1808 he was secretary of the Pennsylvania State Land Office, and from 1812 until his death held the chair of mathematics at West Point Military Academy. He published a *Journal* in 1803. He died at West Point, New York, August 28, 1820.

[1] Pierre Charles L'Enfant, born in 1755, a French officer who came to America with Lafayette in 1777 and joined the American Army. His skill as a designer of fortifications attracted the attention of Washington, who made him chief of engineers with brevet of major of engineers. In 1791 he planned the city of Washington under the direction of George Washington and with aid in the way of plans of foreign cities from Thomas Jefferson. The commissioners in general charge of the work advertised a sale of lots for October, 1791, and requested L'Enfant to furnish his plan to be engraved and published. This he refused to do, and for this insubordination Washington ordered his dismissal March 1, 1792. The execution of his plan for Washington was continued by his assistant, Andrew Ellicott. L'Enfant died in Prince George's County, Maryland, June 4, 1825.

missioners under the Residence Law to meet me, I found Mr. Johnson one of them (& who is Chief Justice of the State) in waiting — & soon after came in David Stuart, & Danl. Carroll Esqrs. the other two. — A few miles out of Town I was met by the principal Citizens of the place and escorted in by them; and dined at Suter's tavern (where I also lodged) at a public dinner given by the Mayor & Corporation — previous to which I examined the Surveys of Mr. Ellicot who had been sent on to lay out the district of ten miles square for the federal seat; and also the works of Majr. L'Enfant who had been engaged to examine & make a draught of the grds. in the vicinity of George Town and Carrollsburg on the Eastern branch making arrangements for examining the ground myself tomorrow with the Commissioners.

Tuesday, 29th.

In a thick mist, and under strong appearance of a settled rain (which however did not happen) I set out about 7 o'clock, for the purpose above mentioned — but from the unfavorableness of the day, I derived no great satisfaction from the review.

Finding the interests of the Landholders about George town and those about Carrollsburgh much at varience and that their fears and jealousies of each were counteracting the public purposes & might prove injurious to its best interests whilst if properly managed they might be made to subserve it — I requested them to meet me at six o'clock this afternoon at my lodgings, which they accordingly did.

To this meeting I represented that the contention in which they seemed engaged, did not in my opinion comport either with the public interest or that of their own; — that while each party was aiming to obtain the public buildings, they might by placing the matter on a contracted scale, defeat the measure altogether; not only by procrastination but for want of the means necessary to effect the work; — That niether the offer from George-town or Carrollsburgh, seperately, was adequate to the end of insuring the object. — That both together did not comprehend more ground nor would afford greater means than was required for the federal City; — and that, instead of contending which of the two should have it they had better, by combining more offers make a common cause of it, and thereby secure it to the district — other arguments were used to show the danger which might result from delay and the good effects that might proceed from a Union.

Dined at Col^o. Forrest's today with the Commissioners & others.

Wednesday, 30th.

The parties to whom I addressed myself yesterday evening, having taken the matter into consideration saw the propriety of my observations; and that whilst they were contending for the shadow they might loose the substance; and therefore mutually agreed and entered into articles to surrender for public purposes, one half of the land they severally possessed within bounds which were designated as necessary for the City to stand with some other stipulations, which were inserted in the instrument which they respectively subscribed.

This business being thus happily finished & some directions given to the Commissioners, the Surveyor and Engineer with respect to the mode of laying out the district — Surveying the grounds for the City & forming them into lots — I left Georgetown — dined in Alexandria & reached Mount Vernon in the evening.[1]

[1] On the day of the President's arrival at Mount Vernon was published the following proclamation:

By the President of the United States of America.

A PROCLAMATION

Whereas, by a proclamation bearing date the 24th day of January of this present year, and in pursuance of certain acts of the States of Maryland and Virginia, and of the Congress of the United States therein mentioned, certain lines of experiment were directed to be run in the neighborhood of George Town, in Maryland, for the purpose of determining the location of a part of the territory of ten miles square for the permanent seat of the government of the United States and a certain part was directed to be located within the said lines of experiment, on both sides of the Potomac, and above the limit of the Eastern Branch prescribed by the said act of Congress

"GEORGE TOWN, AND CITY OF WASHINGTON"

From an engraving published in 1812

On March 24, 1791, Colonel Henry Lee,[1] the famous

And Congress by an amendatory act, passed on the 3d day of this present month of March, have given further authority to the President of the United States "to make any part of the territory below the said limit, and above the mouth of Hunting Creek, a part of the said district so as to include a convenient part of the Eastern Branch, and of the lands lying on the lower side thereof and also the town of Alexandria."

Now therefore, for the purpose of amending and completing the location of the whole of the said territory of ten miles square, in conformity with the amendatory act of Congress, I do hereby declare and make known that the whole of the said territory shall be located and included within the four line following that is to say,

Beginning at Jones Point, being the Cape of Hunting Creek in Virginia, and at an angle in the outset, of forty-five degrees west of the north and running in a direction ten miles for the first line; then beginning again at the same Jones-Point and running another direct line, at a right angle with the first, across the Potomac, ten miles for the second line; then, from the terminations of the said first and second lines, running two other direct lines, of ten miles each, the one crossing the Eastern Branch aforesaid and the other the Potomac and meeting each other in a point.

And I do accordingly direct the Commissioners, named under the authority of the said first-mentioned act of Congress, to proceed forthwith to have the said four lines run, and by the proper metes and bounds defined and limited, and thereof to make due report under their hands and seals; and the territory to be located, defined and limited, shall be the whole territory accepted by the said acts of Congress as the district for the permanent seat of the Government of the United States.

In Testimony whereof I have caused the Seal of the United States to be affixed to these presents, and signed the same with my hand. Done at George town aforesaid, the 30th day of March in the year of our Lord 1791, and of the Independence of the United States the fifteenth.

GEORGE WASHINGTON.

By the President
THOMAS JEFFERSON.

[1] Henry Lee, born in Leesylvania, Prince William County, Virginia, January 29, 1756. Pursued classical studies and was graduated from Princeton in 1774. On motion of Patrick Henry, he was commissioned captain of a company of Virginia dragoons, June 18, 1776. Joined Washington's army in Pennsylvania, September, 1777. By a special act of Congress, April 7, 1778, in recognition of his brave and distinguished services, was promoted to a major commandant and authorized to augment his corps by the enlistment of two troops of horse; received a gold medal and the thanks of Congress "for remarkable prudence, address, and bravery" in the affair at Paulus Hook. By act of October 21, 1780, his battalion was designated "Lee's partisan corps"; which came to be known as "Lee's

" Light Horse Harry " of the Revolution and son of Washington's first love—the "Lowland Beauty," of whom he was enamoured when only sixteen years of age—wrote Washington the following affectionate letter from Alexandria:

My dear General

Permit me to tell you that I have waited to the last moment in my power in the fond hope of seeing you.

My necessitys force me away this day, or the satisfaction I covet, should not be lost. Deprived of what is so grateful to my feelings, I must use this mode of manifesting my happiness on your second return to our native state, on the confirmed health you enjoy, and on the lasting affection of your fellow citizens.

Let me hope you will not forget the pestilential effects of the southern sun in the hot season and that the month of May will not pass, before you revisit the potomac. I wish you an agreable journey & safe return, & beg your acceptance of my most affectionate & respectful regards.

I have the honor to be
My dear General
Your most devoted h: servt.
Henry Lee

legion" and its young commander as "Light Horse Harry." He was promoted to lieutenant-colonel, November 6, 1780; and served until the end of the war. On July 19, 1798, was commissioned major-general, United States Army; and was honorably discharged June 15, 1800. Delegate in the Continental Congress, 1785–1788; and supported Madison and Marshall in the Virginia Convention of 1788, winning distinction for his eloquence. Member of the Virginia Legislature, 1789–91; and governor of Virginia, 1792–95. Commanded the Virginia forces against the whiskey insurgents. Elected to the Sixth Congress as a Federalist (March 4, 1799, to March 3, 1801). At the request of Congress he delivered a eulogy upon Washington at the time of his death, in which he uttered the famous characterization: "first in war, first in peace, and first in the hearts of his countrymen." Injured in a street riot in Baltimore in 1812, receiving injuries from which he never recovered. By his marriage, during the Revolution, to Matilda, daughter of Philip Ludwell Lee, he came into possession of Stratford House, where he spent the latter part of his life. Died in Cumberland Island, Georgia, March 25, 1818.

CHAPTER III

THE FIRST STAGE

Virginia: Fredericksburg, Richmond, Petersburg

WASHINGTON reached home on the 30th of March — gladly greeted by family and retainers. The welcome relaxation from cares of State had an added balm — for when he started forth again, he was not to return to the national capital, but to make a triumphal tour through the southern portion of the vast domain over which he presided. With the shrewd eye of the skilled agriculturist, Washington inspected his plantation each day, made pertinent inquiries, carefully investigated the costs of everything, and gave precise directions regarding every detail of management. At this time, he had one hundred and fifteen "hands" on the Mount Vernon estate, besides house servants; and De Warville, describing his estate in the same year, speaks of his having three hundred negroes. In this congenial task — for Washington loved no rôle quite so well as that of the prosperous country gentleman — he spent a full week at Mount Vernon.[1]

[1] The following description of Mount Vernon at this time appeared in the *General Advertiser and Political, Commercial and Literary Journal* of Philadelphia, April 20, 1791:

"Mount Vernon, the celebrated seat of general Washington, is pleasantly situated on the Virginia bank of the Potowmack, where it is nearly two miles wide, and is about 280 miles from the sea. It is 9 miles from Alexandria, and 4 above the beautiful seat of the late col. Fairfax, called Belleview. The area of the mount is 200 feet above the surface of the river, and after furnishing a lawn of five acres in front, and about the same in

Perhaps he did not wholly regret, as he states in his diary (March 31), that he

Was obliged also, consequence of Col°. Henry Lee's declining to accept the command of one of the Regiments of Levies and the request of the Secretary at War to appoint those officers which had been left to Col°. Lee to do for a Battalion to be raised in Virginia East of the Alligany Mountains to delay my journey on this account — and after all, to commit the business as will appear by the letters & for the reasons there mentioned to Col°. Darke's management.[1]

rear of the buildings, falls off abruptly on those two quarters. On the north end it subsides gradually into extensive pasture grounds; while on the south it slopes more steeply, in a shorter distance, and terminates with the coach house, stables, vineyards and nurseries. On either wing is a thick grove of different flowering forest trees. Parallel with them, on the land side, are two spacious gardens, into which one is led by two serpentine gravel walks, planted with weeping willows and shady shrubs. The mansion house itself (though much embellished by, yet not perfectly satisfactory to the chaste taste of the present possessor) appears venerable and convenient. The superb banqueting room has been finished since he returned from the army. A lofty portico, 96 feet in length, supported by eight pillars, has a pleasing effect when viewed from the water; and the tout ensemble (the whole assemblage) of the green house, school house, offices and servants halls, when seen from the land side, bears a resemblance to a rural village, especially as the lands in that side are laid out somewhat in the form of English gardens, in meadows and grass grounds, ornamented with little copses, circular clumps and single trees. A small Park on the margin of the river, where the English fallow deer, and the American wild deer, are seen through the thickets, alternately with the vessels as they are sailing along, add a romantic picturesque appearance to the whole scenery. On the opposite side of a small creek to the northward an extensive plain, exhibiting cornfields and cattle grazing, affords in summer a luxuriant landscape to the eye; while the blended verdure of woodlands and cultivated declivities on the Maryland shore, variegates the prospect in a charming manner. Such are the philosophic shades to which the late commander in the American armies retired from the tumultuous scenes of a busy world."

[1] Colonel Darke was an active officer in the Ohio country, in the Indian wars in that region from 1792 to 1794; and Darke County was named in his honor. He was with the Virginians at Braddock's defeat; was in the war for independence; was a member of the Virginia Convention in 1788; was with St. Clair in his unfortunate campaign in 1791; and died in 1801. (B. J. L.) Cf. Washington's Letter to Colonel John Darke, written

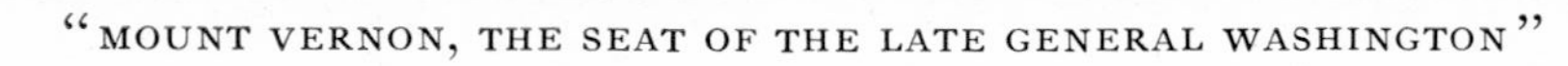
"MOUNT VERNON, THE SEAT OF THE LATE GENERAL WASHINGTON"

TWO VIEWS OF MOUNT VERNON AS IT IS TO-DAY

Virginia

Although there were no telegraphs, telephones, or wireless stations in those days, it was just as important as it is to-day for the members of the Cabinet to have exact knowledge of the movements and the whereabouts of the President. The letter marked: "To the Secretaries of the Departments of State, Treasury, and War," Mount Vernon, April 4, 1791, displays the customary prudence and foresight of this man of glorified common sense:

As the public service may require, that communications should be made to me during my absence from the seat of government by the most direct conveyances, and as, in the event of any very extraordinary occurrence, it will be necessary to know at what time I may be found in any particular place, I have to inform you that, unless the progress of my journey to Savannah is retarded by unforeseen interruptions, it will be regulated, including days of halt, in the following manner. I shall be on the 8th of April at Fredericksburg, the 11th at Richmond, the 14th at Petersburg, the 16th at Halifax, the 18th at Tarborough, the 20th at Newbern, the 24th at Wilmington, the 29th at Georgetown, South Carolina; on the 2d of May at Charleston, halting there five days; on the 11th at Savannah, halting there two days. Thence, leaving the line of the mail, I shall proceed to Augusta; and, according to the information which I may receive there, my return by an upper road will be regulated.

The route of my return is at present uncertain, but in all probability it will be through Columbia, Camden, Charlotte, Salisbury, Salem, Guilford, Hillsborough, Harrisburg, Williamsburg to Taylor's Ferry on the Roanoke, and thence to Fredericksburg by the nearest and best road.

After thus explaining to you, as far as I am able at present, the direction and probable progress of my journey, I have

from Mount Vernon on April 4th, in which he gives a summary of the forces to be employed in the projected expedition against "certain tribes of western Indians" under the command of General St. Clair, and requests Colonel Darke to superintend the engaging of recruits.

to express my wish, if any serious and important cares (of which the probability is but too strong) should arise during my absence, that the Secretaries of the Departments of State, Treasury, and War, may hold consultations thereon, to determine whether they are of such a nature as to demand my personal attendance at the seat of government; and, should they be so considered, I will return immediately from any place at which the information may reach me. Or should they determine, that measures, relevant to the case, may be legally and properly pursued without the immediate agency of the President, I will approve and ratify the measures, which may be conformed to such determination.

Presuming that the Vice-President will have left the seat of government for Boston, I have not requested his opinion to be taken on the supposed emergency; should it be otherwise, I wish him also to be consulted.

The deep personal affection felt for Washington throughout the country found expression in the public prints. The sensibility of our ancestors is admirably illustrated in what passes for a news item: "The President of the United States set out from *Philadelphia*, on a tour, through the Southern States, on the 21st. ult. He *was* accompanied by a number of respectable characters; but best of all, he *is* accompanied by the prayers and wishes of the people over whom he presides; who will not cease to supplicate the *Throne of Grace*, that his health may be preserved; and that in that, he may enjoy every earthly felicity!"

Before starting off from Mount Vernon, Washington received a letter from Jefferson (Philadelphia, March 27th), expressing concern for his safety in travelling. "I shall be happy to hear that no accident has happened to you on the bad roads you have passed, and that you are both prepared for those to come by lowering the hang of your carriage, and exchanging the coachman for two postilions, circumstances which I confess to you appeared to me essential for your safety, for which no one on earth more sincerely prays, both from public and private regard, than he who has the honor to be etc." To which solicitous inquiry, Washington replied: "No accident has yet happened, either from the high hanging of the carriage, or the mode of driving. The latter I must continue, as my postilion is still too much indisposed to ride the journey." Singularly enough, Jefferson's warning was prophetic; for on the very day of Washington's departure from Mount Vernon, with "horses apparently much refreshed and in good spirits," an accident of an extraordinary nature occurred. Had it eventuated disastrously, it might have delayed, if not wholly prevented, the tour of the Southern States. Washington thus relates the singular occurrence in his diary:

In attempting to cross the ferry at Colchester with the four Horses hitched to the Chariot by the neglect of the person who stood before them, one of the leaders got overboard when the boat was in swimming water and 50 yards from the shore — with much difficulty he escaped drowning before he could be disingaged — his struggling frightened the others in such a manner that one after another and in quick succession they all got overboard harnessed & fastened as they were and with the utmost difficulty they were saved & the Carriage escaped been dragged after them, as the whole of it happened in swimming water, & at a distance from the shore — Providentially — indeed miraculously — by the exertions of people who went off in Boats & jumped into the River as soon as the Batteau was forced into wading water —

no damage was sustained by the horses, Carriage or Harness.

After this startling accident — an apparently untoward beginning of his tour — Washington proceeded to Dumfries, where he dined, apparently without demonstration on the part of the populace; and after dinner he visited and drank tea with his niece Mrs. Thomas Lee.[1] This restful visit was but the interlude to the long succession of receptions, greetings, dinners, and balls which began on the morrow and lasted uninterruptedly for well-nigh two months. There was incomparable fitness in the real inauguration of his tour at Fredericksburg on April 8th. With that simplicity and selflessness which marked the man Washington, he gave no advance notice of his prospective visit to his boyhood home. Arising at six o'clock, he set off at once from Dumfries and breakfasted *en route* at Stafford Court House, where his coach was readily recognized and the people left their daily tasks to pay their respects to the revered guest. Not being apprized of his approach, the citizens were "disappointed in the opportunities of evincing their respect to this illustrious character, by meeting him previous to his arrival." No sooner had his chariot

1 Thomas Lee, of "Parke Gate," near Dumfries, Virginia, was the eldest son of Richard Henry Lee and Anne Aylett, his first wife. He was born at "Chantilly," his father's home, on October 20, 1758, and died of consumption in 1805 at "Belmont," the home of his brother, Ludwell Lee, near Leesburg, Virginia. Thomas Lee was twice married, first about October 15, 1788, to Mildred, daughter of John Augustine and Hannah (Bushrod) Washington, his wife. John Augustine was a younger brother of President George Washington. Mildred was born at "Bushfield," the home of her parents in Westmoreland County, about 1760. Thomas Lee's will, 1805, named his wife Eliza Ashton Lee and daughter Elinor Lee.

FIELDING LEWIS

and entourage swept through the quiet village overlooking the placid river than the place was all agog with the news: "The President is here! He arrived at one o'clock and is staying at the home of his sister, Elizabeth, Mrs. Fielding Lewis." [1] How charged with memories, grave and gay, must have been those hours he spent this day and the next in company with his sister Bettie, as he called her, at lovely "Kenmore!" Almost in sight across the river was Pine Grove, on the Ferry Farm where Washington as a lad played with his little neighbor, Jane Strother, one of his early sweethearts. Here grew that apochryphal cherry-tree which fell beneath the mischievous hatchet; and here, too, if tradition doth not lie, he threw the Spanish dollar across the river. A quizzical smile must have flitted across that grave countenance now as he visited the "Rising Sun Tavern," built and owned by his brother Charles, where he had lost at cards "as usual," as he somewhere records in his diary, to those Fredericksburg fellows who were "too smart for him." Fredericksburg had seen him often through the quiet as well as the eventful years of his

[1] His sister Elizabeth married Colonel Fielding Lewis. Their son, Lawrence Lewis, was Washington's favorite nephew. He married Nelly Custis, Mrs. Washington's granddaughter, and resided with her at Mount Vernon at the time of Washington's death. (B. J. L.)

Fielding Lewis, second son of John Lewis and Frances Fielding, born 1725, married: first (1746), Catherine, daughter of John Washington and Catherine Whiting and first cousin of General George Washington; and second (1750), Bettie Washington, only sister of General George Washington. He was not in field service during the Revolutionary War, being over the military age, but was engaged during the struggle in manufacturing arms for the patriot army. His home was "Kenmore," Fredericksburg, Virginia. He died in 1781. From *Genealogies of Lewis and Kindred Families* by J. N. McAllister and L. B. Toody. Compare also *Historic Periods of Fredericksburg, 1608-1861*, by Mrs. Vivian Minor Fleming.

career; here he had foregathered with the young bloods of the town; here he had reviewed the independent companies; and here he had often attended cotillions and country dances, at which he invariably paid chief court to the most beautiful and attractive ladies of those in attendance. Here in November, 1789, his mother accompanied him to a reception held in his honor; and here at the close of the Revolution was given the famous Peace Ball at which Mary, his mother, "occupied a slightly elevated position from which she could overlook the floor and see the dances." It was at this time that the Mayor of the Corporation, William McWilliams, delivered the address of welcome in which were spoken with unaffected emotion these words: "Although you have laid aside your official character, we cannot omit this first opportunity you have given us of presenting, with unfeigned hearts, our sincere congratulations on your returning in safety from the noisy clashing of arms to the walks of domestic ease. And it affords us great joy to see you once more at a place that claims the honor of your growing infancy, the seat of your venerable and amiable parent and worthy relatives."

As he passed down the main street of the town, his eyes turned to the Masonic Lodge, No. 4, where on November 4, 1752, he became a member, and on August 4, 1753, was "raised a Master Mason." Upon the minutes of this same lodge are spread these sentiments, recorded shortly after Washington's death: "He was early initiated in this venerable Lodge, in the mysteries of our ancient and honorable profession; and held it in the highest and most just veneration. . . . As a man he was frail, and it would be a compliment to which human nature cannot aspire to suppose him free from peculiarities or exempt from error. . . . In the offices of private life he was most endeared to those who were most in his familiarity and intimacy. . . . He is gone forever from our view, but gone to the realms of celestial bliss, where the shafts of malice and detraction cannot penetrate, where all sublunary distinctions cease, and merit is rewarded by the scale of unerring justice."

Washington must have enjoyed this first day with the Lewises, especially making and renewing acquaintances with the children of his sister Bettie, who had thirteen all told. But preparations were going rapidly forward for a reception and public dinner at which due honor was to be paid to the beloved and honored guest who was regarded almost as a native son of Stafford. "An elegant dinner was prepared at the Town Hall," says a contemporary print; and at two o'clock Washington was "waited on by some of the officers and principal inhabitants of the corporation, conducted to the place of entertainment, received by the Mayor, and introduced to those present." After the greetings and introductions, marked by unusual heartiness and cordiality, were over, William Harvey, the Mayor, on behalf of the Corporation, then publicly delivered the following "affectionate congratulatory address":

We, the Mayor, Aldermen, and Common Council of the corporation of Fredericksburg are happy in tendering you the sincere and unanimous congratulations of the citizens on your arrival in this town.

The inhabitants of Fredericksburg, Sir, as they can boast

the first acquaintance with your virtues, claim a peculiar pleasure in testifying to the world your exalted merit; and in joining with the rest of America, to express their entire approbation of your conduct thro' life; which has been so productive of blessings to the citizens.

The long and fatiguing journey you have undertaken will further manifest your unremitted attachment to that country, whose obligations to you can be better felt than described, and we trust will not only influence the present generation to admire public and private virtues, from your example, but teach your successors how to watch over the welfare of this extensive union.

We have the fullest confidence in Divine Benevolence, that the Dispenser of all good will will be graciously pleased long to continue you in health, and reward you here and hereafter with blessings adequate to your merit, which he alone can give.

In terms consonant with the spirit of the address, the President made the following gracious reply:

To the Mayor, Aldermen and Common Council of the Corporation of Fredericksburg,

Gentlemen,

At all times flattered by the esteem, and grateful for the good wishes of my fellow citizens, I am particularly so, when, to my respect for their public worth, is united the endearments of private acquaintance.

In this regard, I have the pleasure to receive your congratulatory address on my arrival in Fredericksburg, and, thanking you with sincerity for the sentiments it expresses, I desire to assure you of the affectionate gratitude which they inspire.

With unaffected enjoyment in having in their midst so famous a figure who was also a friend and familiar, the banqueters proposed toast after toast, fifteen in all, which were greeted with resounding applause; last of all the

President won every heart by proposing the following highly popular sentiment: "The town we are in, and prosperity to its inhabitants." It is stated in a contemporary print that "the whole was conducted with the utmost regularity and decorum and the evening concluded with every mark of festivity and cheerfulness."

In his diary of the journey, Washington records on this day:

Was informed by Mr. Jno. Lewis, who had, not long since been in Richmond, that Mr. Patrick Henry had avowed his interest in the Yazoo Company;[1] and made him a tender of admission into it, whch, he declined — but asking, if the Company did not expect the Settlement of the lands would be disagreeable to the Indians was answered by Mr. Henry that the Co. intended to apply to Congress for protection — which, if not granted they would have recourse to their own means to protect the settlement — That General Scott had a certain quantity of land (I think 40,000 acres in the Company's grant & was to have the command of the force which was to make the establishment — and moreover — that General Muhlenburg had offered £1000 for a certain part of the grant — the quantity I do not recollect if it was mentioned to me.

On the morning of his departure, Washington had a taste of the inconveniences of form; for despite the early hour of his departure — "about 6 o'clock" — he was attended for some miles out of town by a "large company

[1] The first legislature of Georgia, after the adoption of the Federal Constitution, undertook to sell out, to three private companies, the preëmption right to vast tracts of land west of the Chattahoochee River, unmindful of any rightful claims of the Indians. They were called Yazoo Land Companies. They sold to the South Carolina Company 5,000,000 acres, for $66,964; to the Virginia Yazoo Company, 7,000,000 acres, for $93,742; and to the Tennessee Yazoo Company, 3,500,000 acres, for $46,875. These companies not complying with the requirements of the sale, a succeeding legislature declared the bargain a nullity. Some of the purchasers contested the claims, and litigations arose, which became still more complicated when the same lands were sold to other companies. (B. J. L)

of gentlemen." The necessity for conversing with this company and maintaining the responsibilities of his high office — perhaps somewhat irksome at sunrise — as well as the nuisance of choking clouds of dust raised by the cavalcade, thus gave him at the very beginning of his tour a distaste for early morning escorts. The day's travel was uneventful, as is shown by Washington's own record: "Left Fredericksburg about 6 o'clock, — myself Majr Jackson and one Servant breakfasted at General Spotswoods [1] — the rest of my Servants continued on to Todd's Ordinary where they also breakfasted. — Dined at the Bowling Green — and lodged at Kenner's Tavern 14 miles farther — in all 35 m."

The events of Monday, April 11th, are also set out with almost painful brevity in the following bare recital of the diary: "Took an early breakfast at Kinner's — bated at one Rawling's half way between that & Richmond, and dined at the latter about 3 o'clock. — On my arrival was saluted by the Cannon of the place — waited on by the Governor [2] and other Gentlemen — and saw the City illuminated at night."

[1] Alexander Spotswood was the oldest son of John Spotswood, who was the oldest son of the colonial governor, Alexander Spotswood. The General Spotswood mentioned by Washington was commissioned Major in the 2d Virginia Regiment, August 17, 1775; Lieutenant-Colonel, May 7, 1776; Colonel, February 21, 1777; resigned October 9, 1777. He was a Brigadier-General in the State line, whence he derived his title. He and Washington were intimate friends, and frequently corresponded on agricultural matters. He died December 20, 1818.

[2] Beverley Randolph, son of Peter and Lucy (Bolling) Randolph, was born at "Chatsworth," Henrico County, Virginia, in 1754. He was graduated from William and Mary College, of which he was appointed a visitor in 1784. An ardent patriot, he was a member of the Virginia

GENERAL ALEXANDER SPOTSWOOD
Brother of Colonel John Spotswood

ELIZABETH WASHINGTON
Who became Mrs. Alexander Spotswood

The genuine interest attaching to the James River Navigation Company makes memorable the tour of inspection of the Canal which Washington made on the following day. A brief account of the origin and operations of the Company may find excuse for being in the close association of Washington with its interests.

As early as October, 1765, there was passed by the General Assembly of Virginia an act looking to the extension of the navigation of the James River, from Westham downwards through the great falls, and commissioners were designated to arrange for the digging and opening of such canals and aqueducts as might appear necessary. It was not until May, 1784, however, that the General Assembly passed an act making it lawful to "open books in the City of Richmond for receiving and entering subscriptions to the amount of one hundred thousand dollars," the said subscribers to be known as the "James River Company" in case fifty thousand dollars or more should be raised. On his return from the long journey through the Western Country, Washington wrote from Mount Vernon (October 10, 1784) to Governor Benjamin Harrison as follows:

I shall take the liberty now, my dear sir, to suggest a matter which would mark your administration as an important era in the annals of this country — if it should be recommended by you and adopted by the Assembly.

Assembly during the Revolution. In 1787 he was chosen President of the Executive Council of Virginia. On December 1, 1788, he succeeded his relative, Edmund Randolph, as Governor of Virginia. He served three consecutive terms of one year each. His administration was notable for Indian depredations and the relations of Virginia to Pennsylvania. He died at his home, "Green Creek," in Cumberland County, Virginia, in February, 1797.

It has long been my opinion that the shortest, easiest and least expensive communication with the invaluable country back of us, would be by one or both of the rivers of this State. A combination of circumstances makes the present juncture more favorable for Virginia, than for any other State in the union, to fix these matters. It is my opinion that Commissioners be appointed to make an actual survey of the James River from tide-water to its source.

It is well known that when Washington went to Richmond to meet the Marquis de Lafayette on November 15, 1784, he had conferences with certain members of the Assembly on the subject of opening the James River; and it has been stated[1] that the chief object of his visit was to further the projects outlined in his letter, above quoted, to Governor Harrison. At the session of the Assembly, January, 1785, acts were passed for clearing and improving the navigation of the James and Potomac; and one hundred shares of stock, of an estimated value of twenty thousand dollars, was voted to Washington, as Governor Harrison wrote him, "in commemoration of your assiduous care to promote your country's interests."[2] After mature reflection, Washington, who was sincerely touched by this "noble proof of the good opinion, affection, and disposition of my country," wrote the following letter to Governor Harrison, which was communicated to the General Assembly in session in October, 1785:

[1] *Richmond in By-Gone Days:* chapter "The James River Canal," by Samuel Mordecai. 1856.

[2] The preamble to the act reads: "Whereas it is the desire of this Commonwealth to embrace every suitable occasion of testifying their sense of the unexampled merits of George Washington, esquire, toward his country." (Hening's Statutes, col. 11.)

Your Excellency having been pleased to transmit me a copy of an act appropriating to my benefit certain shares in the James River Company, I take the liberty of returning the same to the general assembly with the profound and grateful acknowledgements, inspired by so signal a mark of their beneficient intention toward me. With these sentiments in my bosom I need not dwell on the anxiety I feel in being obliged in this instance, to decline a favor which is so affectionate in itself. When I was first called to the station with which I was honored during the late conflict for our liberties, I thought it my duty to shut my hand against every pecuniary recompence, and I do not consider myself at liberty to depart from such a course. Should it please the general assembly to permit me to turn the destination of this fund to objects of a public nature, it will be my object in selecting these, to prove the sincerity of my gratitude for the honour conferred on me.[1]

As a matter of fact, Washington donated his shares of the James River Company stock to Liberty Hall Academy, the seed from which sprang the flourishing Washington and Lee University of to-day. In 1775 the Hanover Presbytery in Virginia established near present Fairfield, Rockbridge County, a seminary of learning known as Mount Pleasant Academy. The next year this academy, often spoken of as Augusta Academy, was moved to a site near the present stone Timber Ridge Church, about seven miles from Lexington; and given the new name, Liberty

[1] Hening's Statutes, vol. 12. In a letter (Mount Vernon, July 30, 1785) to Edmund Randolph, acting President of the James River Company, Washington says: "I have therefore decided to hold the shares which the Treasurer was directed to subscribe on my account in trust for the use and benefit of the public. If agreeable to the Assembly I should like to establish a school on the James River for the education and support of the children of the poor — particularly for the children of those men who have fallen in defence of the rights and liberties of their country."

Hall Academy. At some time during the year 1780, the operations of the academy were wholly suspended, and were never resumed at Timber Ridge. In October, 1782, the trustees had the legislature pass an act incorporating the academy; and it was newly located on the edge of the farm of the Reverend William Graham, the first principal, near Lexington. The academy continued its functions until 1795, when a turn of good fortune materially increased the prospect for the future. The stock in the James River Company, which Washington held in trust for endowing some seminary of learning, had remained unproductive for ten years. When at last these shares gave promise of becoming productive, Washington began to consider donating them to some worthy institution. An address to Washington was prepared by friends and trustees of Liberty Hall Academy, urging its claims. In September, 1796, Washington officially communicated to Robert Brooke, Governor of Virginia, his decision in favor of Liberty Hall Academy. The letter acknowledging the gift drew from Washington the following reply, addressed to the "Trustees of Washington Academy," the name which had been given Liberty Hall Academy following Washington's donation:

MOUNT VERNON, *June 17th*, 1798

GENTLEMEN, —

Unaccountable as it may seem, it is nevertheless true, that the address with which you were pleased to honor me, dated the 12th of April, never came to my hands until the 14th instant.

To promote literature in this rising empire, and to encourage the arts, have ever been amongst the warmest wishes of

VIEW OF RICHMOND

From a painting in the Valentine Museum

my heart. And if the donation, which the generosity of the Legislature of the Commonwealth of Virginia has enabled me to bestow on Liberty Hall, now by your politeness called Washington Academy, is likely to prove a means to accomplish these ends, it will contribute to the gratification of my desires.

Sentiments like those which have flowed from your pen excite my gratitude, whilst I offer my best vows for the prosperity of the academy and for the honor and happiness of those under whose auspices it is conducted.

GEO. WASHINGTON

It was not until March, 1802, that the James River Company stock, which had a par value of twenty thousand dollars, paid its first dividend: six hundred dollars.[1]

On October 20, 1785, the stockholders of the James River Navigation Company met and elected George Washington as president, and John Harris, David Ross, William Cabell, and Edmund Randolph as directors. Owing to the pressure of many other obligations, Washington declined the "active presidency,"[2] and during the term of Washington's nominal presidency the active duties of the office were performed by other men, the first of whom was Edmund Randolph, afterward Attorney-General of the United States. Washington was a stockholder of the company for ten years, and was always deeply interested in its

[1] Consult *Washington and Lee Historical Papers*, No. 1 (1890).

[2] Writing to Edmund Randolph (Mount Vernon, September 16, 1785), Washington says: "I feel very sensibly the honor and confidence which has (sic) been reposed in me by the James River Company; and regret that it will not be in my power to discharge the duties of the office of President of the Board of Directors, with that punctuality and attention which the trust requires."

welfare.[1] It must be recalled that both the James River Company and the Potomac Company were incorporated in 1785, for the purpose of improving the navigation of the two rivers. Washington was selected as president of both companies, accepted the active presidency of the Potomac Company and served in that capacity until he resigned to become President of the United States. On the 29th of September, 1789, the members of the legislature of Virginia were invited to take a trip up the canal and through the locks. The canal was then opened from Westham to Broad-Rock, a short distance above the city.

In Washington's diary, Tuesday, 12th, 1791, appears the following entry:

[1] On October 5, 1795, on the retirement of Washington from the presidency of the company, William Foushee was elected as his successor, and held the office until 1818. Foushee was succeeded by J. G. Gamble, who in turn was succeeded by W. C. Nicholas, in 1819. By the act of 1785, the first James River Company was required to make the river navigable for vessels drawing one foot of water at least, from the highest place practicable to the great falls beginning at Westham, and thence to make such canal or canals, with sufficient locks, as would open navigation to tidewater. On February 17, 1829, the State took over the company as a state "enterprise" by the passage of an "Act for clearing and improving the navigation of the James River, and for uniting the eastern and western waters by the James and Kanawha rivers." The James River Company was under the control of the State Board of Public Works from 1823 until 1835, when the State sold out its interest to a new company, known as the James River and Kanawha Company, which proceeded to dig the canal from Richmond to Buchanan, in Botetourt County. This company sold out to the Richmond and Alleghany Railroad in 1880, and the James River Division of the Chesapeake and Ohio Railroad now runs along the old tow-path of the canal. (Compare *Richmond in By-Gone Days*, by Samuel Mordecai: chapter, "The James River Canal.") I am indebted for information to Professor W. F. Dunaway, State College, Pennsylvania, who has published a *History of the James River and Kanawha Company* (in Columbia University Studies in History, Economics, and Public Law. Longmans, Green & Co., New York, 1922, 251 pages).

> In company with the Governor,—the Directors of the James River Navigation Company—the Manager & many other Gentlemen—I viewed the Canal, Sluces, Locks, & other works between the City of Richmond & Westham.—These together have brought the navigation to within a mile and half, or mile and $\frac{3}{4}$ of the proposed Bason; from which the Boats by means of Locks are to communicate with the tide water navigation below.—The Canal is of sufficient depth every where—but in places not brought to its proper width; it seems to be perfectly secure against Ice, Freshes & drift wood—The locks at the head of these works are simple—altogether of hewn stone, except the gates & cills—and very easy & convenient to work,—there are two of them, each calculated to raise and lower 6 feet—they cost according to the Manager's, Mr. Harris acct. about £3000 but I could see nothing in them to require such a sum to erect them.—The Sluces in the River, between the locks and the mouth of the Canal are well graduated and easy of assent—To complete the Canal from the point to which it is now opened, and the Locks at the foot of them, Mr. Harris thinks will require 3 years.

During his stay in Richmond, it is most probable that he had his quarters at the home of Colonel Edward Carrington[1]—a soldier of the Revolution and a friend for whose

[1] Edward Carrington, son of George and Anne (Mayo) Carrington, was born in Goochland County, Virginia, February 11, 1749. Member of the County Committee in 1775–76; quartermaster-general in the Revolution, having been commissioned lieutenant-colonel of artillery November 30, 1776. Second in command to General Nathanael Greene in the Southern campaign, and was taken prisoner at Charleston, South Carolina. Commanded the artillery at Hobkirk's Hill and Yorktown. He was the brother-in-law of Chief Justice Marshall and the confidential friend of Washington. He was distinguished for personal prowess, imposing appearance, and dignity and sternness of manner. He was a member of the Continental Congress, 1785–86; mayor of Richmond; marshal of the United States District Court of Virginia, 1789–   ; foreman of the jury in the trial of Aaron Burr for treason in 1807. Was recommended by Washington for commander-in-chief of the American army, in the event of a war with France. He died in Richmond, Virginia, October 28, 1810.

good judgment Washington entertained genuine respect. Perhaps, too, while on this visit Washington once again visited the "Old Stone House," originally built by Jacob Egé and said to be the first dwelling erected within the city limits as then laid out — a house which had harbored beneath its sheltering roof Washington, Jefferson, Madison, and Monroe.[1] And as he passed that old wooden building, the *City Tavern*, his mind may have turned again, to that ball of the long ago, where "Minuets, Reels and Congos" were danced in his honor and for his delectation. On the afternoon of Tuesday, the 12th, Washington received an address from the Mayor, Aldermen, and Common Council of the City of Richmond — a ceremony which doubtless took place at the City Hall, although no mention of the place where the ceremony occurred is found in Washington's diary. This address of the Corporation of Richmond is interesting as an expression of the veneration with which Washington had come to be regarded by the great masses of the people. However factions might rage and political frenzy aim poison darts at the leader of the federation (without a capital letter!), the great masses of the people — sound and wholesome in their judgment — continued with increasing fervor to honor and to reverence Washington as the author of their liberties and as the founder of a nation.

The address, which was delivered at three o'clock, is as follows:

[1] See Egé Genealogy in the library at the College of William and Mary, Williamsburg, Virginia.

EDWARD CARRINGTON

Virginia

To George Washington, Esq., President of the United States.

Sir,

If in you the Mayor, Aldermen, and Commonalty of Richmond, beheld only the chief Magistrate of the United States of America, they would indeed feel all that respect which is due to the ruler of a free people; but when they contemplate those virtues which have excited the universal approbation of your own country, and the admiration of all mankind, they cannot approach you without emotions of veneration too big for utterance, — too pleasing to be suppressed.

If the voice of the people be the trumpet of the Almighty, the universality of that gratitude which pervades every bosom in America, will ever remain an incontestable proof of the plaudit of Heaven on the fortitude and wisdom which secured to our common country independence and empire, and which now leads her to wealth and glory.

We well know that to a mind like yours, fraught with benevolence and affection for all mankind, the gratitude and love of the nation, which you have saved must be the best and most pleasing reward; yet we are aware that to such a mind nothing could be more painful than that servility which would convert the sentiment of love into the language of adulation; we shun therefore the expression of the one, lest we should incur the imputation of the other; and while we beg leave to congratulate you on the astounding success which has heretofore attended all your endeavours for promoting the public welfare, we look forward with confidence and joy to the continuance of that administration, which, through the blessings of the Supreme Being, hath been already productive of so much general happiness to the American empire; and we implore that Being, propitiously to smile on all your future designs, to guard and protect you in your intended tour, to grant you every earthly good, and that, when his providence shall see fit to summon you hence, you may be wafted to the regions of eternal happiness, lamented by men and welcomed by angels.

Even the most confirmed admirer of Washington would wish that in this instance the fervor and obvious sincerity of the address might have inspired him to at least a warmer expression than that embodied in the following specimen of punctilious and lifeless propriety:

GENTLEMEN,

The very distinguished manner in which you are pleased to note my public services, and to express your regard towards me, demands and receives a grateful and affectionate return.

If to my agency in the affairs of our common country may be ascribed any of the great advantages which it now enjoys, I am amply and most agreeably rewarded in contemplating the happiness, and receiving the approbation of my fellow citizens, whose freedom and felicity are fixed I trust for ever on an undecaying basis of wisdom and virtue.

Among the blessings which a gracious providence may be pleased to bestow on the people of America, I shall behold with peculiar pleasure, the prosperity of your city, and the individual happiness of its inhabitants.

The home of Colonel Edward Carrington, fronting on Clay Street, was on the same square with his office, a very humble edifice shaded by a catalpa tree at the northwest corner of Marshall and Eleventh Streets. For his soundness of judgment and reliability as an officer in the Revolution, Colonel Carrington had won the respect and regard of Washington; and it is worthy of record that in 1798, when war with France was imminent, Washington selected him to be Quarter-Master-General. At the time of Washington's visit in 1791, Colonel Carrington was a United States Marshal for a large district in Virginia; and this "man of dignified deportment, which was well sustained by his tall and massive figure" — fit companion for the majestic Washington — was in a position to give the President accurate information regarding the state of public sentiment and opinion on national and political issues. In his diary (Tuesday, 12th), Washington records:

> In the course of my enquiries — chiefly from Col°. Carrington — I cannot discover that any discontents prevail among the people at large, at the proceedings of Congress. — The conduct of the Assembly respecting the assumption [1] he thinks is condemned by them as intemperate & unwise — and he seems to have no doubt but that the Excise law — as it is called — may be executed without difficulty — nay more, that it will become popular in a little time — His duty as Marshall having carried him through all parts of the State lately, and of course given him the best means of ascertaining the temper & disposition of its Inhabitants — he thinks them favorable towards the General Government — & that they only require to have matters explained to them in order to obtain their full assent to the measures adopted by it.

It is obvious that Colonel Carrington painted conditions in Virginia *couleur de rose*, and that Washington was only too ready to credit what he greatly desired to be true. In a letter to his friend, Colonel Humphreys, upon his return to Mount Vernon, Washington somewhat credulously voices his satisfaction: "Each day's experience of the government of the United States seems to confirm its establishment, and to render it more popular. A ready

[1] A part of Hamilton's financial scheme for the United States was the assumption of the respective State debts by the general government. This gave rise to violent opposition, and was the chief cause of Jefferson's bitter hostility to Hamilton. Out of the party feelings engendered by the assumption scheme grew the Republican party, that, during the latter years of Washington's administration, gave him much trouble because of the unkind spirit of opposition to the measures of the government. (B. J. L.)

acquiescence in the laws made under it, shows in a strong light the confidence which the people have in their representatives, and in the upright views of those who administer the government. At the time of passing a law imposing a duty on home made spirits, it was vehemently affirmed by many, that such a law could never be executed, particularly in Virginia and North Carolina. As it came in force only on the first of this month, little can be said of its effects from experience; but from the best information I could get, on my journey, respecting its operation on the minds of the people, (and I took some pains to obtain information on this point) there remains no doubt but it will be carried into effect, not only without opposition, but with very general approbation, in those very parts where it was foretold it would never be submitted to by anyone."

The record for Wednesday, 13th, is singularly brief, considering the fact that Washington appeared in public at a dinner tendered him by the Corporation of Richmond. This dinner to Washington by the Corporation of Richmond was held at the famous old Eagle Tavern,[1] which stood on Main Street, between what are now Twelfth and Thirteenth Streets. No other record of the events of this day has as yet come to light. Washington's diary reads as follows:

[1] Here, on March 4, 1805, the Democratic Republican Party gave a dinner to celebrate the inauguration of Thomas Jefferson for a second term as President of the United States. Here, too, on October 21, 1809, Jefferson himself was entertained by the citizens of Richmond at the close of his second term. In later years it was the scene of many historic banquets and entertainments.

Fixed with Col°· Carrington (the supervisor of the district) the surveys of Inspection for the District of this State & named the characters for them — an acct. of which was transmitted to the Secretary of the Treasury.

Dined at a public entertainment given by the Corporation of Richmond.

The buildings in this place have encreased a good deal since I was here last, but they are not of the best kind, — the number of Souls in the City are ——.[1]

After an early breakfast, on Thursday, 14th, the President set off for Petersburg. At Manchester the people were out in force to greet the traveller who embodied the dignity and distinction of the new republic; and full honors were paid the general in the salute of cannon. Indeed, to the President's surprise, he found drawn up at Manchester, to attend him as far as Osborne's,[2] the cavalry of Chesterfield County under the command of Captain David Meade Randolph.[3] Had Washington consulted his

1 In 1790 the population of Richmond was 3761. In 1800 the population was 5735. An approximate figure for the population in 1791 is 4000.

2 A point between Richmond and Petersburg, where troops under the traitor Arnold, and the republicans, had a severe skirmish in April, 1781. A prisoner captured by Arnold at that time was asked by him, "If the Americans should catch me, what would they do with me?" The soldier promptly replied, "They would bury with military honors the leg which was wounded at Quebec and Saratoga, and hang the remainder of you upon a gibbet." (B. J. L.)

3 David Meade Randolph (born 1760, died September 23, 1830) was the son of Richard Randolph, 2d, of "Curles," and his wife Anne, daughter of David Meade. He served in the Revolution as Captain in Bland's Dragoons; and was United States Marshal for Virginia. He lived first at "Presqu'ile," Chesterfield County, near Osborne's, and later at the corner of Fifth and Main Streets, Richmond (the house afterwards owned by Mrs. Allan, at the time Edgar Allan Poe was at the University of Virginia). Mrs. Randolph was Mary, daughter of Thomas M. Randolph, of "Tuckahoe." The Randolph establishment in Richmond was dubbed "Moldavia," after Molly and David, its mistress and master. "Mrs. Randolph," says Mordecai, "was one of the remarkable and distinguished

own personal inclinations, he would doubtless have chosen to leave the cavalcade and accompany Captain Randolph to his fine plantation "Presqu'ile," of which the Duc de La Rochefoucault-Liancourt thus speaks at length in his "Travels":[1]

PRESQU'ILE, MR. DAVIES RANDOLPH'S PLANTATION

At Petersburg I had met Mr. Davies Randolph, for whom I had a letter; and, in consequence of his invitation, I went to his house and there spent a day. He lives at City-Point or Bermuda-Hundred, the place where the river Appomattox discharges its stream into James-River. Here the water is sufficiently deep to admit ships of any tonnage: and this in the place where the larger vessels discharge their cargoes into lighters, and thus forward to Richmond and Petersburg the merchandize which they have brought. City-Point is the spot where the custom-house is established for those two places. If the towns of Richmond and Petersburg had been erected at City-Point, their commerce would have been more considerable, their intercourse with Europe more direct, and Norfolk would not, as now is the case, have engrossed almost the entire trade of that part of Virginia. But City-Point lies low, and is surrounded by swamps. The air in the vicinity is not salubrious; and, in all probability, the detriment which the inhabitants must have suffered in point of health would have been sufficient to counterbalance the advantage of superior opulence.

persons of her day.... The friend who had named Moldavia, now [after she had opened a boarding-house on Carey Street, following her husband's removal from office by Jefferson] conferred on her the title of Queen.... The Queen soon attracted as many subjects as her dominions could accommodate, and a loyal set they generally were. There were few more festive boards than the Queen's. Wit, humor, and good-fellowship prevailed...." (Consult Mordecai: *Richmond in By-Gone Days;* also *William and Mary Quarterly*, IX, 182, 183, 250–52.)

[1] *Travels through the United States of North America, the Country of the Iroquois, and Upper Canada, in the years 1795, 1796, and 1797.* Vol. II. (London, 1799.)

MRS. DAVID MEADE RANDOLPH

DAVID MEADE RANDOLPH

Virginia

At a half-mile from the custom-house stands the habitation of Mr. Davies Randolph, in one of those long windings which James-River forms in this part: from which circumstance it is that this plantation bears the name of Presqu'ile (or Peninsula).

Mr. Davies Randolph is fully entitled to the reputation which he enjoys of being the best farmer in the whole country. He possesses seven hundred and fifty acres of land, of which three hundred and fifty are at present susceptible of cultivation; the rest are all swampy grounds, which may probably be drained at a considerable expence, but which have not yet undergone that process. Eight negroes (of whom two are little better than children), two horses, and four oxen, cultivate those three hundred and fifty acres, which he has divided into fields of forty acres inclosed. Of those three hundred and fifty acres, only forty, which are subdivided into six portions, are alternately dunged; the remainder never has been so.

The common rotation of culture in the country is, Indian corn, wheat, fallow, and thus again in regular succession. The lands produce from five to eight bushels of wheat per acre, and from twelve to fifteen of Indian corn, according to their quality. Mr. Randolph has deviated from this system of culture on his estate: that which he pursues is as follows — Indian corn, oats, wheat, rye, fallow; and he raises from ten to twelve bushels of wheat per acre, and from eighteen to twenty-five of Indian corn. The rise in the price of wheat has induced him to vary the rotation of his crops, and to substitute that of wheat, oats or rye, wheat, two years' fallow. By pursuing this method, he reaps from thirteen to sixteen bushels of wheat. He separately cultivates the Indian corn in one or two fields according to his former rotation. He has proved by experience that manuring with dung triples the produce. His lands are good; and, compared with the rest of the country, they are kept in very excellent condition, though very indifferently in comparison with the most ordinary husbandry of Europe. He keeps no cows except for the purposes of the dairy, and to furnish him with calves for his own consumption. His cows are very fine, and of his own rearing. His labouring oxen are of a small breed; and it is thought in the country that those of larger size could not stand the heat. He purchases those labouring oxen at thirty dollars the pair. Mr. Randolph feeds thirty sheep, but merely for the supply of his own table.

He declares that each of his negroes last year produced to him, after all expences paid, a net sum of three hundred dollars, although he sold his wheat for no more than a dollar the bushel. He expected that they would this year have cleared him four hundred dollars each; but the fall in the prices of produce will disappoint his hopes.

The situation of his house gives him also the means of annually selling eight or nine hundred dollars' worth of fish — sturgeon, shad, and herrings, which he salts.

His swampy grounds supply him with abundance of timber for fuel and fences: but they produce a still greater abundance of noxious exhalations which prove a source of frequent and dangerous diseases. Mr. Randolph is himself very sickly; and his young and amiable wife has not enjoyed one month of good health since she first came to live on this plantation. Accordingly Mr. Randolph intends to quit it, and remove to Richmond, where moreover he has frequent business in consequence of his office, which is that of marshal to the state. He wishes to sell this plantation, which, in the worst years, has brought him in eighteen hundred dollars, and which, for the last two years, has yielded him three thousand five hundred. It is in very good condition: but he cannot find a purchaser for it at the sum of twenty thousand dollars, which he demands. This fact furnishes a proper idea of the low price of land in Virginia. I have been assured, that, although some of the lands have doubled their value during the last twenty years, a much greater portion have fallen in their price.

At Osborne's, the company was swelled by the addition of the cavalry of Prince George and Dinwiddie Counties, and a considerable number of the citizens of Petersburg.

Much interest had been displayed by the people of

Petersburg long in advance of Washington's coming. On March 22d, at the house of Robert Armistead (which was used both by the Hustings Court and the Common Council of the town of Petersburg), a meeting of the Common Council was held; present: Joseph Westmore, Esq., Mayor, and Samuel Davies, Thomas G. Peachy, Rob. Bate, Joseph Weisiger, Archibald Gracie, Gentlemen Aldermen; James Geddy, William Durrell, John Story, Benjamin Smith, and Daniel Dobson, Gentlemen of the Common Council. In the records of this meeting appears the following: "The Hall having received information, that the President of the United States is expected shortly to pass through this place on his way to the Southward — It is thought proper in order to shew the sense and respect of this Corporation to his Excellency's person and character, that an address ought to be presented to him on his arrival in this place." The address finally delivered is spread upon the minutes of this same day. In the records of Wednesday, April 13th, appears the following:

It being represented to this Hall that the President of the United States is expected to arrive in this town to-morrow, and from certain circumstances that have taken place, it may be expected that a public dinner is to be provided for the occasion — It is therefore ordered, that Mr. Robert Armistead be requested to provide a public dinner to-morrow, to be paid out of the subscriptions obtained for that purpose — and, it is ordered that a Ball be also provided (out of the subscriptions already obtained) on Friday next. That the President and his suit be invited thereto, and that they also, together with the Judges of the District Court be invited to Dine on Friday with the members of the Common Hall, at Mr. Durell's — Mr. Davis, Mr. Gracie & Mr. Buchanan are appointed to contract for, and to provide dinner on Friday and to adjust the ceremonies etc. No member is to invite more than two gentlemen to dinner Friday, and is to pay for the gentlemen they may invite.—And whereas, It hath been recommended, heretofore, by the Common Hall that a General Illumination should be on the evening of the arrival of the President of the United States in this Town—But upon reconsideration the Common Hall taking into view the dangerous consequences which might attend a general illumination of the Houses, being chiefly of wood, in this Town, Do Request the Inhabitants to refrain from Illuminating either their Dwelling Houses or Stores on any evening during the stay of the President in this Town.[1]

As Washington mounted the high bluffs overlooking Petersburg, now called Colonial Heights, and saw the fair town stretched out before him, he may have thought of the famous Colonel William Byrd, founder of both the city he had recently left and the town he was now approaching. After visiting his plantation, called "The Land of Eden" and located on the Roanoke River in North Carolina, in 1733, Byrd recorded in his journal: "When we got home we laid the foundation of two large cities—one at Shocco's, to be called Richmond, and the other at the foot of Appomattox River, to be called Petersburg.... These places, being the uppermost landing of James and Appomattox Rivers, are naturally intended for marts, where the traffic of the outer inhabitants must centre. Thus did we build not castles only, but cities in the air." As the President entered the town, he passed beneath triumphal arches which had been erected for the occasion; and was con-

[1] Robert Armistead was the proprietor of Armistead's Tavern, afterwards known as Powell's Tavern.

ducted to the house of Robert Armistead, "where an elegant entertainment was provided, at which the President was pleased to favour the citizens with his presence. After dinner a number of patriotic toasts were drunk, attended by a discharge of cannon." [1] Owing to the fact that the President was to be in town only on Thursday, the dinner at Durell's Tavern on Old Street — once famous as the Golden Ball Tavern, where the British officers had been quartered during the Revolution — which had been planned for Friday, was of necessity abandoned. However, a committee from the Common-Hall, headed by the Mayor, Joseph Westmore, waited upon the President, and delivered the following "Address of the Mayor, Recorder, Aldermen, and Common Council, of the town of Petersburg." This address is significant, in that it expressly states that the people of Petersburg look upon Washington as "the Father of his Country" — which gives a clue to that veneration which Washington had inspired in the people everywhere.

To the President of the United States
Sir

We avail ourselves of the earliest opportunity that your presence has afforded us, to offer you our sincere and affectionate respects; to welcome you, most cordially, to this place, and to assure you, which we do with confidence of the high regard and great affection the inhabitants of this town entertain for your person, and your many virtues. We look upon you, Sir, as the father of your country, and the friend of mankind, and when we contemplate your character in that light, we feel ourselves impressed with the purest sentiments of gratitude, respect and veneration. May you long continue at the head

[1] *Virginia Herald, and Fredericksburg Advertiser*, April 28, 1791.

of our government, honoured, respected and beloved, as you are at present, and we pray, most ardently, that the all-wise Director of human events, may prolong your life to a far distant period of time, and may bless you to your latest breath, with health uninterrupted, and with that happy tranquility of mind which ever flows from a conscious rectitude, and from a heart always anxious to promote the happiness of the human race.

We sincerely wish that the tour which you are about to make, may be an agreeable one, and that it may afford you every imaginable satisfaction.

The President made the following conventionally phrased, yet doubtless sincerely felt reply:

Gentlemen,

Receiving with pleasure, I reply with sincerity to your flattering and affectionate address. I render justice to your regard, and to my own feelings, when I express the gratitude which the sentiments it contains have inspired, and you will allow me to say, that gratitude so impressed, must be lasting.

The government of the United States, originating in the wisdom, supported by the virtue, and having no other object than the happiness of the people, reposes not on the exertions of an individual — yet, as far as integrity of intention may justify the belief, my agency in the administration will be consonant to your favourable opinions; — and my private wishes will always be proffered for the prosperity of Petersburg and the particular welfare of its inhabitants.[1]

In addition to the public dinner given by the Mayor and Corporation, Washington in the evening attended an "Assembly" or ball at the Mason's Hall at which, according to his diary, there were present "between 60 and 70 ladies." It is plain that Washington was wholly uninter-

[1] Washington's reply to the address of welcome appears upon the town records, beneath the entry: "At a court of Common Council held in the town of Petersburg on Thursday 14th of April 1791."

ested in the number of men who were present, as he does not refer to them!

Agriculture and commerce always constitute the main points of interest with Washington, as the following entry indicates:

> Petersburg which is said to contain near 3000 Souls is well situated for trade at present, but when the James River navigation is completed and the cut from Elizabeth River to Pasquotanck effected it must decline & and that very considerably. — At present it receives at the Inspections nearly a third of the Tobacco exported from the whole State besides a considerable quantity of Wheat and flour — much of the former being Manufactured at the Mills near the Town — Chief of the buildings, in this town are under the hill & unpleasantly situated, but the heights around it are agreeable.
>
> The Road from Richmond to this place passes through a poor country principally covered with Pine except the interval lands on the River which we left on our left.

Perhaps it is worthy of record that Pollock, in his "Guide,"[1] observes: "From this it will be seen that Washington was by no means an infallible prophet, for neither did the population of Petersburg fall off nor was his beloved scheme of James River navigation ever 'completed.'" The brevity of Washington's visit doubtless prevented a visit to that "most unique memorial in America," Old Blandford Church — "standing in quiet beauty amid acres of heroic dust" — concerning which the Irish tragedian, Tyrone Power, it is believed, penned the lines:

[1] *Historical and Industrial Guide to Petersburg, Virginia,* by Edward Pollock. Petersburg, 1860.

O! could we call the many back
Who've gathered here in vain, —
Who've careless roved where we do now,
Who'll never meet again:
. . . .
How would our very souls be stirred,
To meet the earnest gaze
Of the lovely and the beautiful
The lights of other days!

Petersburg enjoys the unenviable distinction of being the scene of the departure of Washington — for the only historically recorded occasion — from the strait and narrow path of strict veracity. The preceding day, the dust kicked up by the numerous cavalry of Chesterfield, Prince William, and Dinwiddie had got into the eyes, throat, and nostrils of the long-suffering *pater suæ patriæ* — and made him most uncomfortable. How endeared we are to the supposed "hero of the cherry-tree story," to the improbable person who "could not tell a lie," by this thoroughly human trait — the truth of the incident being attested by the fact that it is recorded by Washington himself in his diary!

Friday, April 15th.

Having suffered very much by the dust yesterday — and finding that parties of Horse & a number of other Gentlemen were intending to attend me part of the way to-day, I caused their enquiries respecting the time of my setting out, to be answered that, I should endeavor to do it before eight o'clock; but I did it a little after five, by which means I avoided the inconveniences above mentioned.

With Jesuitical piety, the hero-worshipping Edward Everett apologetically observes: "The President started

DRY-POINT ETCHING BY JOSEPH WRIGHT

from Petersburg practicing a little artifice as to the time of his departure — of which I recollect no other instance in his whole career — and which, involving no departure from the strictest truth, and resorted to for the best of reasons, will not be blamed"!

CHAPTER IV

THE SECOND STAGE

North Carolina: Halifax, Tarborough, Greenville, New Berne

TO Washington, who always rejoiced when his conduct evoked the plaudits of the nation, must have come a sense of gratification amounting to elation on observing the popular approbation of the Southern tour. The President was heartily commended in the press of the day for combining "the pleasant" and "the useful"— for taking an outing which would be not merely beneficial to his health and a pleasing relaxation from the weighty affairs of government, but primarily designed for the benefit of the people at large. "Perhaps as the former King of Spain," comments a representative writer, "he might have chosen to sport away an hour now and then in bobbing for gudgeon, or shooting snipe — Or like the King of France regularly a fourth part of the day in stag hunting, or something similar — Or in imitation of the King of Great Britain, have indulged betimes in the amusement of a Fox-Chase; but let our WASHINGTON *set* the example — already it is followed — The Secretary of State, and a distinguished member of the federal legislature, have spent some time in a tour thro part of the eastern states. Their observations, and the information they will collect in their journey, will probably be turned to good account. . . . What satisfaction must it afford every citizen of these United States, to observe the pains our

PRESIDENT has taken, since the dissolution of the last federal legislature, to improve the interval between it and the next, for the good of the people over which he presides, by visiting the Southern extremity of the confederated republic." [1]

Everywhere, as Washington's chariot with its outriders and baggage-wagon passed along, it was recognized by the farmers working in the fields, by the slaves, by the children. When the shout went up: "The President is coming! The President is coming!" farmers left their ploughshares, negroes dropped shovel, rake, and hoe, housewives left their duties — all rushed down to the road-side and, as the majestic and awe-inspiring Washington in his impressive-looking chariot passed along, waved their hats and handkerchiefs and shouted "Huzza" and "Long live the President" with fervent enthusiasm. We must imagine these scenes, for they assuredly occurred — and frequently; but Washington makes no mention of them in the pages of his diary. The following extracts deal with two singularly uneventful days — there being no towns or cities along the way and no formal demonstrations of any kind taking place:

Friday, 15th. . . .

I came twelve miles to breakfast, at one Jesse Lee's, a tavern newly set up upon a small scale, and 15 miles farther to dinner; and where I lodged, at the House of one Oliver, which is a good one for horses, and where there are tolerable clean beds. — For want of proper stages I could go no farther. — The Road along whch I travelled today is

[1] *The General Advertiser* (Philadelphia).

through a level piney Country, until I came to Nottoway,[1] on which there seems to be some good land, the rest is very poor & seems scarce of Water.

Finding that the two horses wch. drew my baggage waggon were rather too light for the draught; and, (one of them especially) losing his flesh fast, I engaged two horses to be at this place this evening to carry it to the next stage 20 miles off in the morning, and sent them on led to be there ready for me.

Saturday, 16*th.*

Got into my Carriage a little after 5 o'clock, and travelled thro' a cloud of dust until I came within two or three miles of Hix's ford when it began to Rain. — Breakfasted at one Andrews' a small but decent House about a mile after passing the ford (or rather the bridge) over Meherrin River. — Although raining moderately, but with appearances of breaking up, I continued my journey — induced to it by the crouds which were coming into a general Muster at the Court House of Greensville, who would I presumed soon have made the Ho. I was in too noizy to be agreeable. — I had not however rode two miles before it began to be stormy, & to rain violently which, with some intervals, it contind. to do the whole afternoon. — The uncomfortableness of it, for Men & Horses, would have induced me to put up; but the only Inn short of Hallifax having no stables in wch. the horses could be comfortable, & no Rooms or beds which appeared tolerable, & every thing else having a dirty appearance, I was compelled to keep on to Hallifax; 27 miles from Andrews — 48 from Olivers — and 75 from Petersburgh — At this place (i.e. Hallifax) I arrived about six o'clock, after crossing the Roanoke; on the South bank of which it stands.

This River is crossed in flat Boats which take in a Carriage & four horses at once. — At this time, being low, the water was not rapid but at times it must be much so, as it frequently overflows its banks which appear to be at least 25 ft. perpendicular height.

[1] The Nottoway and the Meherrin Rivers unite to form the Chowan River, which empties into Albemarle Sound.

North Carolina

The lands upon the River appear rich, & the low grounds of considerable width — but those which lay between the different Rivers — namely Appomattox, Nottaway, Meherrin and Roanoke are all alike flat, poor & covered principaly with pine timber.

It has already been observed that before the Rain fell, I was travelling in a continued cloud of dust — but after it had rained some time, the Scene was reversed, and my passage was through water; so level are the Roads.

From Petersburg to Hallifax (in sight of the Road) are but few good Houses, with small appearances of wealth. — The lands are cultivated in Tobacco — Corn, — Wheat & Oats, but Tobacco & the raising of Porke for market, seems to be the principal dependence of the Inhabitants; especially towards the Roanoke. — Cotton & Flax are also raised but not extensively.

Hallifax is the first town I came to after passing the line between the two States, and is about 20 miles from it. — To this place vessels by the aid of Oars & Setting poles are brought for the produce which comes to this place, and others along the River; and may be carried 8 or 10 miles higher to the falls which are neither great nor of much extent; — above these (which are called the great falls) there are others; but none but what may with a little improvement be passed. This town stands upon high ground; and it is the reason given for not placing it at the head of the navigation there being none but low ground between it and the falls — It seems to be in a decline & does not it is said contain a thousand Souls.[1]

1 " Halifax, on the Roanoke," says McRee, "is the centre of one of the most fertile regions in America; it was long noted for the opulence, hospitality, fashion and gaiety of its citizens." It was at Halifax, on April 12, 1776, that the Provincial Congress of North Carolina "Resolved, That the delegates for this colony in the Continental Congress be impowered to concur with the delegates of the other colonies in declaring independency . . ." North Carolina was thus the first colony to "vote explicit sanction to independence." In his Journal (1783), General Nathanael Greene says "Halifax is a little village, containing about fifty or sixty houses, on the banks of the Roanoke, one hundred miles from the sea. . . . Mr. Wily Jones has the only costly seat in or about this place, and is one of its principal inhabitants."

At Halifax resided two men of eminence who had played important rôles in the dramatic struggle over the ratification of the Constitution by North Carolina — William Richardson Davie and Willie Jones. At the Hillsborough Convention in August, 1788, Jones had triumphed in masterly fashion in face of the eloquence of Davie, the sanity of Iredell, the wisdom of Steele — North Carolina rejecting the Constitution by a vote of 184 to 84. Jones was greatly embittered when, the following year, North Carolina ratified the Constitution. It is said that, on being asked to act as chairman of the committee concerned with the entertainment of Washington during his stay in Halifax, Jones declined with the observation: "I shall be glad to greet General Washington as soldier and man; but I am unwilling to greet him in his official capacity as President of the United States." [1]

At Halifax Washington was doubtless greeted and with especial warmth, by his Masonic brethren of the famous Royal White Hart Lodge [2] — the second oldest Masonic

[1] Willie Jones was a personality of strange eccentricity, as well as of great gifts. At one time he was President of the Council of Safety, and so acting Governor of North Carolina until the election of Governor Richard Caswell in 1776. Elected in 1787, he declined to serve as delegate to the Convention at Philadelphia to adopt the Constitution of the United States, which he vehemently opposed. Among other curious clauses in his will is the following: "My family and friends are not to mourn my death even by a black rag; on the contrary I give to my wife and three daughters each a Quaker colored silk to make them hoods on the occasion"! Cf. W. C. Allen: *History of Halifax County* (Boston, 1918).

[2] At the meeting of the Royal White Hart Lodge, December 27, 1799, notice having been given of the "death of our beloved Brother George Washington, Grand Master of the United States," it was:

"Resolved unanimously, that this Lodge go into the usual mourning for the day & that the members thereof wear a white Crape around their left

lodge in North Carolina and chartered by the Revolutionary patriot, Cornelius Harnett. Here somewhat earlier dwelt the distinguished citizen, Joseph Montfort, sometime Master of this lodge, who held from the Duke of Beaufort, Grand Master of England, a commission as "Provincial Grand Master of and for America." [1] One of his daughters, Mary, was the wife of Willie Jones; the other, Elizabeth, the wife of Colonel John Baptista Ashe.[2] On Sunday, 17th, "Col^o. Ashe the Representative of the district in which this town stands, and several other Gentlemen," records Washington in his diary, "called upon, and invited me to partake of a dinner which the Inhabitants were desirous of seeing me at & excepting it dined with them accordingly." The local tradition

arm for the space of one month, in testimony of their respect & affection for the said dec'd & in remembrance of his many patriotic and masonic virtues."

This resolution was ordered published; and on the following February 22d, the Lodge ordered a "funeral oration" to be delivered, which was duly done by the brother, the Reverend James L. Wilson.

For this information I am indebted to Sterling Marshall Gary, Esq., Clerk of the Superior Court, Halifax County.

[1] The original document, which is unique in Masonic history, is preserved in the archives of Masonry in North Carolina. See *Proceedings of the Grand Council Royal and Select Masters of North Carolina* (1911).

[2] John Baptista Ashe, born at Rocky Point, North Carolina (1748), was the son of Governor John Ashe and Mary (Porter) Ashe. Fought at the Battle of Alamance in 1771. Early in the Revolution was appointed captain in the Sixth Regiment of Continental Troops. Served under General Greene at the Battle of Eutaw Springs. Attained rank of lieutenant-colonel. Member of the North Carolina Society of the Cincinnati. Was married to Elizabeth, daughter of Colonel Joseph Montfort, October 7, 1779. Member of the Continental Congress (1787–88), and of the First and Second Congresses under the Constitution (1789–93). Member of North Carolina House of Commons (1786), of the State Senate (1789, 1795). By the Legislature in 1802 he was elected Governor of North Carolina, but died before being inaugurated.

runs that he was royally banqueted at the Eagle Hotel,[1] near the river in the lot almost opposite the Allen home, which is still standing.[2] A Revolutionary soldier, particularly distinguished for his action at the battle of Eutaw Springs, Colonel Ashe had already endeared himself to Washington — an additional tie being Ashe's enthusiastic advocacy of the adoption of the Constitution by North Carolina in 1789. At the banquet he probably regaled Washington with the anecdote of the retort of his wife to Colonel Banastre Tarleton during the Revolution when General Leslie and the British troops were quartered at Halifax. Tarleton often indulged his sarcastic wit in the presence of Mrs. Ashe at the expense of Colonel William Washington, her favorite hero. On one occasion, Tarleton vauntingly observed to her that he would like to have an opportunity of seeing this great hero, who he had understood was a very small man. "If you had looked behind you at the Battle of Cowpens, Colonel Tarleton," she retorted quick as a flash, "you would have had that pleasure" — a taunt which utterly humiliated the British swashbuckler. Mrs. Ashe made another famous retort to Tarleton, who on one occasion said that he understood Colonel Washington was so illiterate that he could scarcely sign his name. "At least he can make his mark," retorted Mrs. Ashe, pointing to Tarleton's hand which

[1] The Eagle Tavern is advertised for sale in the *North Carolina Journal* (Halifax), November 18, 1805.

[2] In a letter to the Honorable James Iredell, Esq., Philadelphia, written from "Hayes," May 23, 1791, Samuel Johnston writes: "The Reception of the President at Halifax was not such as we could wish tho in every other part of the Country he was treated with proper attention."

JOHN BAPTISTA ASHE

THOMAS BLOUNT

RICHARD DOBBS SPAIGHT

JOHN SITGREAVES

still bore evidence of Washington's sabre-cut. Thirty-four years later, when the Marquis de la Fayette visited Halifax, he called upon this famous lady's sister, the equally talented Mrs. Willie Jones, on learning that she was too feeble to attend the reception in his honor. "The meeting of the General and this venerable lady," says a contemporary print, "was truly affecting. There was not a dry eye in the room. The aged frame of Mrs. Jones was convulsed with feeling, and the General sank into a chair, overpowered with various and conflicting emotions." [1]

Monday, the 18th, seems to have been an unusually uneventful day; but we are grateful to it for one of the few traces of humor which the diary exhibits — Washington's tribute to the lone cannon which was so energetic in saluting him upon his arrival at Tarborough. The diary for the day reads as follows:

Set out by six o'clock — dined at a small house kept by one Slaughter, 22 Miles from Hallifax and lodged at Tarborough 14 Miles further.

This place is less than Hallifax, but more lively and thriving; — it is situated on the Tar River which goes into Pamplico Sound and is crossed at the Town by means of a bridge a great height from the water, and notwithstanding the freshes rise sometimes nearly to the arch. — Corn, Porke, and some

[1] Cf. Mrs. Ellet's *Women of the American Revolution;* B. J. Lossing's *Field Book of the Revolution.* It is claimed by the most reliable biographers of John Paul Jones that, out of gratitude to Mr. and Mrs. Willie Jones, who had befriended him in a dark hour in his early career, the young John Paul took the name of Jones. (Consult Mrs. R. DeKoven's *John Paul Jones.*)

The second anecdote related above has been attributed to Mrs. Jones; but the Honorable William H. Bailey, in his "Provincial Reminiscences" (*North Carolina University Magazine*, 1890, N.S., x) states that the "family tradition in writing credits Mrs. Ashe therewith."

Tar are the exports from it. — We were recd. at this place by as good a salute as could be given by one piece of artillery.[1]

In his diary of April 19th, Washington records:

> At 6 o'clock I left Tarborough accompanied by some of the most respectable people of the place for a few miles — dined at a trifling place called Greenville 25 miles distant — and lodged at one Allan's 14 miles further a very indifferent house without stabling which for the first time since I commenced my Journey were obliged to stand without a cover.

The name of the town of Martinborough, by an act incorporating Pitt Academy there in 1786, was changed to "Greenesville" in honor of General Nathanael Greene. The "one Allan" to whom Washington here refers was Shadrack Allen, whose place was known as Crown Point.[2] Here was located one of the earliest of Masonic Lodges established in North Carolina; in the records of a Quarterly Communication of the Grand Lodge of Massachusetts, held at the Royal Exchange in Boston on October 24, 1766, it is referred to as the "First Lodge in Pitt County." During his stop at Allen's, he was doubtless visited by

[1] As early as 1758 seven merchants, one of whom was Edward Telfair, afterwards Governor of Georgia, were selling merchandise at the village, Tar Burrow. In 1760 trustees were appointed by the Legislature of North Carolina to lay off a town, known as Tarborough. It quickly became a center of trade. It is said that Washington was cordially entertained at the "beautiful residence overlooking Tar River" belonging at the time to Major Reading Blount. In his diary, entry for August 30, 1783, General Nathanael Greene records: "We dined at Mr. Blount's in Tarborough, a small village situated upon the banks of the river. Our reception was polite and entertainment agreeable." For a sketch of Reading Blount, consult *Biographical History of North Carolina*, I.

[2] At this period Crown Point Inn, just south of Turkey Swamp, was a famous hostelry on the highway from Halifax via Greenville to New Berne.

some of the Masonic fraternity and congratulated upon the state of the country and his own achievements.[1]

Washington's diary of the 19th continues:

> Greenville is on Tar River and the exports the same as from Tarborough with a greater proportion of Tar — for the lower down the greater number of Tar makers are there — This article is contrary to all ideas one would entertain on the subject, rolled as Tobacco by an axis which goes through both heads — one horse draws two barrels in this manner.

No doubt Washington heard the latest political news from Allen, who was prominent in the county; indeed he had represented it in the Convention at Hillsborough, November, 1789, which ratified the Constitution of the United States.[2]

The house at which Washington dined in Greenville, if tradition is to be relied upon, is still standing; it is pointed out to the curious visitor and the transient motorist who perhaps stops for a chicken and waffle dinner. "On the weatherboarding near the front door can yet be seen some marks, which are what time has left of President Wash-

[1] The members of the Masonic Lodge at Crown Point, June 24, 1767, were as follows: Thomas Cooper, Master, Peter Bliss, John Simpson, Richard Evans, James Hall, Thomas Hardy, James Hill, Richard Richardson, William Pratt, George Miller, John Leslie, Nathaniel Bliss, Peter Richardson, James Glasgow, Robert Newell, Peter Johnson, William Brown, Bolen Hall, John Barber, William Kelly, Robert Bigwall, George Evans, Lenington Lockart, William McClennan, and Thomas Hall. (Cf. *The Beginnings of Freemasonry in North Carolina and Tennessee*, by Marshall De Lancey Haywood, Raleigh, N.C., 1906.)

[2] The patriotism of the people of Greenville is attested in the following resolution passed at a meeting, August 15, 1774:

"Resolved, that as the Constitutional Assembly of this province are prevented from Exercising their Right of providing for the Security of the Liberties of the People, that Right again Reverts to the people as the foundation from whence all power and Legislation flow."

ington's name, said to have been written by him on that occasion." [1]

In Greenville the tradition still survives that at Shadrack Allen's or at his brother John's, farther on, Washington met a young girl to whom he was at once greatly attracted. He is said to have taken her with him in his chariot to New Berne; and to have escorted her with him to the dance at the Palace that night. This was probably the daughter of Colonel John Allen.

On this day Washington broke his ironclad rule not to accept private hospitality, under any circumstances, on the tour. The situation arose through a misunderstanding; and Washington violated his oft-enunciated rule rather than offend the hospitable feelings of warm-hearted and unaffected admirers. "Left Allen's before breakfast," Washington records on Wednesday, 20th, "& under a misapprehension went to a Col°. Allan's, supposing it to be a public house; where we were very kindly & well entertained without knowing it was at his expence, until it was too late to rectify the mistake."

Imagine the surprise of Colonel John Allen and family, bright and early on a Wednesday morning, to see a handsome coach with outriders turn into the yard (near Pitch Kettle in Craven County) and draw up at the door. Lord Erskine, famous English advocate, afterwards Lord Chancellor of England, once wrote to Washington this startling panegyric: "I have a large acquaintance among

[1] Cf. *Sketches of Pitt County*, by Henry T. King, Raleigh, 1911. About the reliability of such tradition, there is always room for doubt; l.c., p. 101. This house is now occupied by Mrs. Henrietta Williams.

the most valuable and exalted class of men, but you are the only human being for whom I have felt an awful reverence." If so astute a judge of human species as Lord Erskine could address Washington in a tone of such impressive humility, then you may picture the excitement and flurry, amounting to consternation, of Mrs. Allen on learning that the majestic Washington wanted a little breakfast. Colonel Allen invited the guests in with simple and hearty hospitality; and Mrs. Allen summoned all the "cullud" help to assist her in preparing the breakfast. In an hour or so, the meal was ready, the bell was rung, and all filed out to the plain dining-room, where stood a board literally groaning with the very best the country could afford. On the table were a young pig, a turkey, fried chicken, country ham, sausages, eggs in every style, waffles, batter-cakes, and hot soda biscuits. Washington looked over the whole table, and ordered — one hard-boiled egg and a cup of coffee with a little rum in it! The others, however, fell to with a will and showed their appreciation of Mrs. Allen's repast by the havoc which they wrought.

When Washington asked the proprietor of what was afterward known as the "Cat Tail Plantation" for his bill, Colonel Allen explosively responded: "Bill! Why, you can never make a bill at my house for anything I can do for you." Washington, who until now had thought "Allen's" a place of public entertainment, yielded gracefully in face of the vehement sincerity of Allen, and cordially thanked his host and hostess for their homely and bountiful hospitality.

In after years Mrs. Allen was frequently twitted on the subject of the President's frugal repast — but, being a "good sport," she took the teasing good-naturedly, and invariably declared: "Well, there was glory enough anyway in having General Washington as my guest!" [1]

Having long since been apprized by his brother, the famous William Blount, of Washington's intended tour of the Southern States, General Thomas Blount [2] was eager to show every civility to the President. The following letter explains itself:

TARBOROUGH, 17*th April*, 1791.

GEN. SAMUEL SIMPSON
Ft. Barnwell.

DEAR SIR: — By a letter this evening received from Col. Ashe, I am informed that the President of the United States arrived last night at Halifax and the inference is that he will pass through this Town: but on that head my informant is altogether silent. I give you this information at the request of

[1] Colonel John Allen's plantation was on the north side of the Neuse River, about twenty miles from New Berne, and ten miles above Street's Ferry, where Washington was met by a delegation from New Berne. Compare "George Washington's Visit to New Berne and Vicinity," in *The Journal* (New Berne), May 1, 1891.

[2] Thomas Blount, fourth son of Colonel Jacob Blount, of Blount Hall, Craven County, and his wife Barbara Gray, was born 1759. He died in 1823, and was buried in the Congressional Cemetery, Washington, D.C. Served as ensign in the Revolution; was taken prisoner and sent to England. Represented Edgecombe County in State Assembly, 1792, 1798, 1799. Member of Congress, from Edgecombe District, 1803, 1809–11, 1821–23. Married, first, Martha Baker, of South Quay, Virginia; had one son, died in infancy; married, second, Mary Jacqueline Sumner, daughter of General Jethro Sumner, no children. One of the Commissioners to fix the State capital at Wake Court House, now Raleigh; and there a principal street, "Blount Street," is named for him. His residence in Tarborough was one of the show places of its day. His wife, Mary Sumner, enjoyed society and they entertained with generous hospitality. She survived him and made large bequests to Christ Church, Raleigh, and to Calvary Church, Tarborough, where she is buried.

Major Gerrard who is gone to Hillsborough, and expects you will repair to this place with your Troop of Horse to escort his Excellency through Pitt County.

If he should come this way, it is probable he will reach here on Tuesday night at the farthest. If you cannot bring your whole Troop it is my opinion that it will be proper to come by that time with as many as can be ready.

Yours sincerely

THOMAS BLOUNT.[1]

In his account of Edgecombe County, Jeremiah Battle says: "Adjacent to the Town [of Tarborough] is the county seat of General T[homas] Blount, where he has lately built a very good house, the best that is in the county. This is a beautiful eminence overlooking the town. An extensive grove surrounds the house; back of which is a tract of 20 or 30 acres of rich swamp, well ditched and drained; and is in a high state of cultivation."[2]

Colonel John Allen accompanied Washington from Greenville to New Berne, as did also the Pitt Light Horse under the command of Captain Samuel Simpson, who waited upon the President as instructed by General Blount. Evidently Washington was as shy of dust as ever,

[1] This letter was the property of Mrs. Henry R. Bryan, of New Berne, North Carolina, a descendant of General Simpson; and this copy was supplied me, as was also the portrait of General Thomas Blount, by Miss Lida T. Rodman, of Washington, North Carolina, a descendant of the Blounts. The original is preserved in the Hall of History, Raleigh, North Carolina. General Samuel Simpson, the son of Colonel John Simpson of Pitt County, North Carolina, the Revolutionary patriot, was a member of the Convention at Fayetteville, North Carolina, November, 1789, which adopted the Federal Constitution. He is referred to by William Blount in a letter already printed in full (Chapter I.)

[2] From *Thomas Henderson's Letter-Book*, in archives of North Carolina Historical Commission, Raleigh, North Carolina. Battle's account bears the date June, 1812.

for in his diary he records: "Another small party of horse under one Simpson met us at Greensville, and in spite of every endeavor which could comport with decent civility, to excuse myself from it, they would attend me to Newbern." At one o'clock on the 20th, the cavalcade was met at the landing of West's Ferry on the Neuse River by a number of "the most respectable inhabitants" of New Berne and by the Craven Light Horse under the command of Captain Williams. This delegation of the "principal Inhabitants of Newbern," as Washington describes them, was headed by John Sitgreaves, who had recently been appointed by Washington United States District Judge. This distinguished man, who served during the Revolution and at one time was aide-de-camp to General Richard Caswell, afterwards Governor of North Carolina, had been Speaker of the North Carolina House of Commons and a member of the Continental Congress, and actively favored the ratification of the Constitution when it was rejected by the Convention which met at Hillsborough, North Carolina, July 21, 1788.[1]

The delegation from New Berne, which consisted of

[1] John Sitgreaves, born in New Berne, North Carolina, about 1740. Studied law, was admitted to the bar, and began practice in his native town. In the Revolution, was appointed a lieutenant in 1776, and attained the rank of major-general. Represented New Berne in the North Carolina Assembly, 1786–89. Member of the Continental Congress, 1784–85. "He was a clever gentleman," says G. J. McRee, "and esteemed a good lawyer." His wife was a sister of the wife of General William Richardson Davie. He served as United States District Attorney for North Carolina from 1789 until his death. Upon his tombstone in Halifax is the inscription: "Beneath this stone rest the remains of the Hon.ble John Sitgreaves, Judge &c. After spending a life of honor and integrity in the service of his country he ended his days on the 4th of March 1802."

North Carolina

John Sitgreaves, James Coor, Samuel Chapman, Isaac Guion, Joseph Leech, Ben Williams, Dan Carthy, and William McClure,[1] received the President at the ferry

[1] James Coor, Representative of Craven County in the North Carolina House of Commons, 1773 (January), 1773–74, 1775; State Senator, 1777–87; Speaker, 1786; Member of the Council of State, December 20, 1776, (December 18) 1792, (January 20) 1795. Member of the House of Commons from New Berne, 1791. Member of the Council of Safety for New Berne, May, 1776; Commissioner in various capacities: Port of Beaufort (1781), on depreciation of currency, on printing of State certificates (1781), Port of New Berne (1776), for completing fortifications on Neuse River. Member Provincial Congress from Craven County, April, 1775, August, 1775, April, 1776, November, 1776. Member of the Provincial Council for New Berne District, September 10, 1775; Member of the Council of Safety for New Berne District, May 11, 1776.

Samuel Chapman, a prominent citizen of New Berne. Commissioned lieutenant (November 28, 1776) in the Eighth Regiment, North Carolina Continental Line. Received the rank of captain, Fourth Regiment, North Carolina Line (commission dated April 5, 1779). In 1782 he was established in New Berne as a merchant.

Isaac Guion, member of the North Carolina House of Commons from New Berne, 1789, 1790, 1793, 1795; borough member from New Berne in the Convention of 1788. Member of the North Carolina Council of State, (1779, 1780).

Joseph Leech, borough member from New Berne in the General Assembly, 1760, 1761, 1762 (April); Representative for Craven County, 1762 (November); Representative for Craven County in the State Convention of 1788; member of the Council of State, December 20, 1776; April 18, 1778; May 3, 1779; 1780; December 10, 1785; December 18, 1786.

Benjamin Williams, son of John Williams and Ferebee Pugh, was born in North Carolina, January 1, 1752. Pursued classical studies. In 1774 served as a delegate from Johnston County in the first North Carolina Provincial Congress. Also represented Johnston County in the Provincial Congress at Hillsborough, August, 1775. Elected (September 9, 1775) member of the Committee of Safety for the district of New Berne. Elected by the Provincial Congress (September 1, 1775) lieutenant in the Second North Carolina Regiment; and on July 19, 1776, was promoted to the rank of captain. Served under Washington, and in campaigns against Lord Dunmore and Sir Henry Clinton. On July 12, 1781, was elected by the North Carolina Assembly colonel commandant of North Carolina troops. Resigning from commission as captain of Continentals, January 1, 1779, he represented Craven County that year in the North Carolina House of Commons; and years later (1788) represented the same county in the House of Commons. He represented Johnston County in the House in

landing with the utmost cordiality and respect. The Mayor of the Corporation of New Berne, Joseph Leech, thereupon read to the President the following "Address of the inhabitants of New-Berne":

SIR,

With hearts impressed with the most lively emotions of Love, Esteem and Veneration, We meet you at this time to express the joy We feel in your visit to the State of North Carolina.

We Sympathize with you in those delightful sensations, which you now so fully experience when We reflect with you on our past difficulties and dangers during a long and arduous War, and contrast these with the bright, the glorious prospects which present themselves — of our beloved Country's enjoying in perfect peace, the inestimable blessings of Civil and Religious Liberty. Our Souls overflow with gratitude to the bountiful Dispenser of all good Gifts, that He has committed to your hands the reins of Government in that Coun-

1785 and 1789; in the Senate in 1780, 1781, 1784 (April and October), and 1786. He represented Moore County in the House of Commons in 1807 and 1809. Was elected to the Third Congress (March 4, 1793, to March 3, 1795). He was four times Governor of North Carolina — from November 24, 1799, until December 6, 1802; and from November 24, 1807, until December 12, 1808. He was married on August 10, 1781, to Elizabeth Jones, half sister of the distinguished Revolutionary patriots Willie and Allen Jones. He died in Moore County, North Carolina, July 20, 1814.

Daniel Carthy, member of the North Carolina House of Commons from New Berne, 1794, 1810, 1811. Agent of Messrs. Royal Flint & Co., merchants, of New York, through whom thousands of pounds of "Public Tobacco" were sold by the State. Member of the North Carolina Council of State (elected November 28, 1795).

William McClure, chirurgeon to the Sixth Regiment, North Carolina Provincial troops (April 17, 1776); surgeon to the Second Regiment, May 1, 1776, continuing in service until the end of the Revolution. Captured by the British at Charleston, South Carolina, May 12, 1780. Member of the North Carolina Council of State (December 10) 1785, (December 18) 1792, (December 19) 1793. Trustee and Director of the New Berne Academy (1784); Commissioner on Pension Claims (1785). Invented a new type of boat "calculated to improve inland navigation." Member of the State Senate from Craven County, 1795, 1796, 1797.

try during peace, of which you have been so lately the defence against the Arm of Despotism and Arbitrary Sway. —

May Almighty God prolong that Life, which has been so eminently useful to the Human Race, for it is not America Alone — but the World shall learn from your example to what a stupendous height of Glory, a Nation may be elevated—whose freeborn souls are fired with a sincere love of Liberty. —

It is our most earnest Prayer to the throne of Heavenly Grace that the divine Benediction may accompany you here and hereafter.

Because of the culture of its inhabitants, New Berne was known as the "Athens of North Carolina." It was beautifully situated upon the River Trent, memorialized in the lines

> Regretful waves, well may you weep and sigh
> For this bright Eden as you pass it by,
> For wander where you may, you ne'er will kiss
> A shore so bright, so beautiful as this.

In his diary (April 20th) Washington records: "This town is situated at the confluence of the Rivers Neuse & Trent, and though low is pleasant. Vessels drawing more than 9 feet water cannot get up loaded. — It stands on a good deal of ground, but the buildings are sparce and altogether of Wood; — some of which are large & look well — The number of Souls are about 2000. — Its exports consist of Corn, Tobacco, Pork, — but principally of Naval Stores & Lumber." [1]

[1] In his *Travels* the Duc de La Rochefoucauld-Liancourt records: "Newbern is situated near the confluence of the river Nuse with the Trent, at a distance of one hundred miles from the sea. Vessels from one hundred and eighty to two hundred tons burden, sail twelve miles above Newbern, and smaller vessels proceed a hundred miles father up the river. The exports of Newbern were estimated in 1795, at seventy-three thousand six hundred and fifty-two dollars."

At the entrance of the town the cavalcade was met by the New Berne Volunteers under the command of Captain Edward Pasteur; and upon alighting at the house designated for his entertainment, the President was saluted by a discharge of fifteen guns from Captain Stephen Tinker's company of artillery, and fifteen volleys and a "*feu de joye*" from the volunteers. Washington described as "exceedingly good lodgings" the famous John Stanly mansion. At the time of Washington's visit the owner was John G. Stanly, who is said to have made a princely gift of $50,000 or more, to General Nathanael Greene for securing supplies and paying the Continental forces under his command.[1] John Stanly, son of John G. Stanly, was but a lad at the time of Washington's visit; he was afterwards famous in North Carolina as legislator and advocate; and is thus described by Stephen Miller: "John Stanly was foremost (among the lawyers of Newbern) in age and natural gifts. His voice was strong, clear and musical, and his manner peculiarly graceful and dignified. In repartee and sarcasm I never saw his equal. His efforts in that line were absolutely withering. The composure of no suitor, witness or rival advocate could survive his pungent criticism. Ever bold and fearless, he at once rose to the breadth of the occasion, always wielding a polished scimiter with the energy of a giant and the skill of an artist." [2]

Writing in 1894, Charles Hallock says of the John

[1] There is reason to believe the story true in general outline. Stanly probably loaned General Greene a large sum of money when the latter was in grave financial difficulties.

[2] *Recollections of New Bern Fifty Years Ago.*

THE JOHN STANLY HOUSE IN NEW BERNE, NORTH CAROLINA

Stanly house: "This building . . . is in excellent repair, with broad concrete walks and ornamental grounds stocked with exotics and semi-tropical plants and fruit trees, the blooms of honeysuckle, cape jessamins, and roses mingling with figs, pomegranates and magnolias. The mansion is of wood but, although much over a century old, remains one of the chief architectural ornaments of the town, with its imposing square front and its interior decorations rich with mouldings and wainscoting." [1] On the wall of the dining-room in this house now hangs a portrait of one said to be a cousin of George Washington, John Washington, the maternal grandfather of the but lately deceased occupant and owner of the house, James A. Bryan, Esq. It is said that Washington was delighted with his entertainment, and had only one complaint to make: that he had been given no griddle-cakes during his stay in New Berne! That evening Washington devoted to rest; but the people celebrated the occasion by having the town "elegantly illuminated."

During the forenoon of the next day, the President walked about the town, accompanied it is believed by Richard Dobbs Spaight,[2] John Sitgreaves, François-Xav-

[1] "President Washington in Newbern," in *The Southern States*, May, 1894.

[2] Richard Dobbs Spaight, born New Berne, North Carolina, March 25, 1758; died there September 6, 1802. Was educated at the University of Glasgow. For a time served as aide-de-camp to General Richard Caswell during the Revolution. Was in the North Carolina Assembly in 1781, 1782, 1783, 1785, 1786, 1787, 1792, 1801. Was appointed by Governor Alexander Martin delegate to the Continental Congress in place of William Blount, who resigned April 25, 1783. Elected delegate to Continental Congress in 1784; and reëlected for year beginning November, 1785. Delegate to the Philadelphia Convention of 1787, and signed the Constitution.

ier Martin,[1] Joseph Leech, Isaac Guion, Samuel Chapman, and perhaps others, viewing the many beauties of the place, hearing the story of Governor William Tryon's extravagance in the erection of the Palace, which helped precipitate the War of the Regulators, and perhaps — who knows? — listening to fanciful tales of the fascinating Esther Wake, who some now say was only a mythical miss! At four o'clock that afternoon he dined with the citizens at a public dinner at the Palace — which Washington describes as "the Government House and a good brick building but now hastening to Ruins." It was pronounced "superior to anything of the kind in British North America" by the historian, F. X. Martin, who said that the unfortunate Don Francisco Miranda, when visiting it in his company, declared it had no equal in South America. A pediment at the front bore the arms of Great Britain; and the rear of the building was finished in the style of the Mansion-House in London. Over the inner door of the entrance hall or antechamber, was a tablet with a Latin inscription, showing that the Palace was dedicated to Sir William Draper, "the conqueror of Manilla," and also some verses in Latin of which F. X. Martin gives the following free translation:

> In the reign of a monarch, who goodness disclos'd,
> A free happy people, to dread tyrants oppos'd,

Elected Governor of North Carolina in 1792; and served in Congress 1798–1801. Killed in a duel with John Stanly on September 5, 1802.

[1] For a sketch of Martin consult *Biographical History of North Carolina*, IV. The contemporary accounts do not confirm the statement therein made that he was a member of "the committee to receive General Washington on his visit in 1791."

Have, to virtue and merit, erected this dome;
May the owner and household make this the loved home,
Where religion, the arts and the laws may invite
Future ages to live in sweet peace and delight.[1]

Although externally much out of repair, it was peculiarly fitted by historic association and original elegance to entertain the great Washington. The following toasts were drunk — with a will, and doubtless with true gustatory appreciation — each toast being announced by a discharge of cannon:

1. The United States.
2. The late Congress.
3. The State of North Carolina — given by the President and greeted with stentorian cheers.
4. The Patriots of America who fell in her defence.
5. The late American army.
6. The King of France.
7. The National Assembly.
8. The memory of Dr. Franklin.
9. The Sieur de la Fayette.
10. The commerce of the United States.
11. The friends of America in every part of the world.
12. The agricultural interests of the United States.
13. The Nations in alliance with us.
14. Universal peace and liberty.

After the President had withdrawn, the fifteenth and final toast of the evening was drunk with all the company standing:

THE PRESIDENT OF THE UNITED STATES[2]

Probably at this juncture the President's aide, Major

[1] For a full description of the Palace, consult B. J. Lossing: *Pictorial Field Book of the Revolution*, vol. 22, p. 364, second edition.

[2] A printed programme of the occasion, containing these toasts, was long in the possession of Mrs. Henry R. Bryan, of New Berne.

Jackson, read to the assembled company, who certainly received its sentiments with expressions of undisguised satisfaction, Washington's fervent reply to the address which had been delivered to him at West's Ferry on the preceding day:

TO THE INHABITANTS OF THE TOWN OF NEW BERN.
GENTLEMEN:

I express with real pleasure the grateful sentiments which your address inspires. I am much indebted, in ever personal regard, to the polite attentions of the inhabitants of New Bern, nor am I less gratified by the patriotic declarations on the situation of our common country. Pleasing indeed is the comparison which a retrospect of the past scenes affords with our present happy condition — and equally so is the anticipation of what we may still attain, and long continue to enjoy. A bountiful Providence has blest us with all the means of national and domestic happiness; to our own virtue and wisdom we are referred for their improvement and realization.

That the town of New Bern may eminently participate in the general prosperity, and its inhabitants be individually happy, is my sincere wish.

G. WASHINGTON.[1]

At New Berne was one of the most active Masonic Lodges in North Carolina, St. John's No. 2. It was founded by a distinguished citizen of Rhode Island, who had emigrated to the colony and established himself on his country estate, "Richmond," near New Berne — Martin Howard, North Carolina's first Chief Justice. This lodge

[1] To John G. Stanly, Esq., at whose house Washington was entertained, he presented the original of this letter. It was printed in a New Berne newspaper edited by the Honorable C. C. Clark prior to the War between the States. It is found in Vass: *The Presbyterian Church in Newbern, North Carolina.*

WASHINGTON AS A MASON

Engraving by A. B. Walter

was instituted on January 11, 1772, the charter being presented by Joseph Montfort, of Halifax, North Carolina "provincial Grand Master of and for America." Some of the earlier meetings of St. John's Lodge were held in the Palace.[1] This lodge afterwards built a two-storey theatre and Masonic Hall. When news of Washington's contemplated visit reached New Berne, the brethren of St. John's Lodge, No. 2, at the stated meeting held on April 1, 1791, passed the following resolution: "Resolved, that an address shall be presented to Brother GEORGE WASHINGTON, in behalf of this Lodge, on his arriving in this town." [2]

During the afternoon of April 20th, after the President had returned to his lodgings, he was waited upon by a committee from St. John's Lodge, No. 2, headed by the Master, Isaac Guion, who read to him the following address:

TO THE PRESIDENT OF THE UNITED STATES OF AMERICA.
RIGHT WORSHIPFUL SIR,

We the Master, Officers, and Members of St. John's Lodge No. 2, of Newbern, beg leave to hail you welcome with three times three.

We approach you not with the language of adulation, but sincere fraternal affection — your works having proved you to be the true and faithful brother, the skilful and expert Craftsman, the just and upright man. But the powers of

[1] In his *Beginnings of Freemasonry in North Carolina and Tennessee*, Haywood says: "Among the many crimes charged against the dark, dangerous and unscrupulous Masons of those old days, was the burning of this building in 1798, when they learned that the State intended to sell it; though, as a matter of fact, the conflagration was caused by an old negro woman with a lightwood torch hunting for eggs among the rubbish in the basement."

[2] Minutes of St. John's Lodge, No. 2, still preserved at New Berne.

eloquence are too feeble to express with sufficient energy the cordial warmth with which our bosoms glow toward you.

We therefore most ardently wish, most fervently and devoutly pray That the Providence of the most high may strengthen, establish, and protect you, in your walk through this life; and when you shall be called off from your terrestrial labours by command of our divine grand master, and your operations sealed with the mark of his approbation, may your soul be eternally refreshed with the streams of living water which flow at the right hand of God, and when the supreme architect of all worlds shall collect his most precious jewels as ornaments of the celestial Jerusalem, may you everlastingly shine among those of the brightest lustre.

We are in our own behalf, and that of the Members of this Lodge,

Right Worshipful Sir,
Your true and faithful brethren
Isaac Guion Master
Samuel Chapman Senior Warden
William Johnston Junior Warden
Solomon Halling,
Edw. Pasteur,
Jas. Carney,
F. Lowthorp
Members of the Committee.[1]

St. John's Lodge No 2.
April 20th, 5791

The President made the following reply to the brethren of St. John's Lodge:

[1] Isaac Guion, Samuel Chapman, William Johnston, and Solomon Halling had all seen service in the Continental Army during the Revolutionary War. Guion served as Surgeon and Paymaster; Chapman, Captain in the 8th North Carolina, served until the close of the war; Johnston, Captain in the North Carolina Militia, fought at King's Mountain; Halling, Surgeon of the 4th North Carolina Regiment, served until the close of the war.

To the Master, Wardens, and Members of St. John's Lodge
No. 2 of Newbern.

GENTLEMEN,

I receive the cordial welcome which you are pleased to give me with sincere gratitude.

My best ambition having ever aimed at the unbiassed approbation of my fellow-citizens, it is peculiarly pleasing to find my conduct so affectionately approved by a fraternity whose association is founded in justice and benevolence.

In reciprocating the wishes contained in your address, be persuaded that I offer a sincere prayer for your present and future happiness.

G. WASHINGTON.[1]

That evening (21st) Washington attended a magnificent ball given in his honor at the Palace.[2] The dancing doubt-

[1] "At the following Meeting of St. John's Lodge, No. 2, April 27, 1791, the Master laid before the Lodge the answer of Brother George Washington and ordered that it be read, which being done, Resolved that it be entered on Minutes of this Lodge." The above entry stands on the original Minutes. Both the address to Washington and his reply are recorded on the Minutes of the Lodge. The original of Washington's reply cannot now be found — and probably disappeared during the War between the States. Consult *Washington's Masonic Correspondence*, by J. F. Sachse (Philadelphia, 1915).

On January 18, 1922, was held at New Berne the one hundred and fiftieth anniversary of the founding of St. John's Lodge No. 2. Elaborate ceremonies were carried out including a pageant in which the reading of Guion's address and Washington's reply constituted the chief feature. The part of Isaac Guion was taken by his great-grandson, Judge Owen H. Guion; that of Washington by Colonel P. M. Pearsall; and that of the Mayor, Joseph Leech, by the late Samuel M. Brinson, Member of Congress. (See the *Charlotte Observer*, January 19, 1922.)

[2] On April 24, 1891, the original occasion was reproduced at a centennial ball in New Berne — "the invitation cards and others of dancing being in *facsimile*, and even some of the identical dresses being worn which appeared in the previous century. General Washington and Lady Washington were personated by Mr. W. P. M. Bryan and Miss Mary T. Oliver, and sixteen leading citizens represented the republican court. The ceremonies took place in the spacious hall of the new courthouse, which was tastefully decorated with flowers, flags, and evergreens. After a few appropriate introductory remarks from Mayor (Genl.) Battle, the ladies and gentlemen of the court, in costumes of 'ye olden times,' were ushered into the room

less took place in the Council Chamber which contained handsome decorations, the chimney-piece being ornamented by Ionic columns below, four columns with composite capitals above, with beautiful entablature, architrave, and frieze. Above the whole were richly ornamental marble tablets, on which were medallions of King George and his Queen. White marble was freely used in the decoration of the Council Chamber, dining hall, and drawing-room.[1] Some sixteen thousand five hundred pounds was expended upon the building; and the passage of the bill for the erection of the Governor's Palace in 1766 has been attributed to the influence with the members of the Colonial Assembly of the beautiful and fascinating Esther Wake, Governor Tryon's sister-in-law. The author of "The Defense of North Carolina" therein first tells this strange story, which appears to be confirmed by a manuscript recently discovered, in which Jones says of Esther Wake: "She was ambitious enough to desire magnificent parlours and boudoirs, wherein to receive the homage of her numer-

and took positions on either side of the dais, General and Lady Washington followed and took places on the platform, the latter in magnificent attire. Under strains of sweet music from the Italian band the courtiers formally presented themselves and were received in the most dignified and courtly manner after the approved régime. Then the court minuet was danced by ten couples of the city's *élite*. The 'Star Spangled Banner' and 'The Old North State' were sung by thirty trained voices; a solo followed, and then a flower dance by young ladies in fairy costumes, each bearing a colored lantern and a basket of flowers. Supper ensued; and the novel affair concluded with the 'Old Virginia Reel' in which nearly everyone present participated. The occasion was most enjoyable and the renaissance instructive and impressive." (From "President Washington in Newbern," by Charles Hallock, *The Southern States*, May, 1894.)

[1] Cf. M. de L. Haywood: *Governor William Tryon* (Raleigh, 1903); B. J. Lossing: *Pictorial Field Book of the American Revolution; Colonial Records of North Carolina*, VIII, 7–8.

TRYON PALACE, NEW BERNE

ous admirers. . . . The heavy taxes levied to complete the edifice [the Palace] contributed to inflame the rebellion of the Regulators, and was more than any other cause the immediate inducement of the famous battle of Alamance on the 16th of May, 1771. . . . It is gratifying to discover the secret source of power, even in the volition of a virtuous woman." And he makes the following quotations from two alleged letters — the one by Colonel John Harvey (January 20, 1771): "What can be said in defense of those Gentlemen of age and experience who to gratify a Governor's wife and to be sure her pretty sister should vote fifteen or twenty thousand pounds to build a palace, when the people were not able to pay even their most ordinary taxes, and what is still worse, then go to war with their countrymen, to enforce the unjust law"; the other from Isaac Edwards, the private Secretary of Tryon, to Judge John Williams (November 6, 1770): "The Palace is finished, and we are in it. The Governor is much pleased with it and the ladies are now ready to give entertainments in a state suitable to their rank and deserts. Miss Wake is in fine humour and is every day planning her party. She has a complete set of new and splendid robes just from home, and when she gets them on, and gets the young assemblymen in the big parlor, she can get a grant of money to build another house for herself." [1] At the brilliant recep-

[1] Manuscript enclosed in a letter from Joseph Seawell Jones to William A. Graham, New Berne, February 28, 1836 — now in the archives of the North Carolina Historical Commission. Little faith is reposed in the statements of Jones by some historians — Haywood, for example, contending that this "rare and radiant maiden," Esther Wake, was none other

tion to Washington, conversation doubtless turned to the famous balls given there by Governor Tryon and his wife, in this "palace worthy the residence of a prince of the blood." The Governor's assumption of royal style, against which "Atticus," who was reputed to be Judge Maurice Moore, turned the full volume of his attack, brought against Tryon this charge: "Your solicitude about the title of *Her Excellency* for Mrs. Tryon and the arrogant reception you gave to a respectable company at an entertainment of your own making, seated with your lady by your side on elbow-chairs in the middle of the ball-room, bespeak a littleness of mind which, believe me, Sir, when blended with the dignity and importance of your office, render you truly ridiculous." [1] What changes had been wrought in human affairs since the scene thus described, in that same ballroom! How solemnly must Washington have reflected upon the mutations of destiny under which the aristocratic Tryon, the Royal Governor, had been driven from this very Palace and where now the highest honors were being paid to that man, "arch rebel and traitor" to his King, who had driven the forces of that monarch to humiliating defeat and disgraceful surrender! In Tryon's office in the Palace were now stabled the horses of Washington!

than a "creature of fancy, brought forth from the realms of Fairyland by the pen of a sentimental writer."

For references consult Haywood's *Tryon*, pp. 74–76; Lossing's *Field Book of the Revolution;* Connor's "Was Esther Wake a Myth?" in *North Carolina Booklet*, XIV, 4.

[1] For the "Atticus" letter, consult Waddell: *A Colonial Officer and his Times* (Raleigh, 1890).

In the spacious Council Chamber of the Royal Governor's Palace, Washington himself was the central, majestic figure. Clad in black velvet with gold buckles at the knee and on his shoes, he held in his hand a cocked hat with a cockade in it, the edges adorned with a black feather. His hair, profusely powdered, was gathered behind in a black silk bag. At his left hip hung a long, slender sword, with finely wrought steel hilt, in a scabbard of white polished leather. He wore yellow gloves; and, contrary to his habit at his own receptions, he graciously greeted with a clasp of the hand those who were presented to him.

Prominent on this occasion was Richard Dobbs Spaight,[1] who had been present in the Continental Congress at Annapolis on December 13, 1783, when General Washington tendered his resignation as Commander-in-Chief; and had also attended as delegate the Convention at Philadelphia, May 14, 1787, and affixed his signature to the Constitution. On the year following Washington's visit to New Berne, he was elected Governor of North Carolina. At the reception, Mrs. Spaight assisted the President in receiving the guests, and danced the first minuet with the stately Virginian. Some verses may summon for us the scene:

Hail to the chief! 'Gainst armèd foes
  No more shall serried ranks advance:
In 'broidered doublet, silken hose,
  Our Washington doth lead the dance.

[1] Some years later Spaight and the younger John Stanly fought a duel in which the former was mortally wounded. Consult John H. Wheeler: *History of North Carolina;* also *Reminiscences.* Consult also Wheeler: *Richard Dobbs Spaight.*

The oaths are said, the seals are set,
The bugle's song is tuned to mirth;
Grave Valor hath with Beauty met
To celebrate a nation's birth.

. . . .

"What homage shall a subject pay,
What can a loyal heart afford,
To him whom millions name to-day
Their Country's Father and their lord?"
Still stepping as the music leads,
The stately Washington replies,
"The guerdon of man's bravest deeds
Is ever found in woman's eyes."

The lady's answering smile is bright.
The dance goes on. How fair the scene!
Earth scarce hath known a happier night,
For day hath never dawned, I ween,
That left such blessings in its track.
How well we love through fancy's power
To bring the glittering pageant back
To us in this centennial hour! [1]

We may be sure that Washington also danced with the young lady who had accompanied him to New Berne, especially to attend the grand ball. According to Washington "abt. 70 ladies were present"; and if he paid full tribute to the goddess Terpsichore, he was more sorely taxed than on many a battle-field — although it is of record that he withdrew at eleven o'clock, while the festivities were at their very height.

Before retiring that night, Washington made the following entry in his diary:

[1] From "Washington Leading the Minuet," by Mary E. Vandyne.

This town by Water is about 70 miles from the Sea — but in a direct line to the entrance of the River not over 35 — and to the nearest Seaboard not more than 20, or 25. — Upon the River Neuse, & 80 miles above Newbern, the Convention of the State that adopted the federal Constitution made choice of a spot, or rather district within which to fix their Seat of Government; but it being lower than the back Members (of the Assembly) who hitherto have been most numerous inclined to have it they have found means to obstruct the measure — but since the Cession of their Western territory it is supposed that the matter will be revived to good effect.

On Friday, 22d, the President recommenced his journey — being escorted by the Craven Light Horse and "many of the principal Gentlemen of Newbern" for some miles from the town. His departure was signalized by a discharge of guns, doubtless by Captain Stephen Tinker's company of artillery. Washington records that he "dined at a place called Trenton which is the head of the boat navigation of the River Trent, which is crossed at this place on a bridge — and lodged at one Shrine's 10 m. farther — both indifferent Houses." At Trenton he was cordially greeted by his Masonic brethren of King Solomon's Lodge, who presented to him the following address:

To the President of the United States of America
Sir

Impressed with the purest Sentiments of Gratitude & Brotherly love, Permit us the Members of King Solomons Lodge at Trenton North Carolina (now in Lodge Assembled) to Hail you Welcome to this State, & Salute you as a Brother

We should feel ourselves remiss in our Duty were we not to Congratulate you on your Appointment to the Head of the Executive department of the United States —

That the Great Architect of the Universe may long preserve your invaluable life to preside over a great & free People & to the Advancement of the United States in Opulence, order & Felicity, is the sincere wish of the Members of this Lodge —

By Order of the Lodge
WM. T. GARDNER Secy.[1]

April 22d AL 5791

Quite the most meagre entry for any day of his tour is that for Saturday, 23d. How Washington must have enjoyed the rest — the refuge from incessant congratulation, from the necessity for playing up to a great and solemn part, from the dust of enthusiastic and persistent escorts! On a day like this, he probably carefully read the despatches from the seat of government which reached him at stages of his journey and pondered over weighty matters of governmental policy. Yet even in so dry and meaningless an entry, one with imagination can fancy the thrill of excitement and the sense of importance which agitated the minds and hearts of the families of "one Everet," "Mr. Foy," and "one Sage." The exiguous entry for the 23d is only this:

Breakfasted at one Everets 12 miles bated at a Mr. Foy's 12 miles farther and lodged at one Sage's 20 miles beyd. it — all indifferent Houses.

[1] See Washington MSS., Letter Books, in Library of Congress.

CHAPTER V

THE THIRD STAGE

Wilmington, North Carolina, and Georgetown, South Carolina

THE Southern tour took place long before the birth of the Associated Press. But the newspapers of America in 1791 eagerly copied from each other long and elaborate accounts of the ceremonies accompanying Washington's spectacular passage at every stage of the journey. Essays on the character of Washington and poems written in honor of his arrival at some particular city reached a truly national audience. Particularly popular was the poem entitled "An Imitation" — being composed "On the Reception of the PRESIDENT at the several Towns and Villages, &c. in his Tour to the South."

An IMITATION.

All tongues speak of him; aged sights
Are spectacled to see him; the prattling nurse
Into a rapture lets her baby cry,
While she views him; the rustic lasses pin
Their richest geer around their sun-burnt necks,
Clambering the walls to eye him: stalls, trees, windows,
Are smother'd up; housetops & ridges fill'd
With various ranks of men, all agreeing
In earnestness to see him — old senators
Do press among the popular throng, & puff
To win a vulgar station; beauteous dames
Commit the war of white & damask, in
Their nicely gauded cheeks, to the wanton spoil
Of Phoebus' burning kisses. Such joyful shouts,
As if the *very* DEITY *who guides him*
Were crept into his human powers
To give him grace and honor!

Making an early start on Sunday, the 24th, Washington breakfasted "at an indifferent house about 13 miles from Sage's." The house, and perhaps the entertainment, was so indifferent, we presume, that the President does not even mention the owner's name — who thus lost perhaps his one and only chance to have his name go down to posterity. On Saturday, authentic information reached Wilmington of the President's approach, and the necessary preparations were made for his coming. So, three miles beyond the aforesaid indifferent house, at a place called the Rouse House, Washington was met by a party of Light Horse from Wilmington under the command of Captain Henry Toomer.[1] At the Rouse House, during the Revolution, was fought a sanguinary engagement between British and Americans, the British General Craig giving no quarter and massacring the patriots with the exception of a boy who escaped.

[1] Henry Toomer was probably of the Welsh emigrant colony from Pennsylvania and Delaware in 1735–37 and subsequently, to which the State of South Carolina made a grant of 173,840 acres along the Peedee River. They were Baptists. For generations the Toomers were prominent in Charleston, South Carolina. Joshua Toomer and his son Henry settled in Charleston, South Carolina, in 1693. This Henry's son, Joshua, with Joshua's son, Henry (the "Captain" here mentioned), removed to Wilmington, North Carolina. Henry Toomer was one of the Gentlemen of Wilmington who signed the paper addressed to the Royal Governor William Tryon (July 28, 1766), which affirmed that "Moderation ceases to be a Virtue when the liberty of British Subjects is in danger." He was a member of the Wilmington Committee of Safety (elected July 6, 1775); and was appointed commissary to a detachment of militia from the Halifax Brigade, under Brigadier-General Ashe. He was appointed by the North Carolina Legislature as Commissioner on Navigation of Cape Fear River (1778), and commissioner to repair Fort Johnston (1778). He was married three times, his third wife being Magdalene Mary de Rosset. Consult Catherine de Rosset Meares: *Annals of the de Rosset Family* (Columbia, S.C., 1906).

GEORGE WASHINGTON ESQ.

PRESIDENT OF THE UNITED STATES OF AMERICA

Engraving by Edward Savage after the portrait painted by him for Harvard College

Wilmington and Georgetown

At a distance of some six miles from Wilmington, the President was met by a committee of prominent citizens and in addition by a large number of the "Gentlemen of the Town" — among whom doubtless were gentlemen bearing such names as de Rosset, Ashe, Moore, Wright, Iredell, Lord, Johnson, Walker, Waddell, and Lillington.

Alighting from his coach, Washington received the greetings of the committee and other gentlemen; and then, mounting one of his horses, was escorted into town in the following order:

Four dragoons from the horse with a trumpet
The President and his aide-de-camp, Major Jackson
The High Sheriff of New Hanover County
with the Committee appointed to attend on the President during his stay
The troop of Light Horse
The Gentlemen of the Town
The President's equipage and attendants.

On reaching Wilmington, about two o'clock, the Wilmington Artillery Company, under the command of Captain Huske,[1] which had previously paraded, now gave a

[1] John Huske, said to have been born in Hull, England, emigrated to North Carolina prior to the American Revolution. He was private secretary to Governor Thomas Burke of North Carolina; and was captured along with him, by the Tory leader David Fanning, and conveyed to Wilmington. He was a confirmed Republican, and actively opposed the ratification of the Constitution. For some years he was clerk of the Superior Court at Wilmington. He was elected member from New Hanover County in the State Conventions of 1788 and 1789. He was married in 1784 to Miss Elizabeth Hogg, of Hillsborough, daughter of James and McDowal

triple "federal salute" — three discharges of fifteen guns each. Over the saluting battery floated the flag of the United States. "The President was then conducted in the same order," says a contemporary print, "to the house provided for his reception, through an astonishing concourse of people of the town and country, whom, as well as the ladies that filled the windows and balconies of the houses, he saluted with his usual affability and condescension. Upon his alighting, the acclamations were loud and universal. The ships in the harbour, all ornamented with their colours, added much to the beauty of the scene."

Thus was Washington escorted into town, and to the "very good lodgings" prepared for him — the tavern kept by a Masonic brother of the President, Lawrence A. Dorsey. At this famous hostelry, known as Dorsey's Tavern,[1] where public banquets were frequently served, the Masonic brethren were in the habit of occasionally gathering around the festive board; and on one historic occasion both the local lodges, St. Tammany and St. John, "proceeded to Brother Dorsey's, where a lecture was delivered by Brother Halling and the lodges called off and dined together in unanimity."[2] The committee were

(Alves) Hogg — occasioning William Hooper's pun: "*Entre nous*, Betsey Hogg will probably change her name before you see her — and, for the sake of a pun — and it is the first I ever made — will substitute the food for the animal." They left two children: John Huske, of Fayetteville, father of the late Reverend Joseph C. Huske; and Annie, who was married to Dr. James Webb, of Hillsborough.

[1] This building stood on what is now the site of the old Fulton House, at present called the Southern Hotel, on the east side of Front Street, between Princess and Market Streets.

[2] Compare *Presidents who have Visited Wilmington, North Carolina*, by

honored by an invitation from the President to dine with him at Dorsey's Tavern, which they did; and after a short repast, he took a walk around the town, being accompanied by the committee and many other gentlemen of the town.

Washington did not have his lodgings at Dorsey's Tavern, as it happened. The house which at first was "intended for him by the inhabitants for his reception and accommodation" was not ready for him; and while the city fathers were in this dilemma, "Mrs. Quince, a widow lady, whose family was then large, cheerfully made an offer to the town of her elegant house and furniture for that purpose, which was gratefully accepted." [1] The patriotic and hospitable Mrs. Quince, who doubtless gave up her house at no little inconvenience to herself, because of being a widow with a large family, was "the wife of Mr. John Quince, a wealthy citizen who has descendants now residing here. They had a very pretentious residence on the southeast corner of what is now Front and Dark Streets, the site whereon now stands the two-story frame house, for so many years occupied by the wholesale grocery house of Adrian and Vollers. Little do we think daily in passing that now unpretentious corner that the immortal Washington tarried there." [2] Not without regret must Washington have learned of the death, a few months earlier, of the courtly Hooper — one of that triumvirate

Iredell Meares, and issued as a souvenir on the occasion of the visit of President Taft, November 9, 1909.

[1] *Columbian Centinel*, June 11, 1791.

[2] *Wilmington Messenger*, April 25, 1901. This building, a brick structure, was destroyed by fire many years ago.

in the Continental Congress, Lee, Patrick Henry, and Hooper, whom John Adams called "the orators"; one who always "feared when Washington was not in command"; and who, when the Revolution was at its height, wrote of Washington in the following strain to Robert Morris: "When it shall be consistent with Policy to give the history of that man, from his first introduction into our service, how often America has been rescued from ruin by the mere strength of his genius, conduct and courage, encountering every obstacle that want of money, men, arms, ammunition could throw in his way, an impartial world will say with you that he is the greatest man on earth." [1] Sad, too, was it to miss that soldier in whom Washington had reposed such particular confidence, the intrepid Robert Howe — the soldier whom Washington, in a crisis in 1781, had sent to quell the mutiny of Pennsylvania and New Jersey troops, a mission so efficiently executed that Washington, in behalf of the country, returned a vote of thanks to General Howe and his troops. And perhaps, too, Washington, associating Wilmington with the days of his youth, affectionately recalled that trustworthy soldier, Colonel James Innes, his comrade in arms at Braddock's defeat.

On Monday, in the forenoon, Washington received a delegation of the citizens; and the leader presented to him the following address, which strikingly predicts the "effectual operation of the new constitution":

[1] Archibald Henderson: "William Hooper," in *Greensboro Daily News*, February 22, 1917.

Wilmington and Georgetown

To the President of the United States.
Sir,

We wait on you to offer the tribute of respect, gratitude and esteem so justly due to your exalted station, your eminent public services, and the extraordinary virtues that adorn your character.

We thank you for the high honour conferred on us by your visit to this place in your tour through the southern states, and salute you with the most cordial welcome to the chief sea-port town of the extensive state of North Carolina.

It may be proper to observe, Sir, that if the progress of agricultural and commercial improvement, in the state of which we are a part, bore any proportion to the great natural resources it contains, this town would probably have surmounted some of the obvious disadvantages of its situation, and become more worthy of the honor it now enjoys by your presence.

Truly sensible, that a system of government, at once benignant and efficient, is the sure source of safety and prosperity to every country where it obtains, We anticipate with great pleasure the effectual operation of the new constitution, persuading ourselves, that the same wisdom, liberality, and genuine patriotism of which there is so illustrious an example in the conduct of our Chief Magistrate, have hitherto influenced and will continue to temper the councils of the nation; We ardently hope that admirable political fabric, reared upon the basis of public virtue, may prove a strong pillar of support to the union of the states, — improved and strengthened by revolving years, may it be as durable as your fame, and extend the blessings of civil liberty to the latest ages.

Accept, Sir, our humble testimony, in addition to the innumerable instances you have experienced, in proof that the same sentiment pervades the breasts of the citizens of the United States universally, that to you, principally (under Providence) our common country is indebted for liberty and independence, that those invaluable acquisitions are become the means of permanent happiness, is equally an occasion of gratitude to you.

May you long continue on earth your country's glory and human nature's great ornament, and finally, in an immortal state receive from the Great Protector of the Universe, the rich reward that awaits the distinguished benefactors of mankind.

Signed WM. CAMPBELL
JOHN BRADLEY
J. FERGUS
G. HOOPER
WM. HILL
ED. JONES
JAMES READ
Committee appointed by the Inhabitants[1]

[1] William Campbell, a man of wealth and a prosperous merchant, was the brother of James Campbell, a prominent Scotch merchant and trader whose enterprises carried him back and forth between Boston and the Cape Fear region. His father, James Campbell, was a resident of Wilmington in the early years of the eighteenth century. He was a leading citizen of Wilmington, a member of the order of Sons of Liberty (1770), sheriff of New Hanover County (1774–75), and served on the Safety Committee of that town with such patriots as Cornelius Harnett, William Hooper, Archibald Maclaine, Adam Boyd, Henry Toomer, and Caleb Grainger. On October 25, 1775, he was elected a member of the Committee of Secrecy and Correspondence, but resigned soon afterwards, presumably because of Royalist sympathies. He lent money freely to leaders of the Revolution, and was solicitous for the welfare of Governor Thomas Burke, when the latter was a prisoner of the British at Wilmington in 1781. He was one of the original subscribers to Thomas Godfrey's *The Prince of Parthia* (completed in Wilmington), the first tragedy ever written by an American.

John Bradley, son of Richard Bradley, of Kendall, England, and Ann Sharpless, of Chester, Pennsylvania. His parents, both Quakers, who were married in 1734, removed from Pennsylvania to Guilford County, North Carolina. Later removing to Wilmington, Richard Bradley became a prominent merchant. During the occupation of Wilmington by Royalist forces, the Bradley family were ousted from their home and otherwise harshly treated by Craig. Richard's son, John, who never married, was also a prominent merchant. His four sisters were married to representatives of leading families of the Cape Fear section: Lord, Green, Wright, Brown. John Bradley was trustee of the Presbyterian Church at Wilmington (appointed 1785), and Commissary of Issues at that port for a time. John Rutherford describes him as a "peaceable and well disposed citizen," a man deserving of "merit in supporting a mother, brother, and several sisters, in ease and comfort, by his industry." In a duel on July 11, 1787,

In his reply, as was his custom, Washington dwells upon the virtues of the general government, and prophesies

he killed Major Samuel Swann. In a Legislative Report regarding this duel, it was stated that he "innocently and unintentionally gave an offence to the deceased Mr. Swann . . . and did everything in his power to avoid the fatal conflict." He was pardoned for this duel by the Legislature of North Carolina in 1789. He died in 1811. Consult McRee: *Life and Letters of James Iredell.*

Dr. James Fergus, a noted physician, was a warm adherent of the Revolutionary cause. He served as surgeon of the Sixth Regiment of North Carolina troops during the Revolution. He was probably the son of Dr. John Fergus, Justice of the Peace for New Hanover County, who is described by McRee, in the *Life and Letters of James Iredell*, as "of stately presence, with velvet coat, cocked hat and gold-headed cane, a graduate of Edinburgh, and an excellent Latin and Greek scholar." Under the title of "Surgeon's Mate," James Fergus appears in a list of the members of the North Carolina Society of the Cincinnati, founded at Hillsborough, October, 1783.

George Hooper was a son of the Reverend William Hooper of Boston, second rector of Trinity Church; and brother of William Hooper, signer of the Declaration of Independence, from North Carolina. He was a graduate of the University of Edinburgh. In a letter addressed to "the distressed inhabitants of the town of Boston" (July 21, 1774), in which occur very strong expressions in regard to the invasion of the rights of the American people, his name stands second in the list of signatures. When the drift toward independence became clear, however, he avowed himself as opposed to the Whig movement. "He was a loyalist from honest conviction," says G. J. McRee, "but took no part in the War of the Revolution, because he could not find it in his heart to imbrue his hands in the blood of his neighbors. . . . His relations with all the Whig leaders on the lower Cape Fear were intimate and cordial, and in despite of his politics, survived the Revolution. Respect for his character was general, if not universal. He possessed a vigorous intellect, was well informed, and reputed to be a good writer." As a merchant, he prosecuted trade for the major part of his life in Wilmington, and acquired a moderate fortune.

William H. Hill, the son of William Hill of Boston and a Harvard graduate; studied law in Boston. He was a brilliant lawyer, an eloquent advocate. In 1789 he was appointed by Washington the first District Attorney of the United States for North Carolina. In the State Assembly, Senate (1794), House (1797). Served in Congress, 1799–1803. Voted for Burr for President. Appointed Federal Judge by Adams, but the appointment was not confirmed. Lived at "Hillton" in the suburbs of Wilmington, and was a successful planter. He was thrice married: to Elizabeth Moore; Alice Starkey; Eliza Maria Ashe. Consult *Life of William Hill*, by A. M. Hooper; also, *Biographical History of North Carolina*, vol. IV.

prosperity for the country under its stable and benign influence.

To the Inhabitants of the Town of Wilmington.
Gentlemen,

Appreciating with due value the sentiments you are pleased to express for my station and character, I should fail in candour and respect not to avow the grateful sensations excited by your address, for which I thank you with unfeigned sincerity.

Reasoning from the rapid progress of improvement throughout the United States, and adverting to the facility which every undertaking must derive from a settled system of government, the obviation of those disadvantages, imposed by situation on your town may, I think, be calculated upon within no very distant period.

Edward Jones, brother of William Todd Jones, the Irish patriot, was born in Lisburn, Ireland, March 10, 1762; settled in Wilmington in 1786. Represented the Town of Wilmington in North Carolina House of Commons (1788–91). In 1791 he was unanimously elected Solicitor General of North Carolina, an office created for him and to which he was elected for life. He attained high distinction as a lawyer, by his talent and learning. Married to Mary Elizabeth Mallett, June 20, 1790. About 1795 he removed to Rock Rest, Chatham County. He died at Pittsborough, North Carolina, August 8, 1841. He was the friend and patron of Johnston Blakely, naval hero of the War of 1812.

James Read was born in Armagh, Ireland. He emigrated to North Carolina and "threw himself heartily into the patriot cause" at the outbreak of the Revolution. Appointed ensign, January 4, 1776; lieutenant, July 7, 1776; and captain, July 8, 1777, First North Carolina Continental Battalion, under the command of Colonel, afterwards General, Moore. He served throughout the war, distinguishing himself under Greene at Guilford Court-House and Hobkirk's Hill. After the war he stoutly opposed the adoption of the Federal Constitution. Was appointed Collector of the Port of Brunswick in 1785, pursuant to an act of the General Assembly (1784). Served as Commissioner on Pilotage of Cape Fear River (1783), Commissioner for the Officers and Soldiers of the Continental Line (1783–85), and trustee of Innes Academy (1788). He was a member of the North Carolina Society of the Cincinnati. In 1790, Wilmington was made the port of entry for the Cape Fear River; and he was appointed collector of that port by Washington in 1790. This office he held until his death in 1802 or 1803. He was never married.

The sanction which experience has already given to the salutary influence of the general government on the affairs of the United States, authorizes a well founded expectation, that every aid which a wise and virtuous legislation can render to individual industry, will be afforded, and creates a pleasing hope, that the happiness of her citizens will be commensurate with the growing dignity and importance of our country.

I express a heartfelt sentiment in wishing to your town and its inhabitants a full proportion of general and particular felicity.

G. Washington

In "The General Advertiser and Political, Commercial and Literary Journal" (Philadelphia, June 4, 1791), the above address to George Washington is dated Wilmington (North Carolina), April 16, and signed "In behalf of the inhabitants of the town of Wilmington, April 26, 1791. Thomas Wright." [1]

[1] Thomas Wright, son of Samuel and Sarah (Pettigrew) Wright, was the great-grandson of Thomas Wright, of Wethersfield, Connecticut, Deputy to the General Court in 1643. He served three years as a private in the Fourth Regiment, North Carolina Continental Line (April 29, 1776, to May 10, 1779). In Wilmington his house stood on the Southwest corner of Market and Third Streets; it was used as headquarters by Lord Cornwallis in 1781. The famous "Fairfield" plantation, on the northeast branch of the Cape Fear River, originally belonged to Humphrey, brother to Gabriel Johnston, Governor of North Carolina; and was purchased by Thomas Wright of the widow of Joseph Wragg. He was appointed by the North Carolina Legislature a Trustee of the Presbyterian Church at Wilmington (1785) and a Trustee of the Innes Academy (1788). He served the longest recorded term as Sheriff of New Hanover County (1782–98). He was married to Anne Grainger, daughter of Joshua Grainger, Jr. Their son, the distinguished Joshua Grainger Wright, was married to Susan Bradley, daughter of John Bradley, already mentioned. For Joshua G. Wright was named Wrightsville, village and beach, a famous seaside resort near Wilmington. Another genealogist states that Thomas Wright (2), was the son of Thomas Wright (1) by his first marriage; that he was married to Ann Winslow, of Fayetteville; and that Joshua G. Wright was the son of Thomas Wright (1) by his second wife, Anne Grainger.

We may be sure, from the evidence of the love of good things and the joy of living which the people of Wilmington have always shown, that Washington enjoyed "the elegant dinner at Jocelin's tavern" given in his honor that day by the gentlemen of the town. In the afternoon there was a "procession," doubtless a military parade, the soldiery under the command of Colonel Brown and Captains Toomer and Huske being reviewed by Washington; and in the evening there was a Grand Ball given at the Assembly Hall, which was sometimes called "Old '76," because it had been built in 1776.[1] At this ball — at which he notes the presence of sixty-two ladies — Washington "appeared to be equally surprised and delighted, at the very large and brilliant assembly, of ladies, whom admiration and respect for him had collected together." The same evening there was a general illumination and bonfires, the ship *Maria* of Boston, festooned with lights — deck, spars, and masts — presenting a rarely beautiful sight. So universal was the participation in the festivities by all the inhabitants that a contemporary print thus comments: "It is scarcely possible to do justice to the zeal with which every description of persons appeared to be animated to do honour and afford satisfaction to the illustrious visitant."

An intimate glimpse of the ceremonies, and of the excitements of these two crowded days, is afforded by a con-

[1] This building stood on Front Street, east side, between Orange and Ann Streets, where now stands the two-story brick tenement house owned by S. Teiler, Esq. It was later used as a sailor boarding-house and was torn down just a century after its erection.

temporary letter, written by Mrs. Anna Jean Simpson to her sister, Mrs. Christian Fleming, of Wilmington, who was then at Brown Marsh, now Clarkton, Bladen County, where her husband had a plantation.

25th April, 1791.

Many thanks, my dear sister, for your kind invitation. Poor Mary is indeed in a very bad way, she has not been out of bed but to have it made for eight days past, though I hope, as her ague has left her and the fever is less, that she will soon get strength to visit you. At present I am afraid she is too weak. I shall let you know by next opportunity when to send.

Great doings this day. General Washington arrived yesterday. The Light Horse went to meet him. The artillery were ready to receive him with a round from the batteries, four guns. This day he dines with the Gentlemen of the town; in the evening a grand ball and illumination; to-morrow takes his leave. I believe the Light Horse are to escort him a day's journey on his way to Chas'ton.

Half-past four — just going to dinner — cannons firing; Chrissy and the children all gone to see the procession. I don't go to the ball this evening as Mary cannot accompany me. She desires me to ask if you have many beaux at the Marsh. Adieu. I must get the candles.

Mrs. Quince has given up her house to the General and she stays with our uncles. . . .

Believe me to be your affectionate sister,

ANNA JEAN SIMPSON.[1]

Surviving down to the present time is the tradition that Washington asked "Lal" Dorsey, the keeper of the inn where he dined the day of his arrival, what kind of water

[1] This letter is owned by Clayton Giles, Esq., of Wilmington, a descendant of Mrs. Fleming. Mrs. Simpson and Mrs. Fleming were the daughters of Mr. William McKenzie, a Scotchman who once lived in Wilmington and subsequently removed to Georgia. Mrs. Simpson was the wife of Mr. John Simpson, of Georgia, who was a member of the King's Council for the Colony of Georgia and, at the date of her letter, is supposed to be visiting relatives in Wilmington.

the people of Wilmington had to drink — as he had noticed the very flat and swampy nature of the surrounding country. The impudent innkeeper, who preceded Volstead by a century and a quarter, replied that he didn't know — as he hadn't drunk any for forty years! Report hath it that, on receiving this reply, the tactful visitor, with a delicate appreciation of the local option then in vogue, made no further inquiries concerning the water during his stay in Wilmington.

In his diary of Sunday, 24th, Washington makes rather lengthy comment upon Wilmington and the surrounding country:

The whole Road from Newbern to Wilmington (except in a few places of small extent) passes through the most barren country I ever beheld; especially in the parts nearest the latter; which is no other than a bed of white sand. — In places, however, before we came to these, if the ideas of poverty could be separated from the Sand, the appearances of it are agreeable, resembling a lawn well covered with evergreens, and a good verdure below from a broom or course grass which having sprung since the burning of the Woods had a neat and handsome look especially as there were parts entirely open — and others with ponds of water, which contributed not a little to the beauty of the scene.

Wilmington is situated on the Cape Fear River, about 30 miles by *water* from its mouth, but much less by land — It has some good houses pretty compactly built. — The whole undr a hill; which is formed entirely of sand. — The number of Souls in it amount by the enumeration to about 1000,[1] but it

[1] The growth of the population of Wilmington was slow. By 1820 Wilmington had only 1098 whites, 1433 slaves, 102 free negroes — a total of only 2633. In 1765 it contained less than eight hundred people. If the increase in population were uniform, the population of Wilmington in 1791 must have been about sixteen hundred.

is agreed on all hands that the Census in this State has been very inaccurately, & Shamefully taken by the Marshall's deputies; who, instead of going to Peoples houses, & there, on the spot, ascertaining the Nos.; have advertised a meeting of them at certain places, by which means those who did not attend (and it seems many purposely avoided doing it, some from an apprehension of its being introductory of a tax, & others from religious scruples) have gone with their families, unnumbered — In other instances, it is said these deputies have taken their information from the Captains of Militia Companies; not only as to the men on their Muster Rolls, but of the Souls, in their respective families; which at best, must in a variety of cases, be mere conjecture whilst all those who are not on their lists — Widows and their families &c. pass unnoticed.

Wilmington, unfortunately for it, has a Mud bank, — miles below, over which not more than 10 feet water can be brought at common tides, yet it is said vessels of 250 Tons have come up. — The quty. of Shipping, which load here annually, amounts to about 1200 Tonns. — The exports consist chiefly of Naval Stores and lumber. — Some Tobacco, Corn, Rice & flax seed with Porke. — It is at the head of the tide navigation, but inland navigation may be extended 115 miles farther to and above Fayettesville which is from Wilmington 90 miles by land, & 115 by Water as above. — Fayettesville is a thriving place containing near Souls[1] — 6000 Hhds. of Tobacco, & 3000 Hhds. of Flax Seed have been recd. at it in the course of the year.

Upon arrival in Wilmington, Major Jackson received a courteous letter from a prominent citizen of Charleston — perhaps Intendant Arnoldus Vanderhorst,[2] expressing the desire that Washington might be lodged at the writer's private house. The writer, presumably in an official ca-

[1] The population of Fayetteville was about one thousand.

[2] The original of this letter has not been found. The reply of Major Jackson, in the Washington MSS., Library of Congress, gives no indication of the name of the person to whom it was addressed.

pacity, had engaged the handsome house of the Honorable Thomas Heyward, Jr., for Washington's "quarters" during his sojourn in Charleston. Major Jackson made the following reply to this letter:

WILMINGTON, *April* 24, 1791.

DEAR SIR,

I had the honor to receive your letter of the 2nd instant; on our arrival here this morning.

The President of the U. S., to whom I have communicated its contents, directs me, as it relates to him to express to you, and through you, to the Citizens of South Carolina, the sensibility with which he learns their intention to receive and to accommodate him — he adds that no subsequent circumstance can lessen his sense of their goodness on this occasion, — But as the uncertainty of his arrival at any given place is greatly encreased by the deep sandy roads, which he is to encounter with horses somewhat exhausted, he is not able to say more than that he will leave Wilmington on tuesday morning, and proceed towards Charleston as fast as may consist with convenience and good speed.

The President's uniform determination to decline private invitations to quarters, which is founded in the desire of avoiding to give inconvenience to private families, prevails over his wish to benefit from the hospitality to which your letter alludes. — He desires me to express his particular obligations to your care in procuring lodgings for him — and to present to you his respects.

On Tuesday morning (26th), having sent his carriage across the day before, Washington made an early start — six o'clock. Prior to his departure, all the necessary preparations and arrangements had been agreed upon. So the programme went off with perfect smoothness. The President went on board the "elegantly decorated" revenue barge, which was manned by six American captains of ships, in which the standard of the United States was displayed; and attended by the boats from the shipping in the harbor, under their national colors, on board of which the committee and other gentlemen of the town embarked, proceeded, to the firing of cannon and the acclamations of throngs of people at the wharves and on the ships, to "Belvidere," the seat of Colonel Benjamin Smith, in Brunswick County. In speaking of the almost universal participation in the festivities at Wilmington, a contemporary print says: "The behavior of the Masters of the vessels above mentioned, does them great honour, and the Commanders of the foreign vessels in the river, are entitled to a considerable share of praise"; with the further bit of news: "The President was pleased, before his departure, to appoint Captain Cook of this town (Wilmington), to the command of one of the Revenue Cutters now building."

According to tradition, when Washington reached the river landing at "Belvidere" he was met by thirteen young ladies, all dressed in white and representing the thirteen colonies, who preceded him up the avenue of old trees leading from the river to the brick residence of General Smith, scattering flowers in the path of the national hero as he approached. Washington greeted with particular pleasure his former aide-de-camp during the hazardous yet masterly retreat from Long Island, the brave soldier who had distinguished himself when the British were driven from Port Royal Island, a most gracious and entertaining host, General Smith. To his host, who at one time was Past Grand Master of the Masonic Grand Lodge of North Carolina, as a mark of friendship, Washington presented a Masonic apron, which a descendant afterwards donated to some Masonic lodge in Pennsylvania. It is said, probably incorrectly, that "when General Smith learned of the illness of Washington he immediately left his house in North Carolina and hastened to the bedside of his chief, where he remained until Washington died." It is not improbable that General Smith went to Mount Vernon on hearing of Washington's death, and was in time to attend the funeral. By an oversight, Washington left his easy slippers behind at "Belvidere," and many years later one of them it seems was presented (such is the interest attaching to even the most trivial thing which once belonged to a celebrity) to the British Museum! [1]

After having breakfast at "Belvidere," Washington took to the road once more, being accompanied for some ten miles by Colonel Brown,[2] commander of the Horse for

[1] Tom Masson, in the *Mobile Register*. General Smith was a great-grandson of Thomas Smith, first landgrave of South Carolina; and his wife, Sarah, the daughter of Colonel William Dry, Collector of the Port of Wilmington, was a descendant of Cromwell's admiral, Robert Blake. The year following Washington's visit, the town which contained the courthouse of Brunswick County was named Smithville in his honor — a name which it bore for a century. It now bears the name of Southport. General Smith was prominent in politics, being repeatedly returned to State House and Senate; a member of the convention which adopted the Constitution of the United States; and subsequently Governor of North Carolina. He was a generous donor to the University of North Carolina, where a building was named Smith Hall in his honor. During Washington's presidency, he was appointed General of Militia (1796).

[2] Thomas Brown, son of John Brown and Lucy Bright, was born in Bladen County, North Carolina, January 7, 1744. Served under General Hugh Waddell in the War of the Regulation, 1771. Member of Committee of Safety for Bladen County, 1774. Participated in general meeting of Committees of Safety of the Wilmington District, June 20, 1775, signing the "Association." About this time he was married to Sarah Bartram,

BENJAMIN SMITH

WILLIAM HENRY HILL

the district, and the Wilmington troop. At his "first stage on the road to Charleston," he was met by the Representative in Congress from Fayetteville, William Barry Grove, Esq., a prominent North Carolina Federalist, Representative from North Carolina in the Second, Third, Fourth, Fifth, Sixth, and Seventh Congresses — the colleague in Congress of such prominent North Carolina Federalists as Archibald Henderson, John Steele, John Stanly, and William H. Hill. Grove, who enjoyed great popularity in his district, was an ardent supporter of the Constitution at the Convention in 1789; and was for many years a member of the National Congress.[1] Before leaving Philadelphia he had learned that Washington contemplated making a tour through the South; and doubtless at his instance, a general meeting of the citizens, pre-

daughter of William Bartram. Appointed lieutenant-colonel of Bladen militia, September, 1775, and participated in the campaign against the Tories and Regulators, terminating in the defeat of General McDonald at Moore's Creek, February 23, 1776. Member of the Provincial Congress which met at Halifax, November, 1776. In the autumn of 1780 was active in procuring supplies for General Gates's army. In August or September, 1781, after the country had been overrun by the Tories, Colonel Brown with about one hundred and fifty Whigs made an attack on the forces under Colonel Slingsby at Elizabethtown, and achieved a striking victory over heavy odds. In 1786 he was elected lieutenant-colonel, commandant of horse, for the District of Wilmington, and was later given the rank of major-general of the State militia. In 1785, 1786, and 1788 he served in the North Carolina Assembly as Senator from Bladen County. Was married a second time, to Lucy Bradley, daughter of Richard Bradley and Elizabeth Ashbridge [or Ann?] Sharpless. He resided at Ashwood, on the Cape Fear River, sixty miles from Fort Johnson. Died in Bladen County, November 24, 1811.

[1] In his *Short History of Cumberland County and the Cape Fear Section*, J. H. Myrover says that Grove was "suave and courtly in manner, but adroit and supple as a politician.... Barry Grove lived in old-time hospitality in a mansion on west Rowan Street, where he profusely and elegantly entertained the Congressmen and other public men...."

sided over by John Hay,[1] was held at Fayetteville at the State House, April 15th, when there was adopted an "Address to the President of the United States of America" by the "Merchants, Traders and principal Inhabitants of the town of Fayetteville," in all probability drafted by Mr. Grove. For some decades, Fayetteville had been a stronghold of the Scotch merchants, the leading market for all the Piedmont region of western North Carolina, and even for the transmontane country of East Tennessee and Southwest Virginia. Here the Legislature of North Carolina met in 1788, 1789, 1790, and 1793; and here for a time on the right hand side of Green Street before you cross Eccles's Bridge, near the intersection of Green and Bow Streets — according to Boswell's "Life of Johnson" — lived the famous Flora McDonald, the protectress of Bonny Prince Charlie. It is said to be the first town in the United States to be named after the Marquis de la-Fayette — the name being changed from Cross Creek to Fayetteville in 1784.[2]

[1] John Hay, of a family associated with the great mercantile interests of Fayetteville, was a brilliant lawyer and talented writer on political subjects. He represented Sampson County in the North Carolina Assembly, October, 1784; and Cumberland County in the House of Commons in 1786, and in the State Convention of 1788. He removed to Fayetteville about 1785, and was a member of the North Carolina House of Commons from the Borough of Fayetteville, 1790, 1793, 1799, 1805. He was a patron of education, a member of the first Board of Trustees of the University of North Carolina. Consult G. J. McRee: *Life and Letters of James Iredell* (New York, 1858).

[2] It is singular that apparently no effort was made to induce Washington to visit the first town ever named for him: Washington, North Carolina. The patriotic fervor of the time, as well as the presence of the armed brig, the *General Washington*, at the wharf, inspired Colonel James Bonner to give to his "intended Township" the name of "Washington" — which he

Wilmington and Georgetown

The news of Washington's arrival at Wilmington did not reach Fayetteville, some ninety miles distant, until the afternoon of Sunday (24th); whereupon Mr. Grove, bearing the address, set off, but reached "Belvidere" on Tuesday morning about an hour after the President's departure. The address, as given below, was delivered by Mr. Grove to the President at his first stop in Brunswick County after leaving "Belvidere." It is conspicuous for its outspoken endorsement of the President for undertaking the tour.

To the President of the United States of America.
Sir,

Although our voice can add little to the general acclamation which attends you, and to your Excellency must be of small moment, yet amidst the warm congratulations on the appearance in this state of their beloved Chief Magistrate, our silence would indicate a want of respect; a silence which would be the more reprehensible in a community so largely interested in trade and navigation, more peculiarly under the directing hand of that government in which you preside.

Could any incident encrease the veneration we feel for your illustrious character, heretofore so fully established as the soldier, the statesman and thc patriot, it is your present expedition, in undertaking at an advanced period of life, a long and laborious journey for the purpose of advising yourself, by personal observations and enquiry, of the true interests of the several states which compose our confederation. From this tour we presage the happy consequence, that those who are not yet satisfied with the tendency, operation and effects of the present constitution of the union, will be convinced of its superior excellency to all former systems of government.

did in the deed to a lot, December 7, 1776. Compare article by Miss Lida T. Rodman in the *Washington* (*N.C.*) *Observer*, February 22, 1921.

Throughout your journey we wish you as much satisfaction as can attend it, and if in its progress we are to be honoured by your visitation, the citizens of Fayetteville will be happy in every attention which may contribute to your pleasure and convenience.

Under the impression of the importance of a life so valuable to our country we commit it to God, with our most fervent prayer, that it may long be preserved as full of happiness as it hath been already full of glory.

Done at the general meeting of the Citizens of Fayetteville, at the State-house, on Friday, the 15th of April, 1791.

JOHN HAY, Chairman

In reply, the President said:

GENTLEMEN,

It is due to your goodness and to my own feelings, that I should express the sensibility excited by your address, and that I should acknowledge the grateful pleasure with which I receive it.

My best services are more than compensated by the affectionate partiality of my fellow citizens, and my most anxious wishes are gratified in observing the happiness which pervades our country.

The very favourable change already manifested in our political system, justifies the prediction that the future operations of the general government will be alike conducive to individual prosperity and national honor.

Should it consist with the necessary arrangements of my journey, I shall be happy in a personal opportunity in confessing my obligations to the regard of the citizens of Fayetteville. In any event I entreat them to be persuaded of my sincere wishes for their welfare. GEO. WASHINGTON

An amusing incident occurred in connection with Washington's journey from Wilmington to Georgetown. On April 5th, Mr. J. Bowman, writing from Peachtree, South Carolina, extended a cordial invitation to the President to "accept of the accomodations" of his house — which was "about 14 miles from Georgetown, & the nearest to the direct road from thence to Charlestown." On the 16th he writes again, saying that he feels it "due" to mention that he is sick, and that he "apprehends his Indisposition to be the Measles"! Although he ventures the hope that Washington and his attendants have already "had that disorder," certain it is that Washington gave Mr. J. Bowman's, for all his hospitality, a wide berth.

The diary for the next three days so fully covers the main events — details of travel and private entertainment — that it is here set down *verbatim:*

Wednesday, 27*th.*

Breakfasted at Willm. Gause's a little out of the direct Road 14 miles — crossed the boundary line between No. & South Carolina abt. half after 12 o'clock which is 10 miles from Gause's — dined at a private house (one Cochran's) about 2 miles farther — and lodged at Mr. Vareen's 14 miles more and 2 miles short of the long bay. — To this house we were directed as a Tavern, but the proprietor of it either did not keep one, or would not acknowledge it — we therefore were entertained (& very kindly) without being able to make compensation.

Thursday, 28*th.*

Mr. Vareen piloted us across the Swash (which at high water is impassable, & at times, by the shifting of the Sands is dangerous) on the long Beach of the Ocean; and it being at a proper time of the tide we passed along it with ease and celerity to the place of quitting it, which is estimated 16 miles, — five miles farther we got dinner & fed our horses at a Mr. Pauley's a private house, no public one being on the Road; — and being met on the Road, & kindly invited by a Doctor Flagg to his house, we lodged there; it being about 10 miles from Pauley's & 33 from Vareen's.

Friday, 29*th*.

We left Doctr. Flagg's about 6 o'clock, and arrived at Captn. Wm. Alston's on the Waggamau to Breakfast.

Captn. Alston is a Gentleman of large fortune and esteemed one of the neatest Rice planters in the State of So. Carolina and a proprietor of the most valuable ground for the culture of this article. — His house which is large, new, and elegantly furnished stands on a sand hill, high for the Country, with his Rice fields below; the contrast of which with the lands back of it, and the Sand & piney barrens through which we had passed is scarcely to be conceived.

Colonel Alston,[1] as he was generally called, lived at Clifton house (long since destroyed by fire), standing among fine trees, some distance from the Waccamaw River, with the rice fields spreading out from the base of the hill. "These fields in early spring," says Mrs. St. Julien Ravenel,[2] "were covered with the young rice, springing green from the dark earth and intersected by innumerable ditches, the water gleaming bright in the sunshine. The President was quite unprepared for such perfection of cultivation, and, the passion of his life being agriculture,

[1] William Alston, who had been one of Marion's men during the Revolution, was now one of the most successful and extensive rice planters in South Carolina. He had recently married as his second wife the beautiful Mary Motte, daughter of Rebecca Motte, one of the South Carolina heroines of the Revolution. He eschewed politics, only once permitting himself to be elected to the South Carolina Senate to assist the political fortunes of his friend, Thomas Jefferson. By his first marriage, to Miss Ashe, daughter of John Baptista Ashe, of North Carolina, he had several children, as well as by his second marriage. In a memorable obituary, written by his son-in-law, the famous Robert Y. Hayne, we are told that "his house was the abode of a refined and elegant hospitality. . . . Courteous in his manners, social in his disposition, surrounded with a large circle of friends and blessed with an ample fortune, his tastes and habits were for many years those of 'a Carolina gentleman of the old school.'" (Consult Grove: *Alston-Allston Genealogy*.)

[2] *Charleston, the Place and the People.*

COLONEL WILLIAM ALSTON

COLONEL WILLIAM WASHINGTON

GENERAL WILLIAM MOULTRIE

was delighted. It won from him one of the few enthusiastic remarks reported of him, for he told his hostess that it 'looked like fairyland.' And afterwards in Charleston he said to the Governor that he had had no idea that anywhere in America was there such perfection of cultivation as he had seen on the large rice rivers which he had crossed."

At Captain Alston's Washington found awaiting him General William Moultrie,[1] Colonel William Washington,[2]

[1] William Moultrie, born in England, 1731; died in Charleston, South Carolina, 1805. Served military apprenticeship in campaigns against the Cherokees. Colonel of Second Colonial Regiment; also in Continental Congress, in 1775. Defended fortress on Sullivan's Island, afterwards named for him, against attack by combined land and naval force in 1776. Soon afterwards was commissioned brigadier-general in the Continental Army. Participated in various engagements. Second in command at defence of Charleston in 1780. His imprisonment, following its fall, lasted nearly two years, when he was exchanged for General Burgoyne. Commissioned major-general by Congress. Governor of South Carolina in 1785 and in 1794. Author of "Memoirs of the American Revolution so far as it related to the States of North and South Carolina and Georgia." In the Journal of the South Carolina Society of the Cincinnati, at the Quarterly Meeting, Oct. 14, 1805, appears an obituary notice of Gen. Moultrie, in which appear these words: "Bold as Leonidas he defended the strait committed to his charge, against a superiority of force, that had been deemed irresistible, and more fortunate than the Spartan hero, lived in honourable old age under the shades of his laurels, to share with a grateful nation the liberty his successful exertion had so happily contributed to establish.... His disposition was frank, liberal, sincere; his manners simple and conciliatory."

[2] William Washington, the noted cavalry leader of the Revolution, was born in Stafford County, Virginia, February 28, 1752. He was educated for the church. Early in the Revolution he received a commission as captain of infantry in the Third Regiment of the Virginia line, and served with credit in the operations about New York, being severely wounded in the Battle of Long Island. Distinguished himself in the Battle of Trenton. After joining army of General Lincoln in the South in 1779, he was promoted to command of a regiment of dragoons, with rank of lieutenant-colonel, March 23, 1780. Was voted a medal by Congress for his gallantry at the Battle of the Cowpens. Later being attached to the army of General Nathanael Greene, he took an active part in the battles of Guilford Court House and Hobkirk's

and Mr. Rutledge, son of the then Chief Justice of South Carolina, who had come as a delegation to accompany him first into Georgetown, and later into Charleston. Colonel Washington was the bearer of the following letter to the President from Governor Charles Pinckney: [1]

Hill. At the Battle of Eutaw Springs, September 8, 1781, he was wounded and captured. Towards the close of the Revolution he was married to Jane Riley Elliott, who acquired the Sandy Hill estate under the will of her father, Charles Elliott, who died in 1781. After the Revolution was elected a member of the South Carolina legislature. In 1798, when the United States was threatened with war by France, George Washington recommended the appointment of his kinsman as brigadier-general, which was done July 19, 1798. After his marriage, he became a planter. He died at Sandy Hill in St. Paul's Parish, South Carolina, March 16, 1810. On the occasion of his death the American Revolution Society of South Carolina adopted resolutions in which he was spoken of as: "Modest without timidity, generous without extravagance, brave without rashness, and disinterested without austerity; which imparted firmness to his conduct and mildness to his manners, solidity to his judgment and boldness to his achievements; which armed him with an equanimity unalterable by the frowns of adversity or the smiles of fortune, and steadiness of soul not to be subdued by the disasters of defeat or elated by the triumphs of victory." Consult H. A. M. Smith: "Grave of Col. William Washington," in *South Carolina Historical and Genealogical Magazine*, x, 243; Garden's *Anecdotes; William and Mary Quarterly*, xv, 132–34.

[1] Charles Pinckney: born in Charleston, South Carolina, 1758; died there October 29, 1824. Grandson of William Pinckney and uncle of Charles Cotesworth Pinckney. Educated for the bar. Taken prisoner at capture of Charleston; remained prisoner until end of war. Elected to Provincial Congress in 1785, and subsequently took an active part in preparing a plan of government for the United States. In 1787 he was a delegate to the Constitutional Convention, Philadelphia; presented there the draft of a constitution, some of the provisions of which were adopted. He advocated ratification of the Constitution in the South Carolina Convention in 1788. Elected Governor in 1784, and presided over State Convention by which the South Carolina Constitution was adopted in 1790; reëlected Governor in 1791, in 1796, and in 1804. In 1798 chosen United States Senator as *Republican.* He was an able speaker and one of the most active supporters of Thomas Jefferson for the Presidency. In 1802–03 he was Minister to Spain. He strongly favored war with England in 1812. He was founder of the old Republican party in South Carolina. Was very liberal in all his views; first Governor of State to advocate establishment of free schools.

Governor Pinckney had a country estate in Christ Church Parish, near

Dear Sir,

Hearing that Colonel Washington will set out in a few days to meet you at Waccamaw I take the liberty of acquainting you that I have requested General Moultrie to ask the favour of yourself & the gentlemen of your family to dine with me on the day of your arrival in Charleston — the arrangements for the other days the General will shew you, & I trust they will prove acceptable. You may be assured that the people of this country feel themselves on this occasion so strongly bound by every principle of gratitude & affection that no exertion will be wanting on their part to render your stay among us as agreeable as possible.

In your way down General Moultrie will request you to make a stage at a little farm of mine in Christ Church a few miles distant from hence. I must apologize for asking you to call at a place so indifferently furnished, & where your fare will be entirely that of a farm. It is a place I seldom go to, or things perhaps would be in better order — but such as they are, they are very much at your service, & I hope you will consider yourself when there as at home — as soon as I know the day you are to be there I shall request a gentleman to go over & meet you.

I am Dear Sir, with esteem

& respect, much obliged

Yours truly

Charles Pinckney

April 26, 1791
Meeting Street.
(Endorsed:)
From His Excelly Govr Pinckney
26th April 1791
Addressed: To the President of the United States
Honoured by Colonel Washington.[1]

---

the parish church, called "Fee Farm," later "Snee Farm." It was here that the British allowed Colonel C. C. Pinckney to reside for a time, when a prisoner of war after the fall of Charles Town. (Consult "The Hon. Charles Pinckney, LL.D.," by W. S. Elliott, in *De Bow's Review.*)

[1] This letter, the original of which is in the Library of Congress, has not hitherto, it is believed, been published.

The whole party dined and lodged at the home of Captain Alston, and set out bright and early next morning for Georgetown.

The boats being in readiness, the President and suite were rowed across the Waccamaw River, descending it for three miles, in an "elegant painted boat" manned by seven captains of vessels, dressed in "round hats trimmed with gold lace, blue coats, and white jackets." On arriving opposite the market, they were saluted by the artillery, with fifteen guns, from the foot of Broad Street. At the landing the Light Infantry Company — "handsomely uniformed," notes Washington — stood with presented arms; and immediately after he passed, fired thirteen rounds. It was very lucky that the father of his country had often been "in the midst of war's alarms" — otherwise he might have proved somewhat gun-shy in times of peace from all the firing which went on, often unexpectedly, all around him —

> Cannon to right of him,
> Cannon to left of him,
> Cannon behind him
> Volley'd and thunder'd.

A committee, appointed to receive and address him, now conducted him to "an elegant house prepared by the inhabitants for his reception" — said to be the old Allston house.[1] At two o'clock, he was waited upon by the same

[1] This house, still in a state of good preservation, is situated on Front Street, between Wood and King Streets. It is on the water front, that is, directly on the Sampit River, toward the western end of the old town. The present owners, the Pyatts, are lineal descendants of Benjamin Allston

PYATT, OR ALLSTON, HOUSE, GEORGETOWN, SOUTH CAROLINA

This is the rear of the house, the part that would be seen from the river

committee, the chairman of which read to him the following congratulatory address of the inhabitants of Georgetown and its vicinity:

SIR

We, the inhabitants of Georgetown, and of its vicinity, beg leave to congratulate you upon your safe arrival in South Carolina, and to assure you, that having ever entertained a high sense of the obligations which you have conferred upon your fellow-citizens in general, we are happy to embrace this opportunity of testifying to you our particular sentiments of gratitude and of affection; We are no less happy, Sir, at being called upon by the laws to obey, and to respect as first Magistrate of the Federal Republic, that person, whom of all men we were most disposed to revere as our benefactor, and to love as the father of his country. Having shared in the distresses of the war, and been exposed to those calamities, and to that loss of property, which were the consequences of it, we have been taught to set a proper value upon the exertions which were made in our behalf, we have experienced the happy influence of your councils, Sir, and have distinguished you as the guardian of our laws, and of our liberties, as an instrument in the hands of providence to protect our dearest rights, and to save us from oppression. The breath of popular applause is fleeting, but the merits of such illustrious actions can never be effaced; they carry along with them their best reward, and we trust, Sir, that in pursuing your progress through this state, you will have the satisfaction to perceive a spirit of freedom, which your services during the war enabled

(born 1765), who originally purchased the house from his nephew. This Benjamin Allston, who as a lad had served under Marion, was called "Big Ben" to distinguish him from the father of Governor Robert Francis Withers Allston, who was designated "Little Ben." It is said that Dorothy Singleton, widow of Colonel Singleton and second wife of Benjamin Allston, was the prototype of the heroine of William Gilmore Simms's novel, *Katherine Walton.* For information concerning this house I am indebted to Miss Minnie Tamplet Hazard, of Georgetown. For a full description of the house, consult Harriette K. Leiding: *Historic Houses of South Carolina.*

us to maintain; a degree of order and tranquility, which your administration has diffused, and a growing prosperity, than which no better proof could exist, of the goodness and efficacy of that government, over which you preside.

Such, sir, are the sentiments with which we approach you upon this occasion, and such the sentiments which we shall in honor, and in gratitude transmit to our latest posterity.

Signed by order of the inhabitants of Georgetown, and its vicinity.

HUGH HORRŸ
JOSEPH BLYTH
E. ROTHMALER
F. KINLOCH
GEORGE KEITH
MATTHEW IRVINE
R. BROWNFIELD
SAMUEL SMITH [1]

[1] Hugh Horrÿ was a dashing cavalry officer and partisan leader under General Francis Marion. He served brilliantly in many engagements throughout the Revolution. In 1782 he was a member of the famous Jacksonborough Convention.

Joseph Blyth was a large landowner and a prominent citizen of Georgetown. He filled with credit many different offices in the county. He was married to Elizabeth Frances, daughter of William and Sabina (Atchison) Allston. He is buried in the churchyard of Prince George's parish.

Erasmus Rothmahler was a descendant of Job Rothmahler, Esq., of Charleston, for many years clerk of the Council of South Carolina. He had large holdings of land near Georgetown. He was connected with the Wragg and Trapier families.

Francis Kinloch, who studied at Eton and Lincoln's Inn, completed his education in France and Switzerland. Handsome, clever, a devotee of society, letters, and art, he was destined for a diplomatic career; but was recalled to America on the outbreak of the Revolution. In that war he served as aide-de-camp to Generals Huger and Moultrie; and was engaged in the fight at Beaufort in 1779, the assault on Savannah, and in other actions. In company with his comrade and close friend, Colonel John Laurens, he served for a time in the field with Washington. During Simcoe's raid he was captured by his cousin, Captain Kinloch of the British army. He was twice married: to Mildred, daughter of John Walker, of Castle Hill, in Virginia; and to Martha, daughter of Governor John Rutledge, the virtual dictator of South Carolina during a critical period of the Revolution. At one time he

To this congratulatory address, Washington made the following felicitous reply:[1]

GENTLEMEN,

I receive your congratulations on my arrival in South-Carolina with real pleasure, and I confess my obligations to your affectionate regard with sincere gratitude.

While the calamities, to which you were exposed during the war, excited all my sympathy, the gallantry and firmness with which they were encountered obtained my entire esteem; to your fortitude in those trying scenes our country is much indebted for the happy and honourable issue of the contest — from the milder virtues that characterise your conduct in peace, our equal government will derive those aids, which may render its operations extensively beneficial.

That your participation of every national advantage, and your prosperity in private life, may be amply proportioned to your past services and sufferings, is my sincere and fervent wish.

GEORGE WASHINGTON.

Immediately following this ceremony came another — conducted by a committee of Masons from Prince George's Lodge, No. 16 (Moderns) of Georgetown. "This Lodge," says Sachse, "was one of the original six Lodges, which had been warrented prior to 1756 in South Carolina, under the Jurisdiction of the Provincial Grand Lodge, and

was a member of Congress; and in 1800 he published a memoir on Washington (quoted elsewhere) whom he had known intimately. He died in Charleston in 1822, and is buried in St. Michael's churchyard.

George Keith and Matthew Irvine were both possessed of large tracts of land in the vicinity of Georgetown and Charleston.

Robert Brownfield, then or afterwards of the High Hills of Santee, was connected with the Sumter family.

Samuel Smith, it appears, was a merchant of Georgetown.

[1] The original of Washington's answer, in the handwriting of Major Jackson and with Washington's autograph signature, is preserved in the archives of the Winyah Indigo Society. For the photographic copy herewith reproduced, I am indebted to W. D. Morgan, Esq.

through it, the Grand Lodge of England. It is the only instance where a Lodge of the 'Moderns' addressed Brother Washington." Follows the address:

TO OUR ILLUSTRIOUS BROTHER GEORGE WASHINGTON,
President of the United States.

At a time when all men are emulous to approach you to express the lively sensations you inspire as the Father of our country. Permit us the Brethren of Prince George's Lodge No. 16 to have our share in the general happiness in welcoming you to Georgetown, and the pleasure of reflecting that we behold in you the liberator of our country, the distributor of its equal laws, and a Brother of our most ancient and most honorable Order.

At the same time indulge us in congratulating you on the truly honorable and happy situation in which you now stand, as the Grand Conductor of the political interests of these United States.

Having by your manly efforts caused the beauteous light of liberty to beam on this western hemisphere, and by the wisdom Heaven has graciously endowed you with established the liberties of America on the justest and firmest basis that was ever yet recorded in the annals of history, you now enjoy the supremest of all earthly happiness that of diffusing peace, liberty, and safety to millions of your fellow-citizens.

As a true reward for your patriotic, noble and exalted services we fervently pray the Grand Architect of the universe long to bless you with health, stability, and power to continue you the Grand Pillar of the arch of liberty in this vast empire, which you have been so eminently distinguished in raising to this pitch of perfection at which we now behold it.

May the residue of your life be spent in ease content and happiness, and as the Great Parent of these United States may you long live to see your children flourish under your happy auspices and may you be finally rewarded with eternal happiness.

We conclude our present address with a fervent wish that

To the Inhabitants of Georgetown and of its vicinity.

Gentlemen.

I receive your congratulations on my arrival in South-Carolina with real pleasure, and I confess my obligation to your affectionate regard with sincere gratitude.

While the calamities, to which you were exposed during the war, excited all my sympathy, the gallantry and firmness, with which they were encountered, obtained my entire esteem ——— To your fortitude in those trying scenes our country is much indebted for the happy and honorable issue of the contest — From the milder virtues, that characterise your conduct in peace, our equal government will derive those aids, which may render its operations extensively beneficial.

That your participation of every national advantage, and your prosperity in private life, may be amply proportioned to your past services and sufferings is my sincere and fervent wish.

G. Washington

you will continue as you have hitherto been, the friend of our ancient and honorable Order, and of all worthy Masons.

I. White
R. Grant
A. Cohen
Jos. Blyth.
J. Carson. — Committee from Prince George's Lodge.

George Town *30th April* 1791.[1]

To this address, the President made the following brief reply:

To the Brethren of Prince George's Lodge, No. 16.
Gentlemen:

The cordial welcome which you give me to George Town, and the congratulations, you are pleased to offer on my election to the chief magistracy receive my grateful thanks.

I am much obliged by your good wishes and reciprocate them with sincerity, assuring the fraternity of my esteem, I request them to believe that I shall always be ambitious of being considered a deserving Brother.

G. Washington.[2]

At four o'clock in the afternoon — how hungry Washington must have been by this time, not to say thirsty, after so long a wait and such long-winded addresses! — he "honoured the citizens with his company at a public dinner." The following toasts were given:

1. The United States of America.
2. The Grand Council of the Union.

[1] Of the above signers, three had served in the War for Independence, namely: Isaac White, Lieutenant in North Carolina Militia at King's Mountain; Reuben Grant, Ensign in the 6th North Carolina Infantry; and Joseph Blythe, Surgeon in 1st North Carolina Regiment; taken prisoner at Charleston, May 12, 1789; exchanged June 14, 1789; in 4th North Carolina in February, 1782, and served to close of war.

[2] Washington MSS.; Letter Book No. II, folio 60–61.

3. The King of France our great and good ally.
4. The National Assembly of France.
5. The memory of Major General Greene.
6. The memory of M. G. Baron de Kalb.
7. The other brave officers and soldiers who fell in the war.
8. The Vice-President of the United States, may the esteem and gratitude of his country be equal to those important services which he has, and continues to render her.
9. Our ministers in foreign countries.
10. The Federal Government.
11. The State of South-Carolina.
12. The Marquis de la Fayette.
13. May the nations of the earth enjoy an equal happiness with us in having rulers equally sedulous to make themselves acquainted with the true interests and situations of the people.
14. The Governors and Legislatures of the respective States.

The President then retired, and the following toast was given:

Our Illustrious President, may calmness, peace and felicity, bless the evening of his life, as his youth and middle age have been glorious by the most exalted achievements of military renown.

The day's festivities were closed with a tea-party in the afternoon, at which Washington was introduced to about fifty ladies who had assembled on the occasion; (why does Washington spell "gentlemen" with a capital *G*, "ladies" with a small *l*?) and with a ball in the evening which the President honored with his company.

In his diary under date Saturday, April 30th, Washington makes the following entry:

George Town seems to be in the shade of Charleston — It suffered during the War by the British, having had many of its Houses burnt. — It is situated on a pininsula betwn. the River Waccamaw and Sampton *Creek* about 15 miles from the Sea — a bar is to be passed, over which not more than 12 feet water can be brot. except at Spring tides; which (tho' the Inhabitants are willing to entertain different ideas,) must ever be a considerable let to its importance; especially if the cut between the Santee and Cooper Rivers, should ever be accomplished.

The Inhabitants of this place (either unwilling or unable) could give no account of the number of Souls in it, but I should not compute them at more than 5 or 600. — Its chief export, Rice.

Accompanied by Major Thomas Pinckney,[1] his good friend and a distinguished American, Washington set out at six o'clock on the morning of Sunday, May 1st. The President's coach had as outriders on this occasion General William Moultrie, Colonel William Washington, and Mr. Rutledge, son of the Chief Justice of South Carolina. The party first crossed the Santee Creek at Georgetown, and, after travelling twelve miles, crossed the Santee River. They were bound for "Hampton," the home of the

[1] Thomas Pinckney, born in Charleston, October 23, 1750; died there November 2, 1828. Educated at Westminster and Oxford. Studied law at the Temple, England. Practised law in Charleston. Joined Continental Army as lieutenant in 1775; was aide-de-camp to Brigadier-General Lincoln, to d'Estaing, and also to General Gates. Was wounded and taken prisoner at Camden, and saw no further service. Governor of South Carolina, 1789. In 1792 he was appointed by Washington Minister to Great Britain. In 1794 he was sent on a mission to Spain and arranged the Treaty of San Ildefonso. He was Federalist candidate for Vice-President in 1796 and was in Congress, 1799–1801. Was appointed Major-General by Madison at the beginning of the war in 1812; took part in the battle of Horseshoe Bend. He succeeded his brother as fourth President General of the Society of the Cincinnati.

widow of Colonel Daniel Horrÿ, who had served during the first five years of the Revolution. This lady was Harriott Pinckney Horrÿ, the sister of Major Thomas Pinckney and General Charles Cotesworth Pinckney. Her mother, who assisted her in entertaining the President, was the remarkable character known in American annals as Eliza Pinckney.

The coach and cavalcade moved in stately procession up the long avenue of a mile or more in length leading to the handsome colonial mansion, "Hampton." It was built in 1730, of yellow pine and cypress, over a brick foundation, by Mrs. Daniel Horrÿ, the widow of the French Huguenot who came to this country in 1686. Standing a mile east of the original Horrÿ house, it faces, says Mrs. Leiding, a "wide lawn dotted by those sentinels of the centuries which, with the white mansion, its lofty portico and its simple, but beautiful pediment supported by heavy columns, in its setting of giant oaks hung with Spanish moss, make a charming and impressive picture." Upon the spacious porch, twenty by forty feet long, stood the ladies in the bright garb of summer — Eliza Lucas Pinckney, famous in our history for charm of personality, force of character, and for her notable contribution to agriculture through the successful introduction of indigo into South Carolina; her daughter, Mrs. Horrÿ, the gracious hostess; her granddaughter, Harriott Horrÿ, and two other granddaughters who made "Hampton" their home, the daughters of General C. C. Pinckney.

After the first greetings were over, the hungry travellers

GENERAL THOMAS PINCKNEY

"HAMPTON"

THE WASHINGTON OAK, "HAMPTON"

were ushered into the great ballroom, occupying the entire east wing of the house and containing an immense carved chimney-place lined with Dutch tiles in which, it is said, five persons could stand. Here the assembled company sat down at a long table, and did full justice to a breakfast consisting of a most bountiful and palatable "best the country could afford." Breakfast over, the party gathered upon the spacious veranda or wandered through the grounds. The General was rarely entertained by Mrs. Pinckney's informing conversation on agriculture and her own successful management of a great rice plantation; and by Mrs. Horrÿ's tales of the Revolution — of the "Swamp Fox," Marion, who made this home his headquarters while in the neighborhood and here once narrowly escaped capture by the British; and of Tarleton, who was once quartered here and on his departure forgetfully carried off a beautiful copy of the Baskerville edition of Milton, bound in crimson and gold!

Pointing to a young and vigorous live-oak growing in front of the house, which, after it had grown older and the branches spread wide, she thought might greatly obstruct the view from the avenue of the fine portico which had just been erected, Mrs. Horrÿ informed the General she intended to cut it down. Looking the spot over carefully, the General replied: "Mrs. Horrÿ, let it stay. It can do no harm where it is and I would not think of cutting it down." This mighty monarch of the forest — just thirty steps from the portico and twenty-six feet around at a height of six feet above the ground and just below the limbs —

still stands as a memorial to the man who, in this way, has made historic reparation for the traditionary felling of a cherry tree early in his career.[1]

Amid such beautiful surroundings and in such charming company, Washington doubtless was reluctant to continue his journey. But after a sumptuous dinner, the party moved on, travelling nineteen miles farther to "Marshlands," the plantation of that cultured gentleman of French Huguenot ancestry, Gabriel Manigault.[2] The Manigault family had long been distinguished for culture, public service, and patriotism in the social and political life of South Carolina. Gabriel Manigault, the grandfather of Washington's host, was for many years a prosperous merchant in Charleston, having succeeded to the business of his father, Peter. Married to Ann Ashley in 1730, he became the father of one son, Peter, who studied law at the Inner Temple, London, and was three times Speaker of the Commons, South Carolina Assembly. He died in London, whither he had gone to regain his health,

[1] For information concerning Washington's visit to "Hampton," I am indebted to the late Colonel H. M. Rutledge, of McClellansville, South Carolina, former owner of "Hampton"; to his son, Archibald Rutledge, Esq.; to Mrs. H. K. Leiding, who has made a special study of the historic houses of South Carolina; and to the delightful book, *Eliza Pinckney*, by Mrs. St. Julien Ravenel. Doubtless Mrs. Pinckney sided with Washington in favor of preserving the tree; for in one of her letters to Mrs. Onslow she says: "I look . . . upon an old oak with the reverencial esteem of a Druid, it staggered my philosophy to bear with patience the Cuting down one remarkable fine tree. . . ." It is worthy of mention that Washington held Mrs. Eliza Pinckney in great esteem; and at his own request acted as pall-bearer at her funeral in Philadelphia, May 27, 1793. The Wedgwood breakfast set, green and white, of very delicate design, which was used for General Washington at "Hampton" is still preserved almost intact.

[2] In his diary Washington speaks of him as "Mr. Manigold."

in 1773; and his father Gabriel dying in 1781, his two sons Gabriel and Joseph became heirs to the extensive property in business, money, and lands. Washington must have been sensibly moved by the touching story of the old Gabriel Manigault, himself seventy-five, appearing with his grandson, Joseph, aged fifteen, upon the ramparts of the defences of Charleston when it was threatened by Provost in 1779 — each with a musket on his shoulder, to assist in the defence of the city. This Gabriel Manigault was Treasurer of the Province of South Carolina; and being possessed of a great fortune, he lent to the State the sum of two hundred and twenty thousand dollars, most of which was never returned.

The house at "Marshlands," which welcomed Washington with open arms, was a fine example of the architecture of the period, spacious and imposing, substantially built, with a brick basement. Washington's host, Gabriel, who had completed his education in Geneva and London, was married to the daughter of Ralph Izard, Washington's trusted friend, and Alice DeLancey of the distinguished New York family. The hostess at "Marshlands" was a woman of cosmopolitan culture and experience, having spent seven years at school in London, Brussels, and Paris. At "Marshlands," she and her husband entertained with all the gracious charm and lavish hospitality so characteristic of the Old South. In this delightful home, situated on the Cooper River about six miles from Charleston, Washington passed a memorable evening — resting the night here before beginning the week of strenuous gaiety and royal entertainment awaiting him in hospitable Charleston.[1]

Among the many eulogies delivered on the occasion of Washington's death, that one delivered at Georgetown by Francis Kinloch, sometime member of Congress, possesses unique interest in its explicit reference to Washington's visit which evidently was attended by every demonstration on the part of the public, of love for and admiration of their Chief Magistrate. The passage in question is quoted:

> It is proper in all nations that those who represent the majesty of the people should be at times encircled with the ensigns of authority, and that the splendour of the government they administer should be in some measure apparent in their persons; and here, my fellow citizens, let me call to your remembrance, for we have possessed him amongst us, let me call to your remembrance the plain, and yet dignified deportment of him whose loss we deplore — it was not a triumphant General who came amongst us, nor yet the semblance of a monarch; it was the first magistrate of a free people, it was a father who visited his children, who delighted in their caresses, and who kindly accepted of their efforts to please, and to entertain him. With what joy was he not received,

[1] For interesting accounts of the Manigault family, consult *South Carolina Historical and Genealogical Magazine*, XII, 116–77; *Transactions of the Huguenot Society of South Carolina*, No. 4 (1897), 48–84; Ramsay's *History of South Carolina*, sketches at end of work. "Marshlands" remained in the Manigault family until comparatively recent years, when it was sold by Gabriel Manigault's grandson, the late Dr. Gabriel E. Manigault, Professor of Natural History. Taken over by the United States Government as part of the Charleston Navy Yard reservation, the house in which Washington was entertained has since been thoroughly restored, and is now used as quarters for officers of the United States Navy. Washington's host, Gabriel Manigault, was born in 1758, and died in 1809. His mother was Elizabeth, daughter of Joseph Wragg, Esq., of Charleston; and she was married to Peter Manigault in 1755.

with what ardour was he not addressed by all ranks and orders of people! And how readily does the public imagination surround him with trophies of victory, and convert the unadorned vehicle which conveyed him into a car of triumph! Behold, said they — but why should I borrow the language of admiration? No, let me rather recall your minds to the melancholy truth, and let us remember, that the father of his country now lies mingled with the dust! The ornaments of eloquence are here unnecessary, the simple accents which proceed from the heart are alone sufficient — you feel for yourselves, your children, your country.

CHAPTER VI

THE FOURTH STAGE

Charleston

IT is entirely in conformity with classic usage that the arrival of the hero should be heralded by pæans of praise from the poets. One can only regret that the poems were not more truly poetic. However, such a poem as the one printed below, which was "written on the expected arrival of our illustrious president by Michael Forrest," helped to create "atmosphere" — whether temperate, torrid, or frigid will be left an open question for debate.

Now let some Shakespear sweep the sounding lyre
Or some brave Milton with prophetic fire
And soar aloft with some new strain sublime,
Beyond the reach of each dull creeping line.
From High Olympus let the gods descend,
And to this poet their assistance lend
While he in strains heroic sings the fame
Of Washington and gilds his noble name.
O let the sacred nine their aid diffuse
In strains sublime t' inspire his chanting muse
And may his song the sleeping echoes raise
From their soft slumber to resound his praise.
Till his glorious theme reaches every soul
From the arctic to the antarctic pole
But if a genius with such matchless strain
Cannot be found to sing our Hero's fame
The *Sons of Freedom* will I hope excuse

Charleston

This imperfect strain from a willing muse
Come then ye sacred nine, inspire my song
With phrase sublime and gliding numbers strong.
Heroic measure teach me to command
And justly praise the glory of this land
George Washington, who though advanced in years,
Disdained subjection to proud British peers;
But when his country loudly called him forth,
Displayed at once his gallantry and worth:
Of her land forces, took the chief command,
And wisely ruled them with his martial hand;
Check'd England's pride — broke her despotic band —
And gained *Freedom* for his native land!
O, could I sing his conduct thro' the whole,
His feeling heart and sympathetic soul;
His love of freedom and his martial skill,
His pride to conquer, his dislike to kill;
His perseverance in his country's cause
To banish *tyrants* and *despotic laws;*
And in a word his patriotic zeal
For his native land and the public weal;
My glorious theme should then on golden wing
Thro' foreign climes and distant nations ring!
But, to do this, requires a wiser hand,
And higher strains, than I can now command.
O, may no trifling bard, with creeping lays
Ever attempt to sing his matchless praise;
But may some Milton full of lyric sound
Whose matchless strain whole nations will astound
To sing his praises speedily be found!
He comes! — He comes! — methinks I see him near;
Now Columbians raise the joyful cheer!
Ye sons of Freedom who revere his name,
Beat loud your drums, and sound the trump of fame![1]

Long before Washington's arrival, the people and the

[1] *City Gazette*, May 2, 1791.

officials of Charleston had been all agog over the great event. The honor of Charleston was at stake — particularly as this was much the most important city Washington was to visit upon his tour. In recognition of Charleston's preëminence, Washington planned to make the longest stay of his journey in this beautiful city of which Josiah Quincy of Massachusetts had written in his diary (1773): "This town makes a beautiful appearance as you come up to it and in many respects a magnificent one. I can only say in general that in grandeur and splendor of buildings, decorations, equipages, numbers, commerce, shipping, and indeed everything, it far surpasses all I ever saw or ever expect to see in America." A very interesting letter to Washington from Governor Charles Pinckney is here published in full:

CHARLESTON *March* 8: 1791

DEAR SIR:

Upon my return to this City I found your obligating Letter of introduction which had been previously left by Col: Trumbull at my house during my absence in attending the meeting of the Legislature at Columbia.

As soon as I am sufficiently recovered from my present indisposition arising from the accident of a fall from my Carriage I shall make a point of seeing him & endeavoring to make this place as agreeable to him as possible. I had an idea at the conclusion of my term of office to have gone to Europe & to have done myself the honor of paying you my respects and those of Mrs. Pinckney, as it was my intention to have embarked by the way of New York, but the establishment of our new Constitution having made me reeligible for two years longer, & it seeming to be the general opinion of the Legislature that I should continue, my sense of public Duty would not permit me to think of refusing — after the end

"A VIEW OF CHARLES TOWN THE CAPITAL OF SOUTH CAROLINA IN NORTH AMERICA"

however of the present two years I am ineligible for four, when I shall endeavor at least to pay a visit to the northward — in the interim we hope much for the honour of your company in this City — it is said you will probably be here about the 20th of April — if so permit me to request that you will stay at my house during your residence where you may be assured no exertions of mine shall be untried to make everything as agreeable as we can. On this point suffer me to request the favour of a Line from you, as your friends are extremely anxious to know whether they are to expect you in the Spring or Fall.

So much has been said on the subject of the Creek Treaty & the Assumption of the State Debts that I shall only observe to you in confidence that they are both measures which very highly meet the approbation, & would I am sure if necessary, very cheerfully receive the support of this State upon every occasion — at least this is my opinion as far as I have been able to collect the sentiments of those who are the most concerned & who speak the most disinterestedly.

You will certainly before this have received Mr. Rutledge's resignation, as a federal judge, on his having been appointed Chief Justice of this State — the reasons which induced this step he has no doubt fully & satisfactorily stated, & if the friendship which you have always honored me with may be considered as giving me a licence to say so much, permit me to wish that his vacancy may be filled by some other Gentleman from this State — I do not say this from any local or partial motives, but from an idea that the very great weight & importance of this country in a commercial view will probably engage more of her citizens in concerns with foreigners than almost any other State in the Union, & that it would I should suppose, always be pleasing to them to reflect that when their suits were taken from the tribunal & carried to another acting under a different authority, that still a citizen of their own was one of the Judges — but to your better Judgement this is very properly left & I trust your goodness will excuse my even having said as much as I have — I know the people of this country wish it — so do I — but both they & I ought with pleasure to acquiesce as I am sure I shall in any appointment you may conceive proper.

With my best wishes for your health & happiness I am with respect and Regard

Dear Sir
Yours Truly
CHARLES PINCKNEY

(Endorsed) From
His Ex[y] Gov[r] Pinckney
8th Mar. 1791

In accordance with his fixed rules concerning accepting hospitalities, Washington declined Governor Pinckney's invitation to be his guest throughout his entire visit, but accepted his hospitality: first in breakfasting at his country seat, "Fee Farm," also the same day dining at the Governor's (in what he called a private way) "with 15 or 18 gentlemen," and finally being entertained later in the week at a magnificent reception at the Governor's house in Meeting Street.

A correspondent writing from Charleston (April 7th) says: "We are making great preparations for the reception of the President of the United States. — There is to be a ball on the night of his arrival. — What think you of 100£: for the rent of a barn six or eight days? Sixty pounds was the lowest it could be obtained for — however I tell them it is wrong to engage one — as the President will not deviate from his rule, which is, not to take private lodgings." The house chosen for Washington's entertainment, as Charles Fraser relates in his "Reminiscences," was "that large three-story house in Church

Street, a few doors north of Tradd, then owned by Judge Heyward, and said to be superbly furnished for the occasion." This house, still standing, is now a bakery, although the owner declares he would never have turned it to such utilitarian uses had he known that it once housed the illustrious Washington. Day after day articles appeared in the local newspapers recommending that various preparations be made — such as that the "commissioners of the roads would display an equally laudable spirit [as that of all others] by having the roads and bridges put in proper repair, which in some places are almost impassable"; and that the citizens of Charleston appoint "a committee from each of their respective professions, to join and consider a mode for forming a procession to meet and receive our great and good President on landing in this city, similar to the one which was formed on the adoption of the federal constitution." Such a committee was appointed; and the report which follows exhibits the high seriousness and civic pride with which the citizens regarded Washington's approaching visit. The prudence which the occasion demanded was exhibited in the additional printed request of the Intendant and Warders that "the citizens will, not on the approaching occasion, exhibit any fireworks or illuminations within the city, as from the long, dry weather, the shingles and wooden buildings are rendered highly inflammable." [1]

[1] Notices from time to time appeared in the *City Gazette*, of which the following are specimens:

Thursday, April 21st.

A committee from the city council appointed to meet the several com-

The lavish preparations being made by the city of Charleston for the entertainment of the Nation's Chief Magistrate attracted wide and favorable attention throughout the country — a circumstance indicative of the universal desire to accord Washington the highest conceivable honors. In the "American Daily Advertiser" of Philadelphia, for example, appeared the striking commentary:

A philosopher, who has contemplated with due seriousness; the aggregate of incidents which have combined to present a novel character, in the history of this chequered planet, its heroes and its monarchs, cannot resist some flow of praise, but rather indulge the stream of panegyric on that ardour we see every hour displayed by the citizens of Charleston to receive the President of the United States with magnificence which his presence will adorn, and with that liberality and splendour which is eminently their characteristics. Every head and every hand are anxiously occupied, each in their proper station, from the governor to the mechanic, devising and executing such preparatory plans as may brighten the lustre of hospitality and display their sensibility and affectionate reverence, not only for virtue so rare, but for qualities "*taken all in all*" without any parallel in the annals of the human species.

mittees from the different professions and occupations will attend at the State house *this morning* at nine o'clock to confer with them in forming the line of procession to receive the president of the United States.

Tuesday, April 19th.

The members of the society of the Cincinnati established in this State intend to pay every respect and honor due to the president of the United States on his arrival in this city; it is therefore to be hoped that those members who may be in the country, will make it a point to be in town at or before the 10th instant, the time when the president may be expected.

April 18th.

Friday, April 22d.

The list of arrangement, taken by ballot from which the different professions and handicrafts are to form the procession, on the president's ar-

MANTELPIECE IN THOMAS HEYWARD HOUSE

The character and magnitude of Charleston's preparations raised misgivings in the minds of some, however; and the charges of monarchist tendencies which Jefferson was always flinging about find their echo in this protest, which appeared in the "Independent Gazette, and Agricultural Repository" (April 30, 1791) of Philadelphia: "We find by the southern papers that the President, on his journey, is still perfumed with the incense of *addresses*. However highly we may consider the character of the Chief Magistrate of the Union, yet we cannot but think the fashionable mode of expressing our attachment to the defender of the liberty of his country, savors too much of monarchy to be used by Republicans or to be received with pleasure by a President of a Commonwealth."

The coming of Washington was heralded by brief notices in the "City Gazette." On April 30th appeared the first notice:

By an express who arrived yesterday from Georgetown with dispatches to the intendant of this city, we learn that the President of the United States was to have been at Wilmington on the 24th instant, and that he was expected in Georgetown yesterday. From whence it is concluded that this illustrious personage will arrive in this city on Wednesday next.

On Monday, 2d, appeared the following:

rival, is left at the printing office for the government of those who intend joining the procession.

Thursday, April 28th.

The standing committee, the committee of arrangements and the other members of the Cincinnati, are requested to meet this evening at 6 o'clock at McCrady's tavern, on business of particular moment to the Society.

From undoubted authority we learn that the President of the United States was at George town on the 30th and was to dine yesterday at Mrs. Horrÿ's. That he intends being in town this day by 1 o'clock and dine in a private manner with his Excellency, the Governor.

The streets being very dry, the citizens are requested to sweep and water before their respective houses early this morning.

The committee of arrangements for the Cincinnati request the members to meet this day at ten o'clock precisely at McCrady's tavern *in their full uniform.*

The celebration of the anniversary of the St. Tammany Society, which was to have been held this day, is postponed to a future day, of which timely notice will be given.

Even the local versifiers burst forth in patriotic poems — notably the long-forgotten (and just as well!) "Address to General Washington on his arrival in Charleston, from *Liberty"[1] [Please note the arresting asterisk referring to fetching allusions in the poem itself]:

Address To

GENERAL WASHINGTON

On his arrival in Charleston,

from *Liberty.

With peals extatic let the welkin ring,
To hail th' approach of him that's more than king;
For having made a gallant people free,
He scorn'd to grasp at regal tyranny;
In war he for them having freedom gain'd,
He still their guardian in peace remain'd;
His care paternal of their rights & laws,
From every grateful heart demands applause;

[1] *City Gazette*, May 3, 1791.

Prudence and courage form my hero's mind,
To every change of fate alike resign'd;
The virtues which illume his daring soul,
Have spread his fame from Indus to the pole.

Then welcome Washington by *me designed,
To make my name rever'd by all mankind;
To snatch the scourge from oppressions hand,
And spread my blessings o'er an injur'd land;
Thy Carolina free'd made great by thee,
T' express her grateful thanks commissions me;
With gratitude each gen'rous bosom beats,
Thy glorious actions every tongue repeats;
The mighty league thro' thee shall be rever'd,
Its friendship courted, its resentment fear'd,
The stripes and stars perpetuate thy fame,
And children yet unborn shall bless thy name;
Follow the glorious course thou hast begun
And prove thyself *my best, my darling son.
When thou hast pass'd th' inevitable doom,
Immortal honors shall adorn thy tomb;
And when thy mortal part to Earth is given,
A cherubim shall waft thy soul to heaven.

The scene of Washington's arrival at Charleston is the brightest, liveliest picture in the gay panorama of the Southern tour. When Washington, accompanied by Major Jackson, reached Haddrel's Point — just across the Cooper River from Charleston — he is greeted most warmly by the Honorable John Bee Holmes,[1] Recorder to

[1] John Bee Holmes, son of Isaac and Rebecca Holmes, was born April 22, 1760. While still a lad he bore arms in the American Revolution; and was an officer in the Charleston Regiment of Militia. In the disastrous attack upon Savannah in 1779, in which he was slightly wounded, he bore the mortally wounded Count Pulaski from the field. He served during the siege of Charleston; and after the surrender was imprisoned on the prison-ship *Pack Horse* with the other officers of his regiment. This was regarded

the city, in his official robes, General Charles Cotesworth Pinckney,[1] Major-General William Moultrie, Major Ed-

as an act of barbarity, as the ship had recently been used as a smallpox hospital. As soon as he came of age, he was admitted to the bar. As a young man he served in the South Carolina Legislature. He won high reputation for ability as a criminal lawyer. "The friendships of the most enlightened men in the State," it is stated in an obituary in the *Charlestown Courier*, "were the first fruits of his manliness and intelligence." On Washington's visit, he steered a boat rowed by eight American captains to meet the President. On November 19, 1783, he was married to Elizabeth Edwards, daughter by his first wife of John Edwards, Mrs. Isaac Holmes's second husband. They had thirteen children. He died very suddenly on September 5, 1827.

[1] Charles Cotesworth Pinckney was born in Charleston February 25, 1746; died there August 16, 1825. Educated at Westminster, Christ Church, Oxford (England); read law in Middle Temple. Nine months Royal Military Academy, Caen, France. Attorney-General of South Carolina; Member of first Provincial Congress of South Carolina, 1775; Captain and Major and Colonel of infantry; aide-de-camp to Washington; took part in the battles of Brandywine and Germantown. Presided over South Carolina Senate, 1779; active in many battles; in council of war he voted "for the rejection of all terms of capitulation and for continuing hostilities to the last extremity." He was taken prisoner on the surrender of Charleston, May, 1780, remaining in rigorous confinement for two years. Exchanged, February, 1782; commissioned Brigadier-General, 1782. He was a member of the convention that framed the Constitution of the United States in 1787. He became a Federalist and served in the convention that ratified it for South Carolina; and in the State Constitutional Convention, 1790. In 1791 he declined the office of Associate Justice of the United States Supreme Court; in 1784, the portfolio of War, and in 1795 that of State. In 1796 he accepted the position of United States Minister to France; but that Government refused to receive him. Federalist candidate for Vice-President, 1800, and for President in 1804 and 1808. At a special meeting of the South Carolina Society of the Cincinnati, held at the court-house, August 18, 1825, the Honorable William Drayton delivered an obituary address in which appear the following words: "His life was extended to extreme old age, yet did he so conduct himself through its whole duration, as not only to obtain the applause of the wise and good, but what is seldom the lot of the illustrious, in such a manner as to avoid the slanders of envy, and the vindictiveness of malice. . . . His was the rare felicity of running an unbroken career of virtue and usefulness; honoured and honourable from the vernal bloom of youth, to the maturity of manhood and the frosts of age." Writing of him, with reference to availability for commander-in-chief of the United States Army, Washington (winter of 1791-

GENERAL CHARLES COTESWORTH PINCKNEY

ward Rutledge,[1] Colonel William Washington, and Colonel Dart, to the accompaniment of the enthusiastic cheers of the many who have come to attend him across the river to Charleston. Entering the elegant twelve-oared barge prepared for the purpose, Washington is rowed across the river by thirteen masters of American vessels, namely: Captain Cochran (cockswain, as senior officer), Cross, Moore, Milligan, Kean, Rea, Lawrence, Drinker, Swain, Congers, Dickenson, Crowly, and Connolly, who were uniformly and neatly dressed ("most elegantly dressed," records Washington) in light blue silk jackets and round black hats decorated with blue ribbons on which were impressed the arms of South Carolina. Properly disposed in two boats close behind were the gentlemen of the Amateur Society who, assisted by Mr. Palmer, Mr. James Badger, Mr. Jonathan Badger, and Mr. Harris, with the

92) records: "A Colonel since Sept[r] 16th 1776; but appointed a Brigadr. by brevet, at the close of the War, only. — In this Gentleman many valuable qualities are to be found. — He is of unquestionable bravery — Is a man of strict honor, erudition & good sense: and it is said has made Tacitus a study."

[1] On this tour occurred a remarkable and unique episode. Washington, writing from Camden, South Carolina, May 24, 1791, addressed the following letter to Charles Cotesworth Pinckney and Edward Rutledge:

GENTLEMEN,

An address to you jointly, on a subject of the following nature, may have a singular appearance; but that singularity will not exceed the evidence, which is thereby given of my opinion of, and confidence in you, and of the opinion I entertain of your confidence and friendship for each other.

The office lately resigned by Mr. John Rutledge, in the supreme judiciary of the Union, remains to be filled. Will either of you two gentlemen accept it? And, in that case, which of you? It will occur to you, that appointments to office in the recess of the Senate are temporary; but of their confirmation in such a case there can be no doubt.

It may be asked, why a proposition similar to this has never been made

choir of St. Philip's Church, made the air sweet with the strains of music, both vocal and instrumental, and delighted the gay throng of richly dressed ladies and gentlemen in more than forty boats who laughed and chattered gaily — rather than listening in silence to the music — on the passage across the river. But all listened intently to the chorus of voices in the song:

> He comes! he comes! the hero comes.
> Sound, sound your trumpets, beat your drums,
> From port to port let cannons roar,
> His welcome to our friendly shore.
>
> Prepare, prepare, your songs prepare,
> Loud, loudly rend the echoing air,
> From pole to pole this praise resound,
> For virtue is with glory crowned.

As the gay flotilla approached Prioleau's Wharf, at the foot of Queen Street, numbers of other boats came to meet and greet the welcome visitor; and cannon boomed a salute in handsome style.[1] As the tall and majestic Wash-

to you before. This is my answer. Your friends, with whom I have often conversed on like occasions, have always given it as their decided opinion, that no place at the disposal of the general government could be a compensation for the relinquishment of your private pursuits, or, in their belief, would withdraw you from them. In making the attempt, however, in the present instance, I discharge my duty, and shall await your answer (which I wish to receive soon) for the issue. Of my sincere esteem and regard for you both, I wish you to be persuaded, and that I am, Gentlemen, &c.

G. Washington

In a joint reply, Mr. Pinckney and Mr. Rutledge declined accepting the proposed appointment. For the grounds of their declination, consult Sparks's *Washington*, XII, p. 165, footnote.

[1] An eye-witness thus describes the scene: "There was such concourse of all ranks on board the several vessels hauled close to the shore as is almost

ington alighted from his barge and walked up the specially erected stairway covered with green cloth, he was accorded official greetings by Governor Charles Pinckney, Lieutenant-Governor Isaac Holmes, Intendant Vanderhorst, the members of the City Council, by name of Mr. Morris, Colonel Mitchell, Mr. Corbett, Mr. Beckman, Captain North, Mr. Cripps, Mr. Lee, Mr. Cole, Mr. Brownlee, Dr. Payas, Dr. Harris, and Mr. Robertson, and by the State Society of the Cincinnati.[1] With solemn mien, the benignant-looking Intendant stepped forward and said:

> The Intendant and Wardens beg leave, Sir, to welcome you to this city. It will be their care to make your stay agreeable — they have provided accomodations for yourself and suite to which they will be happy to conduct you!

With formal dignity the President acknowledged the greeting and bade them lead on. The Fusilier Company [2] then opened their files, and enclosed the following order

beyond description. From superannuated old age to lisping infancy. The crowd was so great there was scarce room to move! On the illustrious personage's approach to the shore, such a buz of approbation — such a shout of joy, took place as that one must see and hear all to have anything like an adequate idea of it. The shore, the streets, the windows, the balconies, all were so crowded, so beset with spectators, that the most attentive observer must fail in an attempt to do justice to the splendid aspect of the whole."

[1] "The uncommonly large concourse of citizens," says a writer in the *Gazette*, "testified their happiness on the arrival of their chief magistrate by reiterated shouts of joy and satisfaction — the Charleston battalion of artillery saluted him with discharges from their field pieces, the bells of St. Michael's Church were rung, and the shipping in the harbour displayed their colors during the day."

[2] The German Fusiliers were organized as a militia company during the Revolution and served with distinction both in that war and in the War between the States. "Their successors," said D. E. Huger-Smith in a letter to me, October 31, 1918, "are to-day serving on the French front in the 30th Division of Pershing's Army."

of procession which moved towards the Exchange, with colors flying, drums beating, fifes playing:

The Sheriff of the City bearing the mace
Messenger and Marshall
Treasurer and Clerk
Recorder
The Wardens, two and two, bearing their wands
The Intendant with his wand
The President and suite
The Governor and Lieutenant Governor
Aids to his Excellency the Governor
Civil Officers of the State
Civil Officers of the United States
President of the Senate
Clergy
Citizens two and two
Officers of the Militia
Members of the Cincinnati.

Banners with "sentiments" inscribed thereon were prominent in the procession; and perhaps the most notable inscription was that on the banner borne by M. Ransier, gunsmith of Charleston:

Arma sunt necessaria
Vis vim repellere licet
Titus vixit pro ipsis
Georgius Washington vivit pro suis
Utinam Nestoris annos recipiat.

On reaching the Exchange, the President was conducted to the platform within the grand balustrade of the Exchange, fronting the Broad Street, where he stood to

INTENDANT VANDERHORST

MORDECAI GIST

await the salutes and discharges from the field artillery. He then reviewed the procession as it passed along; and "politely and gravely bowed" in recognition of the salutations of respect which were rendered to him. The order of the procession was now reversed; the President was escorted to Major Heyward's house, which had been hired from Mrs. Jamieson by the Corporation for his entertainment.[1] The "elegant habitation" was ornamented in front by lamps, and over the portal was a triumphal arch.

[1] The following minutes of the Proceedings of the City Council are worthy of record:

Wednesday, 27th April, 1791. — The Hon. Arnoldus Vanderhorst, Intendant; Col. Mitchell, Mr. Morris, Mr. Corbett, Dr. Harris and Mr. Marshall, Committee to make the necessary arrangements for the reception and entertainment of George Washington, Esq., President of the United States, on his arrival in the City of Charleston, reported, and the said report being read, Ordered, That the said report be taken into consideration immediately, and the same being again read, was agreed to as follows, viz.: The Intendant and Committee appointed to make the necessary arrangements for the reception and entertainment of George Washington, Esq., President of the United States, on his arrival in Charleston, recommend that the house of Thos. Heyward, Esq. in Church Street, at present in the occupation of Mrs. Rebecca Jamieson, be taken for the use of the President during his residence in this city, together with the furniture, for which the sum of £60 be paid, it being the lowest rate at which the said house can be procured. They recommend Mrs. Frances Ramadge for House-keeper, and Margaret Daniel, with other necessary servants for the house, to be paid by the Corporation. Major Peter Bocquet having offered his Barge and Mr. Paul Pritchard agrees to lengthen and put it in thorough repair, gratis, for the purpose of conveying the President of the United States from Haddrel's Point or Hobcau Ferry to the city. Capt. Cochran and twelve other masters of American vessels, viz: Jacob Milligan, Geo. Cross, Charles Crawley, John Connely, Henry Laurence, Thos. Kean, Jeremh. Dickenson, Luke Swain, Thos. Blundel, Wm. Conyers, James Rea, John Drinker, to be handsomely dressed at their own expense, will serve as a volunteer crew.

The Committee advise that their offers be accepted, and that the Recorder in his Robes be directed to attend and present the Barge in the name of the Corporation, to the President at Haddrel's Point, for his accomodation and conveyance to the city; they also advise that the Custom House

During the procession from the wharf to the Exchange and then to his lodgings, the President "with the greatest politeness and attention bowed uncovered to the brilliant assemblage of spectators of both sexes to the right and to the left." "The lodgings provided for me in this place were very good," records Washington in his diary, "being the furnished house of a Gentleman at present in the Country; but occupied by a person placed there on purpose to accommodate me, & who was paid in the same manner as any other letter of lodgings would have been

barge and the Fort boat be procured to assist in bringing over any gentlemen who may accompany the President, and that a temporary pair of stairs be placed at such wharf as may be appointed for his landing.

The Intendant and Committee recommend that a Dinner be given to the President, and such other gentlemen as the Council shall think proper to invite. Mr. Williams of the Coffee House, having made proposals to provide a good Dinner, for six shillings for each person, with a handsome Desert; the best Madeira wine for 5s. per bottle, and other Liquors as usual, but that he cannot find Tables, Seats and Sconces or Candlesticks; it is recommended that his proposals be accepted, and that the Exchange be suitably fitted up with Tables, Chairs, Benches, Sconces and awnings.

It is further recommended that the City Hall be put into proper order, for the purpose of giving a Ball to the President, and the Ladies of the city, with such gentlemen as the Council shall think proper to invite, and that a genteel Supper be provided on the occasion.

The Intendant and Committee further recommend, that a proper stock of liquors, groceries, and provisions, be laid in for the use of the President and his suite, while in the city, and that his horses be properly provided with stables, hay, corn and oats.

They further recommend, that the Bells of St. Michael's Church be put in repair, and proper persons employed for the purpose of ringing a Peal, on the approaching joyous occasion, to be paid by the Corporation.

As a mark of distinction to the Intendant and Wardens, it is recommended that handsome black varnished Wands three-quarters of an inch diameter, and six feet long, be provided. The Intendant's Wand to have a gold head, and the Wardens' silver heads, with the cypher C. C. L. on each to be used on this and other public occasions.

Lastly, they recommend that the expenses which may be incurred in carrying the foregoing or any other necessary arrangements into execution, may be defrayed by the Corporation.

paid." [1] Here he received the "warm congratulations of several of the most respectable characters in the State"; and was individually introduced to the officials of the Corporation, the members of the Cincinnati, and the officers of the Charleston Battalion of Artillery.[2] While the President removed the stains of travel and made ready for dinner at the Governor's, the City Council retired to the Council Chamber, where an address to the President from the Corporation, which had been previously prepared, was

[1] On May 23, 1901, a bronze tablet on the front of Thomas Heyward's husoe in Church Street, then owned by H. W. Fuseler, was unveiled with appropriate ceremonies, the orator of the day being Professor Yates Snowden, of the University of South Carolina, who spoke in Hibernian Hall. The tablet was the gift of Mrs. Edward Willis, Vice-Regent of Rebecca Motte Chapter, Daughters of the American Revolution, of the City of Charleston. The tablet, of diamond shape, bears the inscription:

DURING
HIS VISIT
TO CHARLESTON
MAY 1791
THE GUEST OF THE CITIZENS
PRESIDENT
GEORGE WASHINGTON
WAS ENTERTAINED IN THIS HOUSE
—— * ——
This Memorial erected by a Daughter
of the
American Revolution
A Charter Member
May 1901

Consult *The Exposition*, August, 1901. For the text of Professor Snowden's address see *Charleston News and Courier*, May 26, 1901. Also consult *News and Courier*, May 24, 1901.

[2] The Charleston Battalion of Artillery was a militia command organized about 1757. Throughout the Revolution until the fall of Charleston in 1780, the services of this military organization were continuous and creditable. At the fight on Port Royal Island in 1777 its two companies were commanded by Edward Rutledge and Thomas Heyward, Jr., both signers of the Declaration of Independence.

read and agreed to. It was then "Ordered, that the Recorder do wait on the President of the United States, to know when he would be pleased to receive the Corporation, with their address," and the Recorder, on his return, informed the Council that the President would receive the City address the next afternoon at three o'clock.

At five o'clock that afternoon (May 2d), the President dined with the Governor, at his house in Meeting Street "(in what he called a private way) with 15 or 18 Gentlemen." A description of the Pinckney house, recorded by Fraser, gives color and atmosphere to the picture:

His collection of Paintings, statuettes, medals, etc., rendered his house almost a museum. His fine library occupying an entire suite of three large rooms, the floor and windows of which were richly carpeted and curtained, while the ceilings were worked with classic representations — is supposed to have contained near twenty thousand of the most rare and choice books collected from every part of the Continent and in every known language. The old gentleman was accustomed to receive his friends in a room peculiarly his own — two large old fashioned richly carved and covered chairs stood on either side of the fireplace while a table of ebony wood inlaid with mosaic occupied the centre; Ben Franklin's bust over the door; and in beautiful fresco Ganymede flying, with his cup worked on the ceiling; a heavy carved mahogany case occupied one corner, in which cake and wine were kept, and on the arrival of a visitor always were placed before him. This room overlooked a garden of choicest flowers in which were to be seen two beautiful flamingoes with their rich plumage. . . .

It was in this very house, that, when the third time Governor of the State, he entertained General Washington in a style and manner which has come down to our day — the whole of the large mansion was thrown open and illuminated

MR. AND MRS. JOHN RUTLEDGE

by varied colored lights which burned night and day, the garden was arranged as a promenade — there with music, viands and the dance time was cheated for a week.

It is characteristic of Washington that, after a day of great exertion, which must have taxed him severely, he should nevertheless find time to record before retiring some observations on geography and agriculture:

It may as well in this as in any other place, be observed, that the Country from Wilmington through which the Road passes, is, except in very small spots, much the same as what has already been described; that is to say, sand & pine barrens — with very few inhabitants — we were indeed informed that at some distance from the Road on both sides the land was of a better quality, & thicker settled, but this could only be on the Rivers & larger waters — for a perfect sameness seems to run through all the rest of the Country — on these — especially the swamps and low lands on the Rivers, the Soil is very rich; and productive when reclaimed; but to do this is both laborious and expensive. — The Rice planters have two modes of watering their fields — the first by the tide — the other by resurvoirs drawn from the adjacent lands. — The former is best because most certain. — A crop without either is precarious, — because a drought may not only injure, but destroy it. — Two and an half and 3 barrels to the Acre is esteemed a good Crop and 8 or 10 Barrls. for each grown hand is very profitable; but some have 12 & 14, whilst 5 or 6 is reckoned the average production of a hand — a barrel contains about 600 weight and the present price is about 10/6 & 11/ Sterg. pr. 100.

It will be recalled that the son of the Chief Justice, John Rutledge,[1] had gone to meet the President at "Snee"

[1] John Rutledge, born in Charleston, 1739; died there, 1800. Educated for the bar at the Temple, London. Opposed Stamp Act, advocated colonial union (1765). "By far the greatest orator," according to Patrick Henry, in first Continental Congress. President of the Provincial Government of South Carolina (1776) and head of military forces. Resigned governorship

farm, the country estate of Governor Charles Pinckney, and attended him thence into the city. The Chief Justice had previously made his apologies to the President for his absence on the circuit in the following letter:

Dr Sir —

I am extremely sorry, that official Duty [1] prevents (which nothing but indispensable Necessity should), my going, with my Son to meet you, at the Boundary-Line of North Carolina; He will do himself the Honour of waiting on you, from thence. And I flatter myself, that I shall have an opportunity of paying my Respects, to you, in Person, on you Tour thro' the upper Country, (where I must be for several Weeks, on the Circuit), & of joining my fellow Citizens there, in expressing, and testifying those Sentiments of Affection for your Person, & Veneration for your character, which prevail in every part of this State, as much as in any part of the United States.

I have the Honour to be, with the greatest Esteem & Respect, Dr Sir

Y^r obliged & most obed^t Servt

J. Rutledge /

The President of the United States of America

(Endorsed) From the Honble Jno Rutledge /
15th Ap^l 1791

---

in 1778, reëlected in 1779. When Charleston was besieged by the British in 1780, he supported Council proposal to make South Carolina neutral during remainder of Revolution. Convened legislature at Jacksonborough in 1782. Member of Congress, 1782–83; and in 1784, after declining mission to The Hague, appointed Chancellor of South Carolina. Member of the convention that framed the Constitution. Declined post of Justice of the United States Supreme Court, to accept that of Chief Justice of Supreme Court of South Carolina. On July 1, 1795, was appointed Chief Justice of the United States, over which he presided at the August term; but his nomination was not confirmed owing to mental alienation.

[1] The Court of Chancery prior to 1791 was held only at Charleston for the whole State. In that year the judges of the court were by statute directed to hold courts at stated times in Columbia and Ninety-Six as well, and it was permitted to any one judge to make all interlocutory orders previous to final decree, which could only be made by the whole court. After the resignation of John Rutledge, the last Chief Justice under the old law, no other Chief Justice was elected, but the judges of the State were all

In his absence, Mrs. Rutledge [1] did the honors of the occasion — the President accepting her hospitality by breakfasting with her on the morning of Tuesday (3d). At two o'clock in the afternoon the President held a levée "at which were present a number of ladies and gentlemen of the greatest respectability." [2] The President's diary —

called Associate Judges, and writs were tested in the name of the senior Associate Justice for the time being.

[1] Eliza Grimké, wife of John Rutledge, Governor of South Carolina and known as "the Dictator," was born November 29, 1741. She was the daughter of Frederick Grimké, who in 1733 at the age of twenty-eight emigrated from Germany; and in 1737 was married to Martha Emms Williamson. He died October 20, 1778. By her marriage to John Rutledge (May 1, 1763), Eliza Grimké had five sons and two daughters. When the officers defending Fort Moultrie against British attack advised its evacuation, John Rutledge is credited with saying: "You will not do so without an order from me and I would sooner cut off my right hand than write one." Eliza Grimké died June 7, 1792.

[2] John Rutledge was a warm friend and sincere admirer of Washington, and never permitted him to be attacked or slandered in his presence. In his unpublished diary (Paris, 1787), Rutledge describes a dinner-party he attended in England, at the house of a nobleman, Sir John S——, a large company being present. During the course of the dinner, one of the guests described in detail the hanging of a political prisoner, Argill, at Washington's orders, with many reflections on Washington. "When Mr. G. had finished," records Rutledge, "I said that I was an American. That I had the honor of knowing General Washington, and was well acquainted with all the circumstances attached to Mr. Argill's case. That out of regard to Truth, as well as respect for Genl. Washington's character (which had been very much questioned on this occasion), I came forward to declare that the *whole* of Mr. G.'s information was false, and that *no one circumstance* had happened as by him related. I said I was sure that Mr. G. could not have got his information from Captain Argill, for that I was persuaded that whenever he mentioned the affair, that also he must have mentioned the great delicacy and kindness with which he was treated not only by Genl. Washington but by all the different officers to whose charge, during his confinement, he had been committed. Every body at table seemed pleased with the part I had acted, and I was begged to tell the story — which I did.

"But very differently from what Mr. G. had done. I concluded by saying that I had not related it as a thing I merely believed but which I *knew* to be a fact. And that I would let the credit of my information rest on the word of Mr. G.'s brother, a gentleman I had not the honor to know, but who

written under extraordinarily trying conditions, during snatches of rest between balls, parties, receptions, and addresses, is very dry and succinct, for the most part. But on this occasion a touch of real emotion succeeds in transferring itself to the page of the little diary book: "Was visited about 2 o'clock by a great number of the most respectable ladies of Charleston — the first honor of the kind I had ever experienced and it was as flattering as it was singular." Not Jefferson himself could have expressed more deftly or tersely the sense of combined gratification and surprise which Washington has here expressed in the last eight words. While these festivities were under way, the City Council met according to adjournment and proceeded to the President's house where, at three o'clock, His Honor the Intendant, Arnoldus Vanderhorst, delivered an address in these words:

To the President of the United States:

Sir: The Intendant and Wardens, representing the citizens of Charleston, find themselves particularly gratified by your arrival in the Metropolis of the State. It is an event, the

having been in America at the time must necessarily have known what I mention to be true.

"I added that with respect to the inhumanity of which General Washington had been accused I would appeal for a contradiction of the charge to those officers who had been his prisoners in America; and I was sure (from my acquaintance with some of them, and good opinion of the rest) they would not be satisfied merely with contradictions of it, but they would esteem it a duty they owed their consciences, and to Justice, to go further and declare they never knew a man possessing *more humanity;* and that if anything could have rendered the position of a prisoner agreeable it would have been the very great kindness which Genl. Washington shewed to his.

"When all the company had gone Sir John told me he never in his life was more pleased with anything than the modest and probable manner in which I had related Argill's affair. . . ." For this extract I am indebted to Mr. E. B. Rutledge, The Plains, Fauquier County, Virginia.

THE JOHN RUTLEDGE HOUSE
Where Washington breakfasted

expectation of which they have for some time with great pleasure indulged. When in the person of the Supreme Magistrate of the United States, they recognize the Father of the People, and the defender of the liberties of America, they feel a particular satisfaction in declaring their firm persuasion that they speak the language of their constituents, in asserting, that no body of men throughout this extensive continent can exceed them in attachment to his public character, or in revering his private virtues. And they do not hesitate in anticipating those blessings which must ultimately be diffused amongst the inhabitants of these States by his exertions for their general welcome, aided by those in whom they have also vested a share of their confidence.

Go on, Sir, as you have done. Continue to possess as well as deserve the love and esteem of all your fellow citizens: while millions in other parts of the globe, though strangers to your person, shall venerate your name. May you long be spared to receive those marks of respect which you so entirely merit from a grateful people; and may all who live under your auspices continue to experience that freedom and happiness which is so universally acknowledged to have proceeded from your wise, judicious and prudent administration.

To which the President graciously replied:

GENTLEMEN —

The gratification you are pleased to express at my arrival in your Metropolis, is replied to with sincerity, in a grateful acknowledgment of the pleasing sensations which your affectionate urbanity has excited.

Highly sensible of your attachment and favorable opinions, I entreat you to be persuaded of the lasting gratitude which they impress, and of the cordial regard with which they are returned.

It is the peculiar boast of our country that her happiness is alone dependent on the collective wisdom and virtue of her citizens, and rests not on the exertions of any individual. Whilst a just sense is entertained of their natural and political advantages, we cannot fail to improve them, and with the progress of our national importance, to combine the freedom and felicity of individuals. I shall be particularly grateful in observing the happy influence of public measures on the prosperity of your city, which is so much entitled to the regard and esteem of the American Union.

Not to be outdone, the Charleston Chamber of Commerce had made preparations to present an address to the President, particularly in view of the great importance of Charleston as a commercial centre and port of entry. Accordingly at half-past three, almost before the President could catch his breath, a delegation of the merchants arrived at the President's house, and the following address was presented by the chairman, Edmund Darrell:

Sir,

The merchants of Charleston, entertaining a just sense of the high honour conferred on the City by your Presence, take the earliest opportunity of congratulating you on your arrival.

The obligations which are due to you by every member of the Republic, are acknowledged by all; to enter into detail of them, would be to produce the history of your life, and to repeat what is re-echoed from one end of the Continent to the other. Were it possible, Sir, for your Fellow-Citizens to omit doing justice to your Merits, the Testimony of other Nations would evince their neglect, or ingratitude; the whole world concurring in the same opinion of you.

Convinced as we are of your constant Solicitude for the general Welfare; it must afford you particular Satisfaction to find the progressive Effects of the Federal Government in this State; and that the inhabitants are fast emerging from the heavy Calamities, to which they were subjected by the late War.

Sensible of the numerous blessings our Country has derived from your Wise and judicious Administration, we feel animated with the most lively Sentiments of Gratitude towards you: Suffer us then, on the present occasion, to represent to you the effectionate Sensibility with which we are impressed, by assuring you that we yield to none in sincere Respect and attachment to your Person; and, we earnestly implore the Almighty Father of the Universe, long to preserve a life so valuable and dear to the People over whom you preside.

The reply of the President follows:

TO THE MERCHANTS OF CHARLESTON:
GENTLEMEN:

Your congratulations on my arrival in South Carolina, enhanced by the affectionate manner in which they are offered, are received with the most grateful sensibility.

Flattered by the favorable sentiments you express of my endeavors to be useful to our country, I desire to assure you of my constant solicitude for its welfare and of my particular satisfaction in observing the advantages which accrue to the highly deserving citizens of this State from the operations of the general government.

I am not less indebted to your expressions of personal attachment and respect; they receive my best thanks, and induce my most sincere wishes for your professional prosperity and your individual happiness.

Following the ceremonies, the President at once adjourned to the Exchange, where an "elegant entertainment" was given in his honor by the City Corporation.[1]

The Exchange, which had recently been "fitted up and decorated in very sumptuous style," was well suited for so memorable a company — those invited being the Governor, Lieutenant-Governor, officers of the State, Union and city, consuls of foreign powers, the reverend clergy, members of the Society of the Cincinnati, officers of the

[1] It is so styled in the contemporary *Charleston City Gazette*. But A. S. Salley, Jr., to whom I am indebted for information, states that Charleston was not incorporated as a city until more than forty years after this event. The name was changed from Charles Town to Charleston by act of assembly in 1783.

militia, "gentlemen strangers," and a number of "respectable citizens." The banquet, unusually protracted, was a great success according to the ideas of our leisurely ancestors; and, following custom, fifteen toasts were given after the banquet — each toast being followed by a discharge from the cannon of the Charleston Battalion of Artillery:

1. The United States of America, may they long enjoy freedom in peace.
2. The federal constitution, its friends and supporters.
3. The Vice-President of the United States and members of the Senate.
4. The late members of both houses of Congress; may their successors inherit their wisdom and patriotism.
5. (By the President.) The commercial interests of Charleston.
6. Louis 16th and the National Assembly of France.
7. The navigation of the United States; protected by the strong arm of the federal government, may it increase and flourish.
8. Agriculture and commerce; may their dependence on each other be properly understood.
9. The useful arts of peace.
10. May the merchants of the United States continue to merit the flattering compliments paid them by the President at the opening of the last session of Congress.
11. The National bank; a general diffusion of its happy effects throughout the United States.
12. The defenders of the rights and liberties of the people throughout the world.
13. The Secretary of State; may the important service he has rendered to the commercial interest of his country, endear him to every merchant.
14. The Secretary of the Treasury; may his fame increase with the rising credit of his country.
15. May the mantle of peace and friendship cover the world.
16. The fair daughters of America.

THE EXCHANGE, CHARLESTON

VIEW OF CHURCH STREET, CHARLESTON, SHOWING JUDGE HEYWARD'S MANSION IN CENTRE

And when the President retired —

17. The illustrious President of the United States; long may he live to enjoy the praises of a grateful people.
18. The lady of the President.

At the conclusion of this ceremony, which came at eight o'clock, the "President retired" — whereupon the banqueters enthusiastically and mayhap hilariously drank a last toast to "The President of the United States."

Over the President's head [reads a description in the *Gazette* referring to the place which he occupied at the banquet table] was fabricated, in very ingenious workmanship, a beautiful triumphal arch, from which was suspended a wreath of laurel. It is almost unnecessary to add, that the day and evening were spent with all that hilarity, harmony and happy festivity suitable to the occasion.

The Charleston battalion of artillery performed Military Duty during the entertainment and the privates of that ancient, respectable corps (who in their official capacity have uniformly acquitted themselves with honor) dined in an agreeable manner, in a separate apartment, provided by the corporation. The shipping in the harbour displayed all their colors during the day and St. Michael's bells echoed forth their joyous peals.

An incident worthy of record is associated with this banquet. Commodore Alexander Gillon, a native of Rotterdam, and commander of the ill-fated *South Carolina* during the Revolution, was a figure in the social world of Charleston — owning a handsome residence in Charleston on East Bay, renamed "Batavia," where he and his first wife lived in style prior to the Revolution. Following the battle of Lexington, a volunteer military organization called the German Fusiliers was organized in Charleston

(May, 1775), with Gillon as captain — a post he retained until 1777. During Washington's visit, Gillon played a prominent part — both as former captain of the German Fusiliers and as a leader of society. At the banquet at the Exchange, given by the City Corporation on May 3d, the President was to take in the Governor's lady, of course; but the question was raised by the committee of arrangements: What other fair companions should Washington have? "Leave it to me," said the tactful Gillon, "and I will arrange things quite *comme il faut.*" When the guests were seated, the gallant Commodore's wisdom was universally approved — for at the President's left was seated Miss Claudia Smith, the wittiest woman of Charleston, and immediately before his eyes across the banquet table Mrs. Richard Shubrick, the most beautiful of Charleston's daughters! Distinction, wit, and beauty — what more could even the great Washington desire?

Early on the morning of Wednesday, 4th, the President, accompanied by the Honorable Mr. Izard, Major-General Moultrie, Brigadier-General Pinckney, Major Rutledge, and Major Jackson, viewed the remains of the lines and batteries which had been thrown up for the defence of the city when attacked by the British fleet and army under Sir George Clinton and Admiral Arbuthnot in 1780. Mr. Izard, at this time Senator from South Carolina, was tall, graceful, and unusually prepossessing in appearance. He enjoyed the confidence of Washington in an unusual degree, especially for acumen in judgment of men he recommended to Washington for appointment. It appears from the letters of the period that he influenced the Commander-in-Chief to send General Greene to take command of the Southern Army, for which he received the thanks of the Governor of South Carolina.[1] With a trained eye for military works and fortifications, General Washington rode over the whole ground covered by these works, exhibiting keen interest in an inspection of the localities of the enemy's trenches, batteries, parallels, and approaches. Says a writer in the "City Gazette," the General was "pleased to express great satisfaction at the very gallant defence that had been made by the garrison during the siege." In his diary he records: "I . . . was satisfied that the defence was noble & honorable altho' the measure was undertaken upon wrong principles and impolitic." [2]

On this day, General M. Gist,[3] Grand Master of the

[1] Ralph Izard was born near Charleston, South Carolina. The family residence, "The Elms," was situated in St. James Parish, Goose Creek, about seventeen miles from Charleston. Of English ancestry, he pursued classical studies in Hackney, and was graduated from Christ College, Cambridge. He returned to America; but in 1771 he settled in England, and his home in England was the centre of the most intellectual and cultured society. Later he removed to Paris to live, and was appointed Commissioner to the Court of Tuscany, being recalled in 1779. When Commodore Gillon was sent from South Carolina to Europe to purchase frigates, and was unable to negotiate the requisite loan on the security of the State Government alone, Izard came forward and pledged his whole estate for the loan. He returned to America in 1780. He was a delegate from South Carolina in the Continental Congress, 1782–83. He was elected to the United States Senate, serving from March 4, 1789, to March 3, 1795, and was President *pro tempore* of the Senate from May 31, 1794, to February 20, 1795. Founder of the College of Charleston. Died May 30, 1804, and was buried at the Parish Church of St. James, Goose Creek. Cf. Memoir in *Correspondence of Ralph Izard*, vol. I.

[2] These lines were upon Charleston Neck, extending from the Ashley to the Cooper River, at the junction of which the City stands.

[3] Mordecai Gist was born in Baltimore, Maryland, in 1743, of English

fraternity of the ancient York Masons, "a tall and graceful figure, symmetrical proportions, and expressive features," attended by the other present and past grand officers, waited on their "beloved brother, the president of the United States," and presented the following address:

Sir — Induced by a respect for your public and private character, as well as the relation in which you stand with the brethren of this society, we the Grand Lodge of the State of South Carolina, Ancient York Masons, beg leave to offer our sincere congratulations on your arrival in this state.

We felicitate you on the establishment and exercise of a permanent government, whose foundation was laid under your auspices by military achievements, upon which have been progressively reared the pillars of the free republic over which you preside, supported by wisdom, strength, and beauty unrivalled among the nations of the world.

The fabric thus raised and committed to your superintendance, we earnestly wish may continue to produce order and harmony to succeeding ages, and be the asylum of virtue to the oppressed of all parts of the universe.

When we contemplate the distresses of war, the instances of humanity displayed by the Craft afford some relief to the feeling mind; and it gives us the most pleasing sensation to recollect, that amidst the difficulties attendant on your late military stations, you still associated with, and patronized the Ancient Fraternity.

Distinguished always by your virtues, more than the ex-

parentage. He was elected captain "Baltimore Independent Company" at beginning of the Revolution. In 1776 he was appointed major of a battalion of Maryland regulars, and with them was at the battle near Brooklyn. In January, 1779, he was appointed by Congress brigadier-general in the Continental Army, and took command of the Second Maryland Brigade. He participated in the battle of Camden, 1780. He was present at the surrender of Cornwallis, and joined the Southern Army under Greene. In 1782, when the army was remodelled, he was given the command of the Light Corps. He fought bravely at the battle of the Combahee, August 6, 1782, gaining a decisive victory over the British. After the war he resided at his plantation near Charleston, South Carolina, where he died in 1792.

RALPH IZARD

alted stations in which you have moved, we exult in the opportunity you now give us of hailing you brother of our Order, and trust from your knowledge of our institution to merit your countenance and support.

With fervent zeal for your happiness, we pray that a life so dear to the bosom of this society, and to society in general, may be long, very long preserved; and when you leave the temporal symbolic lodges of this world, you may be received into the celestial lodge of light and perfection, where the Grand Master Architect of the Universe presides.

Done in behalf of the Grand Lodge.

M. GIST, G. M.

CHARLESTON, 2*d May*, 1791.

The reply of the President, which was thoughtfully composed — as indicated by the corrections and deletions[1] — is as follows:

GENTLEMEN:

I am much obliged by the respect which you are so good as to declare for my public and private character. I recognize with pleasure my relation to the brethren of your Society, and I accept with gratitude your congratulations on my arrival in South Carolina.

Your sentiments, on the establishment and exercise of our equal government, are worthy of an association, whose principles lead to purity of morals and are beneficial of action.

The fabric of our freedom is placed on the enduring basis of public virtue, and will, I fondly hope, long continue to protect the prosperity of the architects who raised it. I shall be happy, on every occasion, to evince my regard for the Fraternity. For your prosperity individually, I offer my best wishes.

After these ceremonies were concluded, the President held a short reception, the Grand Master introducing the deputy and other attending brothers.

[1] The original draft of Washington's reply is in the Library of Congress.

This day the President dined — "a very sumptuous dinner" we are told it was — with the members of the Society of the Cincinnati in the Long Room at McCrady's Tavern,[1] which was handsomely decorated with laurel and flowers. In attendance were the Governor, Lieutenant-Governor and civil officers of the State, the Intendant and Wardens of the city, the members of Congress, the consuls of foreign powers, gentlemen strangers, the officers of the artillery, and a number of the most distinguished characters of the State. The officers of the Society of the Cincinnati at this time were: Major-General William Moultrie, President; Major-General Charles Cotesworth Pinckney, Vice-President; John Sandford Dart, Secretary; and Charles Lining, Treasurer. Major-General C. C. Pinckney, who had been Vice-President of the South Carolina Society since 1786, was elected Vice-President-General of the General Society at Philadelphia in May, 1800, after the demise of Washington, first President-General. In May, 1805, following the demise of Alexander Hamilton, second President-General, General C. C. Pinckney was elected President-General of the General Society of the Cincinnati.[2]

After the "sumptuous dinner" was consumed, the fol-

[1] This tavern, which was on the site occupied by the Daggett Printing Company on East Bay (Address of Professor Yates Snowden, May 23, 1901), was conducted by the great-grandfather of Edward McCrady, the historian.

[2] In the *City Gazette* of Charleston, February 10, 1790, appears the "Address to the President of the United States by the Society of the Cincinnati, in the State of South Carolina, voted 17th November, 1789," signed "By order of the Society, William Moultrie, President"; and Washington's reply.

lowing toasts were drunk, followed by a discharge from the field pieces of the Charleston Battalion of Artillery:

1. The United States.
2. The 4th of July, 1776.
3. Louis 16th, King of the French.
4. The national assembly of France.
5. All nations in amity with the United States.
6. Count d'Estaing and officers of the French navy who served in America.
7. Count Rochambeau and the French officers who served in America.
8. The President of the United States.
9. The Secretary of State.
10. The Secretary of the Treasury.
11. The Secretary of the War Department.
12. The Army of the United States.
13. Agriculture and Commerce.
14. The memory of those who have fallen in defence of the Liberties of America.
15. (By the President.) The memory of General Greene and all those officers who have fallen in defence of America.
16. The Patriotic Fair of America.[1]

While the dinner was in progress, a choir of singers entertained the diners with vocal selections.

In the evening Washington attended what he describes with (for him) exceptional praise as a "very elegant dancing Assembly" at the Exchange, given by the City Corporation. The occasion was extraordinarily brilliant; the

[1] The South Carolina Society of the Cincinnati was organized at Charleston, August 29, 1783, with the following officers: Major-General William Moultrie, President; Brigadier-General Isaac Huger, Vice-President; Major Thomas Pinckney, Secretary; Captain Charles Lining, Treasurer; Lieutenant James Kennedy, Assistant Treasurer, Lieutenant Samuel Beekman and John Sandford Dart, Esq., Stewards. Consult the *Original Institution of the General Society of the Cincinnati, together with the Rules and By-Laws of the State Society of South Carolina.* Charleston, 1880.

throng came to enjoy themselves not less than to pay honor to the revered President. In the "City Gazette" the ball is thus described:

The ladies were all superbly dressed and most of them wore ribbons with different inscriptions expressive of their esteem and respect for the president such as: "long live the president," etc. Joy, satisfaction and gratitude illumined every countenance and revelled in each heart, whilst the demonstrations of grateful respect shown him seemed to give him the utmost heart felt satisfaction which nobly displayed itself in his countenance.

The beautiful arch of lamps in front of the exchange was illuminated; and over the entrance there was a superb transparency in the centre "Deliciis Patriae" and at the top G. W.

The fusileer company was drawn up before the exchange to maintain order, and exhibited a very pleasing appearance. In short every circumstance of the evening's entertainment was truly picturesque of the most splendid elegance. At half past ten, the company sat down to supper; at the table were seated more than 250 ladies, besides gentlemen. The brilliancy of the company and elegance of the supper surpassed all conception.[1]

[1] According to Washington's diary, there were present "256 elegantly dressed and handsome ladies" — truly a wonderful group, since the gallant Washington, it will be noted, makes no exceptions — all were "handsome."

CHAPTER VII

THE FOURTH STAGE

Charleston (continued)

ON Thursday morning early, the President, accompanied by Intendant Vanderhorst, Major Butler,[1] Mr. Izard, Generals Moultrie and Pinckney, Majors Rutledge and Jackson, Captain Cochran and Mr. Henry Laurens, Jr.,[2] made a visit to the forts of Charleston — "both of which," notes the President, "are in Ruins, and

[1] Pierce Butler, son of Sir Richard Butler, was born in Ireland, July 11, 1744. He came to America as a member of the British army, and was stationed in Boston. He resigned from the British army in 1773, and settled in Charleston, South Carolina. During the Revolution he was Adjutant-General of South Carolina. He sat in the Continental Congress, 1787–88. He was a member of the convention which framed the Federal Constitution in 1787, and was elected as a Democrat to the United States Senate, and served from March 4, 1789, to 1796, when he resigned. He was again elected to the United States Senate, to fill the vacancy caused by the death of John Ewing Calhoun, November 3, 1802; took his seat October 18, 1803; resigned in 1804. Appointed director of the Bank of the United States, he removed to Philadelphia, where he died February 15, 1822.

[2] Henry Laurens, Jr., the son of Henry Laurens and Eleanor Ball, was born August 25, 1763. In April, 1771, he was sent to London to stay with the Reverend Richard Clarke in Islington for his education. His father sent minute instructions as to his care — "he was to be clad in decent apparel unmixed with any kind of foppery"; "keep him in due subordination ... impress the fear of God upon his mind." His father and brothers followed in July. All three boys were together in Islington for a short time. Later they were taken to Geneva. In 1774 Henry went to Westminster School. When his father was imprisoned in the Tower, Henry was allowed to see him once, "which deeply affected the father who had not seen his 17 yr. old son for 6 years." In 1785, having returned to America, Henry, the only surviving son, went overland with his father to Charleston. He had not been in his native State since he was a child, yet in 1785 he was elected to the Legislature, but did not serve. He was again elected in 1787. On May 26, 1792, he was married to Eliza Rutledge.

scarcely a trace of the latter [Fort Moultrie] left — the former [Fort Johnson] quite fallen." At Fort Johnson on James Island the party partook of an "exceedingly good breakfast," which the commandant, Captain Kalteisen, had all in readiness for them upon their arrival. Under his guidance they inspected the fort and took note of the commanding situation for a battery on the marsh immediately opposite the city. They next visited Fort Moultrie on Sullivan's Island, viewed the remains of the fort and battalions, and the bridge built by General Gadsden. General Washington listened with the keenest interest to the animated recital by that gallant soldier and entertaining conversationist, General Moultrie, of the defeat, on June 28, 1776, by the forces under his command of the British fleet under Sir Peter Parker. After eating lunch — described in the quaint language of the period as "an excelent collation" — the party returned to the city about two o'clock, the President at parting expressing the great satisfaction he had received from the morning's excursion.

At four o'clock Governor Pinckney gave a magnificent reception at his home on Meeting Street,[1] the appointment and decorations being lavish in the extreme. Traditions long survived in Charleston of the exceptional beauty and elegance of this entertainment, which was given to the President and the principal gentlemen of the civil, clerical,

[1] "By the sixties," says Professor Snowden, "this house had been torn down, and the very earth upon which it had been built had been removed to form one of the fortifications on White Point Battery for the defence of Charleston." In 1901 the house standing upon this site was owned by George W. Williams, Esq.

THOMAS SUMTER

PIERCE BUTLER

and military professions. At this entertainment, according to a contemporary account, the following toasts were drunk with gusto, to salvos of applause:

1. United States.
2. Congress of the United States.
3. 4th of July 1776.
4. Lewis Sixteenth.
5. National Assembly of France.
6. Friendly power of Europe.
7. Fair America.
8. Memory of General Greene.
9. Agriculture and Commerce.
10. Arts and Sciences.
11. Friends of freedom in every quarter of the globe.
12. Marquis de la Fayette.
13. Memory of those who have fallen in the defence of the rights of the mainland.

After the President retired, the following was drunk:

14. The President of the United States.

That evening, in the City Hall, was given one of the most brilliant concerts in the history of that justly famous and unique musical and social organization, the St. Cecilia Society. On this occasion the Amateur Society, which had participated in the vocal greetings to Washington upon his arrival, gave their assistance to the St. Cecilia. This Society, even then, had a long and honorable history, having been inaugurated in 1737 by a concert given upon "Thursday being St. Cecilias day," but it was not formally organized until 1762. The hall of the Exchange had recently undergone an alteration; and was most handsomely decorated with various ornaments. The pillars were "ingeniously entwined with laurel"; and about the hall were decorative pieces bearing patriotic devices complimentary to the President: "Hominis jura, defendit et curat"; "Magnus in pace"; "Magnus in bello"; "Vitam imprudere bono"; "Diogène aujourdhui casseroit la lanterne." The most arresting of the lofty "sentiments," which exhibits the marks of feminine sensibility, attracted every eye:

> With grateful praises of the hero's fame,
> We'll teach our infants' tongues to lisp his name.

An excellent band of music played in the orchestra, we are told; and they were "accompanied in the vocal strain by the choir of St. Phillip's Church." [1]

Even the imperturbable Washington, a great admirer of feminine charms, was dazzled by the sparkling scene and beautiful gentlewomen of Charleston: "In the evening went to a Concert at the Exchange at wch. there were at least 400 ladies the number & appearance of wch exceeded any thing of the kind I had ever seen."

Friday, 6th, was a light day for the President. He be-

[1] In his *Journal*, March 3, 1773, Josiah Quincy of Boston described a St. Cecilia concert: "The music was good, the two base viols and French horns were grand. A Frenchman played the first violin, and a solo incomparably better than any one I ever heard. He has a salary of 500 [50?] guineas a year from the St. Cecilia Society. There were upwards of two hundred ladies present, and it was called no great number. In loftiness of headdress, these ladies stoop to the daughters of the north — in richness of dress, surpass them, in health and floridity of countenance vail to them. In taciturnity during the performance, greatly before our ladies; in noise and flirtation after the music is over, pretty much on a par. If our ladies have any advantage it is in white and red, vivacity and spirit. The gentlemen many of them dressed with richness and elegance, uncommon with us: many with swords on." (*Memoir of the Life of Josiah Quincy, Jun.*, by Josiah Quincy. Boston, 1825.)

gan the day by taking a horseback ride through most of the principal streets of the city. Upon his return, the irrepressible "I. H. W." bobbed up in the "Gazette" with a most high-flown eulogy to Washington — of whom the poetaster justly says: "Freedom for all, was all thy soul requir'd." It would be interesting — to say the least — to fathom the emotions of Washington as he sat down after breakfast and indulged in the "luxuries" of a nation's thanks:

> Rome Fabius grac'd for natural prudence fam'd
> And Aristides, Greece, the just surnam'd
> Both heroes with peculiar merits shone
> Their merits meet in Washington alone.
> Great man! When pillar of a drooping land,
> Well did'st thou wield the scepter of command.
> When Great Britannia with her dreadful arms,
> Fill'd thy desponding country with alarms;
> Thru skill with caution all thy deeds display'd
> In dangers cheerful nor by loss dismay'd;
> Till thy unequalled prudence gave the blow,
> Which sav'd unhurt thy brave though vanquished foe
> Thy country's wrongs gave courage to thy breast.
> The sons of Britons tyranny detest.
> To free thy country was thy only aim,
> Thy present action loud this truth proclaim —
> Cæsar when tow'ring on ambitions height,
> Sprung to imperial sway with quick delight,
> But thy transcendent soul no crown desired
> Freedom for all, was all thy soul requir'd.
> When war had yielded to the spring of peace,
> Thy country own'd from thee came such release.
> Though long trained soldiers lov'd thee as their chief
> Ev'n when America had gain'd relief;
> Yet did thy patriotic breast with joy dilate,
> And give their powers to each admiring state

That glorious day repaid thy mortal strife
A nation's thanks are luxuries in life
Well hast thou earn'd thy never fading bays,
The world admits as just thy country's praise.

I. H. W.

This day the President dined "in a private manner" with the Honorable Pierce Butler, one of the Senators from South Carolina, there being present a number of congenial gentlemen. That evening the President attended a ball given by Governor Pinckney at his home, where was gathered a "select company" of ladies and gentlemen. The ladies, sacrificing for the nonce their elaborate floral headdresses and imposing feathers, wore handsome fillets or bandeaux upon which was drawn or painted Washington's portrait, with the national colors entwined. "Every hand that could hold a pencil, professional or amateur," says Fraser, "was enlisted to furnish them." [1] Whatever the great hero's former conquests in peace and war, certain it is that he had never before seen himself go to the heads of so many ladies at one time. Nor must we forget the patriotic sacrifice of these ladies in "killing" the delicate tints of their own gowns of azure and maize and mauve with the primary red and blue of the national colors. The most memorable of the bandeaux were ribbons on which was inscribed in large letters of gold:

Health to Columbia's noblest son
Her light and shield — great Washington.

Before breakfast on Saturday the President, accompanied by the Honorable Pierce Butler, General Moultrie,

[1] Fraser's *Reminiscences*.

CHARLES PINCKNEY

General Pinckney, Major E. Rutledge, and the Attorney-General of South Carolina, and the Intendant, who conducted the party, visited the Orphan House.

In the act, passed in 1783 by the Legislature of South Carolina, incorporating the city of Charleston, the "care of providing for the poor, and maintaining and educating poor orphan children" was imposed upon it. During the next five years, Commissioners of the Poor appointed by the City Council collected orphan children and boarded them out "at several private houses, under the care and direction of different respectable ladies, and educated them at schools in the City, at its expense." In 1788 John Robertson, a merchant in moderate business, and a philanthropic citizen, actively busied himself in the effort to make permanent provision for the care of the orphan poor. As the result of his efforts, the City Council of Charleston passed an ordinance providing for the establishment of an Orphan House in Charleston. The Commissioners appointed by the Council hired from Mrs. Elizabeth Pinckney a commodious building in Ellery Street, later Market Street, on or near the site of the "Sailors' Home" (1855), and collected and domesticated therein upwards of one hundred children. "This asylum has recorded on its journals the interesting fact, that on 25th May, 1791, it was visited by George Washington, president of the United States, then on his southern tour, who expressed great satisfaction at the establishment of such an institution, and invoked a benediction on it and its little inmates. That blessing and prayer have been graciously heard and answered in the prosperity and extensive usefulness of the institution."[1] When the sixth anniversary of the institution was celebrated in 1795, the Reverend Doctor George Buist, pastor of the Presbyterian Church, and the orator of the occasion, speaks of the "Orphan House building of that day, as the most magnificent edifice of the kind of which the new world can boast." According to a Government report, Department of the Interior, this institution has the longest continuous existence of any institution of the kind in the United States.[2]

The President and party were received by the Commissioners — who were doubtless surprised, as Roosevelt's friends used to be, by unusual hours and exceptional actions — : John Mitchell, John Robertson, Richard Cole, Thomas Corbett, Samuel Beckman, and Charles Lining. Mr. Besselieu and all the boys under his tuition were present. The President expressed the "highest approbation" of the institution, after the Commissioners had submitted for his perusal the ordinance for establishing the Orphan House, the rules of the house, the journals of the proceedings of the board, and the register. The President visited the breakfast room, where the children, one hundred and

[1] *The Proceedings of the Sixty-Sixth Anniversary of the Orphan House of Charleston, South Carolina* (Charleston, 1855).

[2] Consult *Centennial Proceedings*, *Charleston Orphan House* (Charleston, 1891). This publication contains illustrations: of the Orphan House as completed, in 1794, located on vacant city land, between Boundary (now Calhoun) and Vanderhorst Streets; and of the new Orphan House as it was in 1890. The Commissioners elected in 1790 were Arnoldus Vanderhorst, Intendant, as Chairman *ex officio;* John Mitchell, John Robertson, Richard Cole, Thomas Corbett, Charles Lining, William Marshall, Thomas Jones, and Samuel Beckman.

seven in all, were assembled; and on his departure "very pathetically pronounced his benediction on them," an antique use of language which, while expressing the fact, provokes a smile over what was doubtless an affecting scene. After partaking of a "genteel breakfast" (whatever that may be!) in the Commissioners' room, the President took his leave — wishing the Commissioners all success in their "laudable and benevolent endeavors." Before returning to his quarters the President ascended the steeple of St. Michael's Church to the balcony, whence he obtained an extensive view of the city, harbor, rivers, and adjacent country. "The whole is seen in one view and to advantage," he notes in his diary, "the Gardens & green trees which are interpersed adding much to the beauty of the prospect."

The festivities of this, perhaps the most socially hectic, week of Washington's career were concluded, fittingly enough, with a "sumptuous entertainment" in the Exchange given to the President by the merchants of Charleston. This was doubtless the most widely representative, in *personnel*, of all of the receptions — being attended by the Governor, Lieutenant-Governor, Senators, Federal, State, and City officers, all the members of both Houses of the Assembly for Charleston District who were in town, Representatives in Congress, the Intendant and Wardens, the clergy of every denomination, and "many respectable strangers."

The description of the decorations, which appeared in the "City Gazette," summons a vivid picture of the scene and gives us an insight into the æsthetic tastes of our ancestors of one hundred and thirty years ago:

> The walls of the exchange were beautifully decorated with flowers & shrubbery, wreaths of laurel encircling the arches, over the president's head was exhibited an emblematical painting representing commerce distributing plenty over the globe. Opposite under the center arch was exhibited a ship in miniature, handsomely decorated and furnished with lamps to the number of 136 which in the evening were lighted up. This at once discovered a beautifully emblematical figure and formed a most happy substitute for a brilliant chandelier; on her stern was painted "The Commerce of Charleston" and the repeated acclamations of the company testified their wishes for her success.

The company assembled to the number of upwards of three hundred in the City Hall;[1] and on the President's arrival — which was the dramatic moment of the day — the ship *America* of Charleston which was moored in the harbor fired a federal salute. About half-past four the company sat down to an elegant dinner — the board groaning with "every delicacy that the country and season could afford" and the wines being "excellent and in great variety." The *America* fired a salute of thirteen guns after each of the following toasts:

1. The United States of America, may they long enjoy freedom in peace.

[1] The City Hall, or, as it was then called, "The Public Offices," was located on the southwest corner of Broad and Meeting Streets where the United States Post-Office building is now located. This location was owned and used for city purposes by Charleston until 1886. President Washington had only two short city blocks to go from the City Hall to the Old Exchange. Consult *The Charleston Directory* (1790), a copy of which is in the Charleston Library. For this information I am indebted to the Reverend William Way, D.D., of Charleston.

2. The federal constitution, its friends and supporters.
3. The vice-president of the United States and members of the senate.
(By the President. The commercial interest of Charleston.)
4. The late members of both houses of Congress; may their successors inherit their wisdom and patriotism.
5. Louis 16th and the national assembly of France; a speedy and successful termination of their labours.
6. Agriculture and commerce; may their dependence on each other be properly understood.
7. The navigation of the United States; protected by the strong arm of the federal government, may it increase and flourish.
8. The useful arts of peace.
9. May the merchants of the United States continue to merit the flattering compliment paid them by the president at the opening of the last session of Congress.
10. The national bank; a general diffusion of its happy effects throughout the United States.
11. The defenders of the rights and liberties of the people throughout the world.
12. The fair daughters of America.
13. The secretary of state; may the important service he has rendered to the commercial interest of his country endear him to every merchant.
14. The secretary of the Treasury; may his fame increase with the rising credit of his country.
15. May the mantle of peace and friendship cover the world.

And when the President had retired:

16. The illustrious president of the United States; long may he live to enjoy the praises of a grateful people.

At eight o'clock the President "retired to the City Hall"; that is, presumably to the portico facing the ocean, whence he had a view of the fireworks displayed on the

America. This ship with its multitude of lanterns stood out a gleaming constellation of lights, the letters "V. W.," for *Vivat Washington,* shining brightly forth in bold outline against the dusky background of the summer night.

In a final flourish of patriotic affection the "City Gazette" epitomizes the common sentiment of the people of Charleston whom Washington graciously described as "wealthy — Gay — & hospitable":

> The harmony and hilarity which prevailed throughout were strongly demonstrative of the general gratitude and joy; and it must have afforded the highest gratification to every true patriot to have observed the man whom we most venerate — *venerated by all.*

One of the most signal tributes paid to Washington during the Southern tour — a tribute compounded of affection, admiration, and regard for posterity — was the decision of the City Council of Charleston to commission John Trumbull, a recent visitor to Charleston, to paint Washington's portrait. On the journal of the City Council for May 7, 1791, appears the following:

> Resolved, unanimously, That His Honor the Intendant in behalf of the City Council and their Constituents, be desired to request of George Washington Esquire, President of the United States, That he will be pleased, when it is convenient to him, to permit his Portrait to be taken by Colonel Trumbull, in order that it may be placed in the City Hall, as the most lasting testimony of their Attachment to his person, to commemorate his arrival in the metropolis of this State, and to hand down to posterity the resemblance of the Man, to whom they are indebted for the blessings of Peace, Liberty and Independence.
>
> PET. BOUNETHEAU: City Clerk

WASHINGTON ON THE EVE OF THE BATTLE OF PRINCETON

By Colonel John Trumbull

GEORGE WASHINGTON

Painted by Colonel John Trumbull for the City of Charleston

A representative of the City Council waited upon the President to prefer this request, to which he readily assented. One of South Carolina's representatives in Congress, William Loughton Smith, gave the commission, which was unlimited, to Colonel Trumbull who, on that account, as he records in his autobiography, undertook it *con amore* —

meaning to give his military character, in the most sublime moment of its exertion — the evening previous to the battle of Princeton; when viewing the vast superiority of his approaching enemy, and the impossibility of again crossing the Delaware, or retreating down the river, he conceives the plan of returning by a night march into the country from which he had just been driven, thus cutting off the enemy's communication, and destroying his depot of stores and provisions at Brunswick. I told the President of my object; he entered into it warmly, and, as the work advanced, we talked of the scene, its dangers, its almost desperation. He *looked* the scene again, and I happily transferred to the canvas, the lofty expression of his animated countenance, the high resolve to conquer or to perish. The result was in my own opinion eminently successful, and the general was satisfied. But it did not meet the views of Mr. Smith. He admired, he was personally pleased, but he thought the city would be better satisfied with a more matter-of-fact likeness, such as they had recently seen him, — calm, tranquil, peaceful.

Oppressed as the President was with business, I was reluctant to ask him to sit again. I however waited upon him, stated Mr. Smith's objection, and he cheerfully submitted to a second penance, adding, "Keep this picture for yourself, Mr. Trumbull, and finish it to your own taste." I did so — another was painted for Charleston, agreeable to their taste — a view of the city in the background, a horse, with scenery, and plants of the climate; and when the State Society of Cincinnati of Connecticut dissolved themselves, the first picture, at the expense of some of the members, was presented to Yale College.[1]

The decision of the City Council adverse to the first picture, as expressed through Mr. Smith, was all the more singular in view of Trumbull's own opinion that this picture was "the best certainly of those which I painted, and the best, in my estimation, which exists, in his heroic military character." The President had so endeared himself recently to the people of Charleston in the benignant rôle of peace President that Mr. Smith's explanation needs no gloss.[2]

The citizens of South Carolina generally — and not merely the inhabitants of Charleston — vied with each other in paying every courtesy to the President. Even the venerable Thomas Sumter, although unable to be present in person, sent his son to represent him, as evidenced in the following letter:

DEAR SIR,

Being informed by my son that he will wait on you in Chas:ton at your arrival, I am happy in having occasion of offering you the sincerest welcome to our State, together with my best wishes for your health & happiness not only at present but in perpetuity.

In your travels you may yet remark the traces of British devastation &, I am afraid, the pernicious effects of impolitic counsels and lax principles. But you will also discern a happy contrast to this representation, in the prospects of

[1] The portrait now in the City Hall, Charleston, was regarded as an excellent likeness by those who had seen Washington about the time it was made. Colonel Trumbull had served as Washington's aide, and had made a close study of his features and person. (Consult Fraser: *Reminiscences.*)

[2] J. Trumbull: *Autobiography, Reminiscences and Letters.* (New York, 1841.)

vigor & prosperity that are now budding from the unity of our American Governments, and which have been so strongly assured to us by the happy management which has characterized the first & most trying period of your Presidency.

I hope, Sir, this freedom will be excused, as I have been moved to it from considerations of the highest esteem & the warmest regard. And likewise to declare how happy the People of this quarter and myself should be made, by having an opportunity of receiving *one* amongst us, who is always thought & spoken of with most affectionate emotion.

We have been led to suggest our desire from a report of your having it in your intention to visit Collumbia & Camden — the first lies opposite to Stateburgh, at 30 miles distance & the latter at not more than 20 — So that the deviation will be, perhaps, more trifling than the pleasure which the view of those Highlands may afford, which have been doubtless described to you.

Allow me, Dear Sir, to subscribe myself with the truest sentiments of respect & regard, y^{r} most obd.^{t} Hb^{e} Ser^{t}

THOS. SUMTER SEN^{r}[1]

12th April 1791
STATEBURGH

A pleasing and significant incident of Washington's visit arose out of the offer by the Charleston Battalion of Artillery of their official attendance upon the President during his stay — as well as regularly to mount guard for the purpose. Washington literally won all hearts by his reply — politely declining the friendly offer and declaring that he considered himself perfectly safe in "the affection and amicable attachment of the people."

Not content with the public festivities in Washington's honor, the thirteen American captains who rowed the

[1] From a copy in the Draper MSS., 8vv48, Wisconsin Historical Society. Draper has written on the margin: "Copied from the original in Simon Gratz's Collection — & by him furnished to me. L. C. D. Sep. 1886."

barge in which the President came in from Haddrell's Point had a special "function" of their own on Monday — an "elegant entertainment" at McCrady's Tavern — to which a number of masters of vessels were invited. The following toasts were drunk, especially significant being those to John Paul Jones and Captain Barry:

Our illustrious president.
United States of America.
The governor and State of South Carolina.
The federal government; may it be equal to time.
The memory of fallen heroes in defence of America.
Lewis XVIth and the national assembly.
The sufferers in the cause of Freedom.
The Marquis de Lafayette, liberty's viceroy.
John Paul Jones.
Captain Barry.
The memories of Biddle and Pickering.
Protection to our commerce.
The family of mankind.

Not to be outdone, a number of young bloods of the city — "gentlemen of various professions" — met and dined on board a ship in the harbor on Saturday afternoon. The facts that the dinner was held on a ship in the harbor (no doubt beyond the three-mile limit), that the name of the ship was carefully withheld, and that the following day was Sunday all seem to have a meaning of their own. Rare enthusiasm must have animated these gay spirits when they drank the fifteenth toast: "May the circuit of the president round the states be as much admired as that of the earth round the sun." The "Correspondent" who inserted the notice of the dinner in the "Gazette" was careful to add the disarming postscript: "About 8 o'clock they broke up after spending the afternoon in the greatest harmony and hilarity." Follow the toasts:

1. The president; may he long live and honour and benefit his country.
2. May the States be ever united.
3. The vice president, may his virtues be continued.
4. Congress of the United States.
5. May every state regard the interest of its sister states.
6. The State of South Carolina.
7. May commerce flourish.
8. May the State of South Carolina be soon the carriers of its own produce.
9. May merchant and planter understand their own interest, and each agree and assist the other in mutual good offices.
10. The memory of General Greene.
11. General Marion.
12. The grateful memory of all who fell in defence of American Liberty.
13. Our worthy ally Lewis the 16th
14. A grateful reception to the president on his arrival in Georgia.
15. May the circuit of the president round the states be as much admired as that of the earth round the sun.

A charming tribute to Washington is found in the following note, preserved in the national archives:

Miss Elliott presents her compliments to The President of the United States, and as a small tribute of her grateful respect, begs that he will Honor her by the acceptance of a Sword knot.
CHARLESTON
May 7, 1791.

On Sunday, by special invitation, the President — formally accompanied by Intendant, Wardens, city officers, Governor, Lieutenant-Governor, and, of course, a number of thoroughly "respectable characters" (for he wasn't allowed even to go to church by himself!) — attended service at St. Philip's Church in the morning; and St. Michael's Church in the afternoon.[1] After morning service he dined at a private dinner, with Major-General William Moultrie — a delightful host and skilled *raconteur*.

Thus ends the story of Charleston's famous entertainment of George Washington — a civic entertainment probably without a parallel, for duration, variety, elegance, and universal cordiality, in the history of this country. A lady of Charleston writing to a friend in Hartford, Connecticut, describes in perfervid terms the events of this memorable week during which "little or nothing like business has been done." She particularly describes the elegant costumes of the romantic ladies of Charleston at the Corporation Ball — "the sashes and ribbons on their heads with *his* picture painted on them, and different inscriptions in gold and silver letters, pertinent and sentimental." Of this same ball she naïvely says: "When he entered the room joy sparkled in every countenance; but more so when, after being seated a few minutes, he rose, went all round the room and bowed to every lady — this gave particular satisfaction, as every one was anxious to have a

[1] On the minute book of the Vestry of St. Philip's appears the following:

At a Meeting of the Vestry & Church Wardens of St Philip's Church 3d May 1791

Resolved —

That the President of the United States, be invited to service in St Philips Church, & the Church Wardens do inform him, That a Pew is ready for his Accomodation on Sunday next, or any other day that he may think proper.

ST. PHILIP'S CHURCH, CHARLESTON
Erected 1723 — Burnt 1835

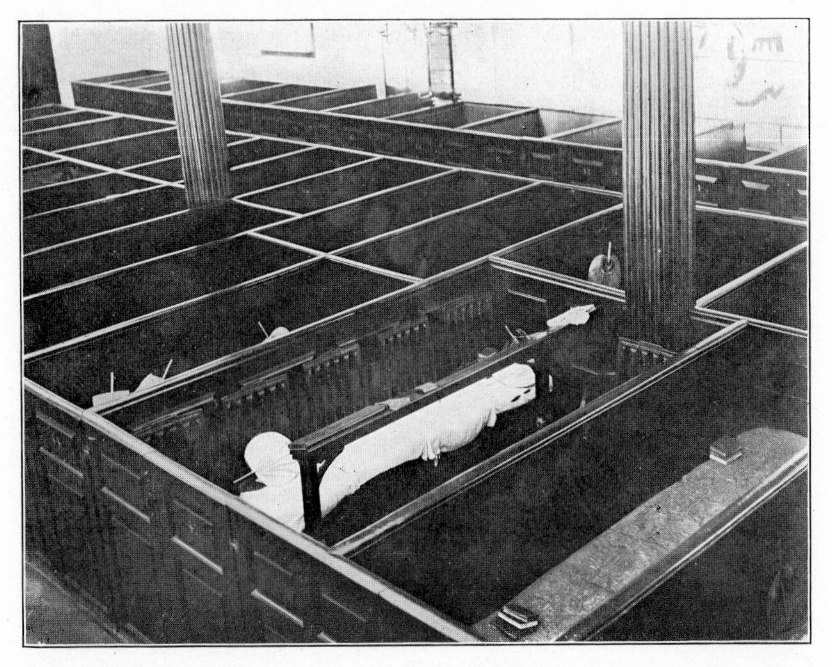

PEW OCCUPIED BY WASHINGTON IN ST. MICHAEL'S CHURCH, CHARLESTON

ST. MICHAEL'S CHURCH, CHARLESTON

good view of him"! The letter concludes with the pious benediction for the President upon his journey: "May every protecting angel be his guardian!"[1]

Washington's observations in his diary (May 7th) merit quotation:

> Charleston stands on a Pininsula between the Ashley & Cooper Rivers and contains about 1600 dwelling houses and nearly 16,000 Souls of which about 8000 are White — It lies low with unpaved streets (except the footways) of sand. — There are a number of very good houses of Brick & wood but most of the latter — The inhabitants are wealthy, — Gay — & hospitable; appear happy and satisfied with the Genl. Government. A cut is much talked off between the Ashley & Santee Rivers but it would seem I think, as if the accomplishment of the measure was not very near — It would be a great thing for Charleston if it could be effected. — The principal exports from this place is Rice, Indigo, and Tobacco; of the last from 5 to 8000 Hhds. have been exported, and of the first from 80 to 120,000 Barrels.

A contemporary commentary on the entire visit, with its ludicrous transition from the cheerful to the lugubrious, may well serve to write "Finis" to this long account:

> We learn from the most respectable authority, that the president of the united states was, from the unrivalled tribute of praise and respect, incessantly preferred to him in South Carolina, impressed with the highest sensibility; this, the lineaments of his countenance evinced in uttering grateful acknowledgments for the honors conferred on him by the fair sex, and homage of the heart by all ranks of the community. — This *surely* is *such a man*, whose primary maxim, the Roman poet, in classic lore reveres.
>
> Hic murus ahenus esto;
> Nil conscire sibi. . . .

[1] *Connecticut Courant*, June 6, 1791.

Long may he live to please a virtuous people!

And at the awful period of *dissolution* — on his mausoleum, *by some kind hand*, may this motto be engraven — George Washington — Hic cinis — ubique fama.[1]

[1] *The South-Carolina Independent Gazette; and Georgetown Chronicle*, May 21, 1791. The quotation is from Horace, and should read:

His murus aeneus esto,
Nil conscire sibi; nulla pallescere culpa.

CHAPTER VIII

THE FIFTH STAGE

Georgia: Savannah

CONSPICUOUS evidence of the development of the democratic feeling in America, and the aversion from titles, comes to light in connection with Washington's Southern tour. When a writer in the "Gazette of the United States" made a strong plea for titular distinctions, he was answered in the "Philadelphia General Advertiser" in vigorous terms:

> What more dignified title could be bestowed on our supreme executive Magistrate than GEORGE WASHINGTON? Would the epithet Honor, or even Excellency, annexed to his name express as much as his Name itself? Does EXCELLENCY call to mind the services he has rendered to his country? and is not GEORGE WASHINGTON synonymous with prudent and brave warrior, profound statesman, defender of liberty, good citizen, great man?

And in the same paper, of another date, appears this "crushing retort":

> The unlimited *respect* which has been paid to the PRESIDENT of the United States, in his southern excursion, is a striking proof that *titles* are not necessary to procure it. But it will be said that this respect is paid to the MAN, and not the *station*. So much the better. Let it teach rulers hereafter to be MEN, if they wish to be treated in like manner. *Titles*, like crowns and bishops in the female dress, or like large cravats and high collars in the dress of gentlemen, were introduced only to supply the absence of real beauties, or to cover some existing defects. When the United States, or any single State

shall have the misfortune to be governed by a *Tyger*, an *Ass*, or a *He Goat*, then let titles be applied to supply the absence of *majesty*, serenity, wisdom or excellency.

On his departure from Charleston at six o'clock on May 9th, the President had a handsome escort as far as Ashley Ferry, consisting of His Excellency the Governor, the Honorable Mr. Izard, the Honorable Major Butler, a Corps of the Cincinnati, and officers of the militia, all mounted on horseback — in a word, as Washington says, "most of the principal Gentlemen of the City." At Boundary Street they were met by the Intendant and Wardens of the City; and here His Honor the Intendant briefly addressed the President as follows:

SIR,

The Intendant and Wardens, in behalf of themselves and their constituents beg leave to offer you their unfeigned thanks for the visit with which you have honored this city, and they are hopeful it will not be the last. They sincerely wish you a pleasant tour and happy return to your mansion; and may health, that most grateful of all temporal blessings, attend you.

To which the President "was pleased to reply":

SIR,

I beg you will accept and offer my best thanks to the Corporation and the citizens of Charleston for their very polite attentions to me. Should it ever be in my power, be assured it will give me pleasure to visit this very respectable city.[1]

[1] In his *Reminiscences*, Fraser says: "Every attention that hospitality, public and private, could devise, was shown him [Washington], and it must have been very gratifying to the citizens of Charleston to receive from General Washington himself, on his departure, the warm acknowledgments which those attentions had won from his heart."

The President then took his leave of the Corporation; and as the cavalcade, joined by the Intendant, moved on, the field pieces of the Charleston Battalion of Artillery boomed forth a federal discharge and the muskets of the Fusilier Company, drawn up some distance from the skirts of the city, fired a parting volley. A triumphal arch, adorned with flowers and laurel, greeted them at Ashley Bridge — and the enthusiasm of the assembled multitude no doubt burst forth in acclamations as the Nation's head passed beneath this graceful arch. At Mr. Fraser's, on the south side of the bridge, the party had breakfast — after which the President bade his escort an affectionate farewell — with the exception of the Governor, Mr. Izard, Major Butler, and Generals Moultrie and Pinckney, who accompanied him some distance farther upon his journey.

After a journey of twenty-eight miles the party reached "Sandy Hill," in the old Parish of St. Paul's, the home of Colonel William Washington. It was about three miles from the highway leading directly from Charleston to Savannah between Charleston and what was then known as Jacksonboro. The stately mansion was formerly the residence of Charles Elliott, Esq., and the large inland rice plantation surrounding it had originally been granted to a member of the Elliott family. A fine avenue led up to the house, which was located in the midst of a group of magnificent live-oaks; and in front of the house was a lawn with ornamental pond. Colonel Washington, who was greatly interested in horse-racing, himself had race-horses; and on the estate, not far from the residence, he laid out a trial race-course for the practice of race-horses. The gallant William Washington, who was known as "the sword of the army," served with great distinction in campaigns in South Carolina. As occasion permitted, he visited the Elliotts at "Sandy Hill," fascinated by the charms of Miss Jane Elliott. It is related that on a hurried visit there while war was at its height, the dashing cavalryman mentioned that his men were without a flag of any kind. The quick-witted Miss Elliott readily improvised a square flag — from a heavy crimson silk curtain, with handsome silk fringe. Attached to a hickory pole as a staff, this famous flag was placed in his hands by the patriotic young girl, with the hope expressed that it would serve his men as a battle standard. This completely won the Colonel's heart; and they were married while the Revolution was still at its height. They were living happily at "Sandy Hill" in 1791; and the President broke his rule not to accept private hospitality because he and William Washington were cousins — John Washington, great-grandfather of William, being own brother to Lawrence, grandfather of George.[1]

At "Sandy Hill" Washington remained the night; and

[1] For a reliable genealogical table, showing this relationship, consult "The Genealogy of William Washington," with accompanying table, in *Proceedings at the Unveiling of the Battle Monument in Spartanburg, S. C., in Commemoration of the Centennial of the Battle of the Cowpens.* 1781–1881. Edited by William A. Courtney (Charleston, S. C., 1896). The cover design is a picture in colors of the flag above mentioned. On April 19, 1827, this historic flag, which was borne at the Cowpens, Guilford Court-House, Hobkirk Hill, Eutaw Springs, and numerous minor engagements, was presented by the widow of Colonel William Washington to the Washington Light Infantry of Charleston. For details concerning "Sandy Hill" I am indebted to the present owner, Judge Henry A. M. Smith.

the following morning (Tuesday, 10th) bade adieu to the friends and attendants who had accompanied him thus far — except General Moultrie who went as far as Purysburg and Major Butler who went all the way to Savannah. This day the President and party breakfasted at Judge Bee's,[1] twelve miles from Sandy Hill, and after a further journey of some eighteen or twenty miles, spent the remainder of the day, and the night, at "Mr. Obrian Smith's." [2]

The President was perhaps prepared, after two quiet days, for a resumption of the bombardment — which was renewed at Pocotaligo,[3] a point some twenty miles from Mr. Smith's, where Washington breakfasted. A large gathering awaited him at Pocotaligo; and he sat down to a handsome dinner prepared by the "Parishioners of Prince William." Here he was presented with the following address by the "Inhabitants of Prince William's Parish":

To the President of the United States

Permit us Great Sir to Welcome you most cordially into this Parish in your progress thro' the State.

We are sensibly affected with the Honour you do us, by this kind condescending visit — And cannot but embrace the Opportunity of declaring that our Hearts are penetrated with

[1] Thomas Bee, born in South Carolina in 1729; a distinguished lawyer, sometime member of the Assembly and of the Privy Council. Served on Council of Safety during the Revolution. Was Lieutenant-Governor of South Carolina, a member of the Continental Congress (1780–82), and later, judge of the United States Court for the District of South Carolina. Author of *Reports of the District Courts of South Carolina* (1810).

[2] O'Brien Smith, a nephew of James Parsons, probably came from Ireland to South Carolina. He lived in St. Paul's Parish, and was married to a Miss Webb in 1785. He died about 1811.

[3] A town on the Combahee River, York District, South Carolina. In his diary Washington comically spells it "Pokitellico."

the Warmest Sense of our Obligations to you Who under God have been the deliverer of the Country and its eminent Benefactor in War & in Peace — May you continue to Enjoy the Exquisite satisfaction that Arises from the Veneration and gratitude of a great People that has been signally benefitted by you as an Anticipation of your heavenly Reward

By the Unanimous Voice of the People of Prince William's Parish The 11th day of May 1791 —

John McPherson
John Heyward
Jno. A. Cuthbert
Felix Warley
James Maine
William Heyward
James E. McPherson

(Endorsed:)
Address of the
Inhabitants of Prince William's
Parish South Carolina
May 1791

To which the President made the following reply:

Gentlemen,

My best thanks for your cordial welcome and affectionate address are not more justly due than they are sincerely offered. I am much indebted to your good wishes which I reciprocate with grateful regard.

After dinner the following 'toasts' were given:

1. United States of America.
2. Federal Constitution.
3. The Parish of Prince William (*given by the President*).
4. Vice-President.
5. The 4th July, 1776.
6. Lewis the Sixteenth.
7. National Assembly of France.
8. Memory of General Greene.
9. Memory of Colonel John Laurens.

THOMAS HEYWARD, JR.

10. Marquis de la Fayette.
11. Governor of South-Carolina.
12. The memory of our friends who fell in the glorious cause of freedom.
13. The patriotic fair of America.
14. Agriculture and commerce of America.

After the President retired, the following was drunk:

15. The President of the United States of America.

That night the President and party dined and lodged at "Judge Hayward's." [1] Here, as also at Mr. Smith's, says Washington, "we were kindly and hospitably entertained." By way of explanation he makes the following statement in his diary for this day:

> My going to Col.º Washington's is to be ascribed to motives of friendship & relationship; but to Mr. Smith's & Judge Hayward's to those of necessity; their being no public houses on the Road and my distance to get to these private ones increased at least 10 or 12 miles between Charleston and Savanna.

On Thursday, as Washington had to ride twenty-two miles before breakfast at Purysburg,[2] he set out from Judge Heyward's at five o'clock. At Purysburg he was

[1] Thomas Heyward, born in St. Luke's Parish, South Carolina, 1746; died March 6, 1809. Signer of the Declaration of Independence. Educated by tutors; read law in Charleston and at the Temple, London, England. Returned home offended by British attitude toward colonists and gained eminence as advocate of freedom. He was a member of the first Assembly which was free from royal influence and of the first Committee of Safety in his province. Member of Congress 1775–78. He took part in the defence of Charleston and was a prisoner for a year. His lands were ravaged and his slaves taken away. He served on the bench till 1799; in 1790 helped to frame the South Carolina Constitution.

[2] This town, on the Savannah River, was named in honor of John Pury, founder of a Swiss settlement in South Carolina. Here, for a time early in 1779, General Lincoln had his headquarters.

greeted by five eminent patriots of the Revolution — the Honorable Noble Wymberley Jones, Colonel Joseph Habersham, the Honorable John Houstoun, General Lachlan McIntosh, and the Honorable Joseph Clay, a committee from the City of Savannah. Between ten and eleven o'clock the President, with the committee, Major Jackson, Major Butler, General Wayne, and Mr. Baillie, went on board a handsome boat elegantly fitted out, and was rowed down the river by nine American masters of vessels, namely, Captains Putnam, Couster, Rice, Fisher, Huntingdon, Kershaw, Swain, McIntire, and Morrison, who were dressed in light blue silk jackets, black satin breeches, white silk stockings, and round hats with black ribbons bearing in letters of gold the device "Long Live the President." At a point two miles below Purysburg, where the horses and carriages were landed for a twelve-mile overland journey to Savannah, Washington, as he quaintly puts it, "called upon Mrs. Green the widow of the deceased Genl. Green, (at a place called Mulberry Grove) and asked her how she did." Washington and Nathanael Greene had been very close friends; and Mrs. Greene had shared with both the privations and sufferings of Valley Forge. In addition to beauty, Mrs. Greene possessed personal charm, intuitive perception, and a very acquisitive intellect. "This power of rendering available her intellectual stores, combined with a retentive memory, a lively imagination, and great fluency of speech," says Mrs. Ellet, "rendered her one of the most brilliant and entertaining of women." [1]

[1] Mrs. E. F. Ellet: *Women of the Revolution.*

MRS. NATHANAEL GREENE

Washington doubtless welcomed the opportunity to tell her of the many tributes to General Greene he had heard upon this journey, demonstrating the secure place he held in the people's affection. And she in turn was glad to thank in person, and most warmly, the generous Washington who had offered to adopt her son and his namesake, give him as good an education as North America could afford, and have him brought up in any of the genteel professions, at his "own cost and charge." Since the death of her husband from sunstroke in 1786, Mrs. Greene had lived here at "Mulberry Grove," an estate which had been presented by the State of Georgia to General Greene in testimony of appreciation for his services in the Southern campaigns of the Revolution.[1]

No doubt it was with reluctance that Washington parted from his delightful hostess and set sail once more. "The wind and tide being both agst. us," he records, "it was 6 o'clock before we reached the City where we received every demonstration that could be given of joy and respect. We were Seven hours making the passage which is often performed in 4, tho' the computed distance is 25 miles." The reception Washington received from the admiring multitude is admirably described in a contemporary print:

[1] Here, little more than a year later, under Mrs. Greene's hospitable roof, a young inventor, Eli Whitney, constructed the first cotton-gin, in its economic influence one of the most epochal inventions of modern times. For an interesting account of this episode and of the life of the Greene family in Georgia, consult "Recollections of Washington and his Friends. As Preserved in the Family of General Nathanael Greene." By Martha Littlefield Phillips: *Century Magazine*, vol. 55, January, 1898.

Within ten miles of the city they were met by a number of gentlemen in several boats, and as the President passed by them a band of music played the celebrated song, "He comes, the Hero comes," accompanied with several voices. On his approach to the city the concourse on the Bluff, and the crowds which had pressed into the vessels, evinced the general joy which had been inspired by the visit of this most beloved of men, and the ardent desire of all ranks and conditions of people to be gratified by his presence. Upon arriving at the upper part of the harbor he was saluted from the wharves and by the shipping, and particularly by the ship Thomas Wilson, Capt. White, which was beautifully decorated with the colours of various nations. At the foot of the stairs where the President landed he was received by Col. Gunn and Gen. Jackson, who introduced him to the Mayor and Aldermen of the city. The Artillery Company saluted him with 26 discharges from their fieldpieces, and he was then conducted to a house prepared by the Corporation for his accommodation, in St. James's Square, in the following order of procession: Light Infantry Company; Field Officers and other Officers of the Militia; Marshall of the City; Treasurer and Clerk; Recorder; Aldermen; Mayor; President and Suite; Committee of Citizens; Members of the Cincinnati; Citizens two and two; Artillery Company.[1]

Upon his arrival the President was at once conducted to "very good lodging which had been provided for the occasion"—the inn on the corner of Barnard and State Streets.[2] The President and his suite dined with the Cor-

[1] *Georgia Gazette*, May 18, 1791. Colonel Gunn, it appears, was the Recorder of Savannah.

[2] Until recent years, this old inn was a landmark of the city. "Its well-worn, time-eaten boards were finally pulled down to make way for the present imposing structure of Odd Fellows Hall." (Consult *Historic and Picturesque Savannah*, by Adelaide Wilson, 1889.) "At the time of Washington's visit," according to the *Historical Record of the City of Savannah*, by Lee and Agnew (1869), "there were no houses beyond South Broad Street, and only five upon that street, all being on the north side. The city limits on the east was Lincoln street, and on the west Jefferson street, although

poration at Brown's Coffee House that evening, being escorted thither by the Mayor, Thomas Gibbons,[1] and by General Anthony Wayne, the President of the Society of the Cincinnati. The following gentlemen were invited to partake of the entertainment prepared: the Judges of the Superior Courts of the State and Inferior Courts of the county, clergy, members of the Legislature, members of the Cincinnati, field officers of the militia, President of the Union Society, the Recorder and Treasurer of the City. The following toasts were drunk, each being succeeded by discharges from the field pieces of the Artillery Company:

1. The United States.
2. The State of Georgia; may she increase in population and wealth. (*By the President.*)
3. The happy Occasion.
4. The Governor of the State.
5. The Vice-President.
6. Louis the XVIth.

there were a number of houses west of the latter named street. Of the five houses then standing on South Broad street four remain, viz: 'Eppinger's house,' on the northeast corner of Jefferson street, now occupied by Mr. S. Davis; the old frame house between Barnard and Jefferson; the frame house at the northeast corner of Whitaker; and the old brick house the third door east of Drayton street, now occupied by John B. Robinson; the fifth house stood where a brick house has just been completed, between Drayton and Abercorn street."

[1] Thomas Gibbons was a lawyer of Savannah, Georgia, who as early as the year 1800 is said to have earned as much as $15,000 per annum from the practice of law. He also engaged extensively in land speculations, and on this question, as well as many others pertinent to the times, was frequently found on opposing sides to Governor James Jackson. Both men being possessed of violent tempers, they finally met on the field of honor, but, though three shots were exchanged between them, neither suffered an injury. An attestation of the esteem in which Thomas Gibbons was held was his election to the Constitutional Convention of 1795 and his representation of Chatham County in the General Assembly for the years 1788, 1789, and 1792.

7. The National Assembly.
8. The Congress of the United States.
9. Agriculture and Commerce.
10. Arts and Sciences.
11. The fair Daughters of America.
12. The Sons of Freedom in every part of the globe.
13. The Marquis de la Fayette.
14. The Memory of Gen. Greene.
15. The Memory of those brave Men who fell in defence of American Liberty.

The President then retired, and a sixteenth toast was given: "The President of the United States." Prior to the coming of the President, the Mayor and Aldermen had requested the citizens to illuminate their houses, and the order was enthusiastically carried out. The result was a beautiful illumination of the city — Alderman Scheuber's house "showing no less than three hundred lights contained in the form of a W in front." It was said that the ship *Thomas Wilson*, with a "great number of lanterns with lights," was conspicuous for its beauty.

At some time during the 13th, presumably in the forenoon, the committee on behalf of the "Citizens of Savannah, and the Inhabitants of its Vicinity," consisting of the Honorable Noble Wymberley Jones,[1]

[1] Noble Wymberley Jones was born near London, England, in 1723. He early removed to Georgia, and took his degree in medicine. After serving for a time, as surgeon, with a company of Rangers, he entered upon the practice of the medical profession. In 1768 he was elected Speaker of the Lower House of Assembly; but in 1770 and 1772, when he was again elected Speaker, his pronounced leanings toward independence caused his rejection by the Governor's dissolving the Assembly. Although elected by the Provincial Congress, January, 1775, a delegate to the Continental Congress, he declined to serve because the Provincial Congress represented only four of the twelve parishes. He assisted on May 11, 1775, in breaking open the magazine and removing the powder stored there. He was a member of

NOBLE W. JONES

ANTHONY WAYNE

JOSEPH HABERSHAM

LACHLAN McINTOSH

WASHINGTON'S HEADQUARTERS IN SAVANNAH

Georgia: Savannah

Colonel Joseph Habersham,[1] the Honorable John Houstoun,[2] General Lachlan McIntosh,[3] the Honorable Joseph

the Provincial Congress of Georgia, July 4, 1775, by which he was elected a delegate to the Continental Congress. He was captured in Charleston, 1780, and sent as a prisoner to St. Augustine. After release in 1781, he settled in Philadelphia; and while residing there, was reëlected by the General Assembly of Georgia to the Continental Congress. He returned to Savannah in 1782. He presided over the Constitutional Convention of Georgia, May, 1795. He was President of the Georgia Medical Society, 1804, and died in Savannah, January 9, 1805.

[1] Joseph Habersham was born in Savannah, Georgia, July 28, 1751. He was graduated from Princeton during the presidency of Dr. Witherspoon. In July, 1775, he was instrumental in capturing a British vessel loaded with gunpowder and other military stores. He rendered valuable service, political and military, during the Revolution, rising to the rank of colonel in the Continental Army. He was twice Speaker of the Georgia General Assembly; delegate to the Continental Congress (1785–86), and to the convention which ratified the Federal Constitution (1788); Mayor of Savannah (1792). Appointed in 1795, he served under Washington and Adams as Postmaster-General of the United States. He was President of the Branch Bank of the United States at Savannah, from 1802 until his death, November 17, 1815.

[2] John Houstoun, son of Sir Patrick Houstoun, Bart., was born in Georgia, in the parish of St. George, August 31, 1744. In July, 1774, along with N. W. Jones, Archibald Bulloch, and others, he called the famous meeting at Tondee's Tavern; and was of the committee then appointed which in August brought in a very independent series of resolutions. In 1775, he was chosen by the Provincial Congress to represent Georgia in the Continental Congress; and was again chosen twice in 1776. He was elected Governor of Georgia, January 10, 1778; and again in 1784; Chief Justice of Georgia in 1786; Mayor of Savannah, 1790. He died at White Bluff, near Savannah, July 20, 1796.

[3] Lachlan McIntosh was born near Raits, in Badenoch, Scotland, March 17, 1724. He emigrated to Georgia with his father in 1735. After serving for a time as cadet in General Oglethorpe's regiment, he went to Charles-Town and worked in the counting-room of the Honorable Henry Laurens. He returned to New Inverness, Georgia, and sat as delegate in the Provincial Congress, Savannah, July, 1775. On January 7, 1776, he was elected colonel of the battalion ordered by the Continental Congress to be raised for the defence of Georgia. He was later promoted by the General Assembly of Georgia to the rank of brigadier-general. On May 16, 1777, he killed Button Gwinnett in a duel. Resigning his command in Georgia, he reported at Washington's headquarters for active service in the Continental Army. After service at different points, he was appointed by the Continental Congress at Washington's request to the command of the Continental forces in Georgia. He was second in command at the siege of Savannah. He retired

Clay,[1] waited on the President and presented to him through its chairman the following address:

SIR,

When, having accomplished the great objects of a war, marked in its progress with events that astonished while they instructed the world, you had again returned to the domestic enjoyments of life, to which you were known to be so strongly attached, there was little probability, in the common order of things, that the People of Georgia, however ardently they might desire, should ever be indulged, the happiness of a personal interview with you — but summoned again, as you were, from your retirement, by the united voice and the obvious welfare of your country, you did not hesitate to furnish one more proof that, in comparison to the great duties of social life, all objects of a private nature are with you but secondary considerations; And to this your ruling passion of love for your country it is that we owe the opportunity now offered of congratulating you on your safe arrival in the City of Savannah — an office we the Committee, under the warmest impressions of sensibility and attachment, execute in the name and behalf of a respectable and grateful number of citizens.

History furnishes instances of some eminently qualified for the field, and of others endued with talents adequate to the intricate affairs of state; but you, Sir, have enriched the an-

with General Lincoln to Charles-Town, and was captured upon the surrender of that city. On his release, he retired with his family to Virginia where he remained until the termination of hostilities. He returned to Savannah in 1782; was elected to the Continental Congress in 1784, and died February 20, 1786.

[1] Joseph Clay was born in Beverley, Yorkshire, England, October 16, 1741. He emigrated to Georgia in 1760; and a few years later engaged in a general commission business, with his uncle, Governor Habersham, in Savannah. He was successful as merchant and planter. He took a prominent part in 1774 in protesting against England's unjust policies. He was a member of the Council of Safety, and of the Provincial Congress, June, 1775; appointed Deputy Paymaster-General in Georgia, August 6, 1777; delegate from Georgia to the Continental Congress, 1778, 1779, 1780; Treasurer of Georgia, 1782. He died in Savannah, November 15, 1804.

nals of America with a proof, to be sent abroad to all mankind, that, however rare the association, the virtues and talents of soldier and republican statesman will sometimes dwell together, and both characters derive additional lustre from a subserviency to the precepts of Religion.

Roused by oppression at home, and inspired by example from America, the people of enlightened nations in Europe are now beginning to assert their rights: And it is observable that those brave men, the subjects of foreign powers, who were votaries to our cause, and companions in your victories, are always found foremost in the struggle for just and equal government.

You have now, Sir, an opportunity of viewing a state which, from its exposed situation, has been peculiarly affected by the calamities of war, but which, under the influence of a happy Government, will rise fast to that rank of prosperity and importance to which her natural advantages so justly entitle her, and which will enable her to reflect back upon the Union all the benefits derived from it.

We shall always take a deep concern, in common with the other citizens of the United States, in whatever regards your personal welfare and happiness. We make it our prayer to Almighty God that you may be long continued to your country her Ornament and Father, and that it may be more and more exemplified in you, Sir, that to know how to conquer, and to improve the advantages of conquest into blessings to a community, are faculties sometimes bestowed on the same mortal.

In the name and on behalf of a number of Citizens of Savannah and its Vicinity, convened for the Reception of the President,

N. W. Jones
Lach. M'Intosh
Joseph Clay — The Committee
John Houstoun
Joseph Habersham

To this address, which contained a notable tribute to Washington as the soldier-statesman, he replied as follows:

GENTLEMEN,

I am extremely happy in the occasion now afforded me to express my sense of your goodness, and to declare the sincere and affectionate gratitude which it inspires.

The retrospect of past scenes, as it exhibits the virtuous character of our country, enhances the happiness of the present hour, and gives the most pleasing anticipation of progressive prosperity. The individual satisfaction to be derived from this grateful reflection must be enjoyed by the deserving citizens of Georgia — a state no less distinguished by its services than by its sufferings in the cause of freedom.

That the city of Savannah may largely partake of every public benefit which our free and equal Government can dispense, and that the happiness of its vicinity may reply to the best wishes of its inhabitants, is my sincere prayer.

G. WASHINGTON [1]

Probably on this same day was presented to the President an address of the Church and Society at Midway (Medway), Liberty County, Georgia. In 1752, some settlers from Dorchester and Beach Hill, in South Carolina, removed to Midway and Newport in Georgia. On August 28, 1754, the society formed at Midway and Newport drew up articles and rules of incorporation. The members of this remarkable society were mostly of a dissenting or congregational persuasion. In their articles and rules of incorporation, it is recorded that: they agreed, each person, "to contribute a reasonable part, according to our ability and circumstances, for the support of a standing Ministry of the Gospel and its ordinances among us"; and, moreover, at their annual meeting and other occasional meet-

[1] The originals of both address and reply are preserved in the De Renne Library of Savannah. The address to Washington is described as "an eloquent address" in the "autograph of John Rutledge."

ings "every common matter of a Secular Nature shall be determined by a majority of Voices or Votes of such convened persons of the Society, who according to their circumstances and capacities, both have been, and continue to be, supporters of, and attenders on a Gospel Ministry among us, and who are agreeable to these our articles of agreement, members of our Society." Further, state the records, "We agree to choose annually, three or more Select Men, more immediately to manage our Public Business, according to the instructions, powers, and restrictions that shall be given them by the Society." [1] The address to the President and his reply are given below:

SIR: We feel ourselves happy in an opportunity of expressing our attachment to your person, and our peculiar pleasure in your selection by the unanimous voice of your country to the Presidency of the United States.

Though situated in the extreme part of the Union, we have gratefully to acknowledge that we already experience the propitious influence of your wise and parental administration. To the troops stationed on our frontiers by your order, and to the treaty lately concluded with the Creek nation under your auspices, we are indebted, under Providence, for our present tranquility. The hatchet is now buried, and we smoke with our Indian neighbours the calumet of peace. This, while it affords a happy presage of our future protection, gives, at the same time, a recent proof how justly you have earned, in your civil as well as military capacity, the glorious title of Father of your Country.

With the laurel, then, be pleased to accept the civic wreath from a grateful people.

We readily conceive how arduous must be the duties, how weighty and complicated the cares of office, in the govern-

[1] Consult: *The Published Records of Midway Church*, vol. 1, edited by the Reverend James Stacy, D.D.

ment of so extensive a Republic as that over which you are called to preside. Impressed with a deep sense of this, we will not fail to implore the Divine blessing in your behalf. May you continue to be directed by that wisdom from above which is necessary to the discharge of the duties of your high and important station; and may you long be preserved the favored instrument of Heaven to secure a free people those invaluable rights which you so eminently contributed to rescue from the hand of oppression. Distant as our situation is from the Seat of Government, permit us to assure you that our influence however inconsiderable in the national scale, shall not be wanting in encouraging submission to the laws of the United States, and thus under God perpetuate the blessings of an efficient Federal Government, now so happily established.

(Signed) James Maxwell
Daniel Stewart
A. Holmes
Henry Wood
John P. Mann
Committee in behalf of the Church and Society.

Midway, Liberty County, *May* 12, 1791.

Gentlemen: I learn with gratitude proportioned to the occasion, your attachment to my person, and the pleasure you express on my election to the Presidency of the United States. Your sentiments on the happy influence of our equal government impress me with the most sensible satisfaction. They vindicate the great cause of humanity. They reflect honour on the liberal minds that entertain them, and they promise the continuance and improvement of that tranquility which is essential to the welfare of nations and the happiness of men.

You overrate my best exertions, when you ascribe to them the blessings which our country enjoys.

From the gallantry and fortitude of her citizens, under the auspices of Heaven, America has derived her independence. To their industry and the natural advantages of the country, she is indebted for her prosperous situation. From their virtue she may expect long to share the protection of a free and equal government, which their wisdom has established, and which experience justifies, as admirably adapted to our social wants and individual felicity.

Continue, my fellow-citizens, to cultivate the peace and harmony which now subsist between you and your Indian neighbours — the happy consequence is immediate — the reflection which arises on justice and benevolence will be lastingly grateful. A knowledge of your happiness will lighten the cares of my station, and be among the most pleasing of their rewards.

George Washington.

Later in the day the President dined with the members of that organization which he had taken so much interest in founding and, in the face of violent criticism, establishing upon a sound footing: The Society of the Cincinnati. On this most enjoyed occasion, which took place at Brown's Coffee House, the following toasts were drunk "under federal salutes from the Artillery Company":

1. The United States of America.
2. The Memory of our worthy deceased Brother Gen. Greene (By the President).
3. The Governor and State of Georgia.
4. May the virtues which inspired the Revolution continue to support the present Establishment.
5. May the principles of a free government be universally disseminated.
6. Agriculture and Commerce.
7. Louis XVI and the French Nation.
8. The powers in alliance with the United States.
9. The Vice President.
10. The Memory of Dr. Franklin.
11. The Non-Commissioned Officers and Soldiers of the late American Army.
12. The Memory of those brave Men who fell in defence of American Liberty.

13. The Members of the Society of the Cincinnati throughout the globe. (By the President.)
14. The American Fair.
15. The Marquis de la Fayette.

At this point the President retired, whereupon a sixteenth toast was drunk with great joviality and gusto: "The President of the United States."

In the evening the President, as he states in his diary, went to "a dancing Assembly at which there was about 100 well dressed handsome ladies." This "dancing Assembly" — an antique phrase quaintly expressive of lightness and motion — was held at the Filature, a building which symbolized a singular phase in the Colony's industrial history. It was a cherished plan of the Trustees to make of Georgia a silk, oil, and wine-growing colony. They offered large bounties (1750) to those who would engage in the growth of silk; and a "filature for that purpose was built the next year to serve as a normal school to the town." [1] This first filature, thirty-six feet long by twenty wide, was built of rough boards; and the green cocoons were spread in a loft above the one floor. The General Assembly, in order to promote the silk culture, actually passed an act to the effect that, after June, 1751, "no inhabitant could be elected a deputy who had not one hundred mulberry trees planted and properly fenced, upon every tract of fifty acres which he possessed." Despite this sustained and persistent effort to interweave the silk

[1] Cf. Adelaide Wilson: *Historic and Picturesque Savannah* (1889). "This building stood on the east side of Reynolds Square where now (1889) stands the block of houses known as Cassell's Row."

culture with the fabric of government, the ultimate result was failure. Although this filature, together with large stores of silk and cocoons, was burnt in 1758, it was rebuilt, and for several years used for the manufacture of silk. The year 1770 saw the death-throes of the silk culture — after which date the Filature was used as a public hall for municipal and social entertainments. It was destroyed by fire in 1839.[1]

In the Long Room of the Filature took place the public ball in honor of the President, thus quaintly described in a contemporary print:

> In the evening a Ball, in honor of the President, was given at the Long Room in the Filature. At half past 8 o'clock the President honored the company with his presence, and was personally introduced by one of the Managers to 96 ladies, who were elegantly dressed, some of whom displayed infinite taste in the emblems and devices on their sashes and head dresses, out of respect to the happy occasion.
>
> The room, which had lately been handsomely fitted up, and was well lighted, afforded the President an excellent opportunity of viewing the Fair Sex of our city and vicinity, and the ladies the gratification of paying their respects to our Federal Chief.
>
> After a few minuets were moved, and one country dance led down, the President and his Suit retired about 11 o'clock. At 12 o'clock the supper room was opened, and the ladies partook of a repast, after which dances continued till 3 o'clock.

[1] Consult *Historical Records of the City of Savannah*, by F. D. Lee and J. L. Agnew (Savannah, 1869). Another interesting act of the Assembly, designed to stimulate silk culture, stipulated that, after June 24, 1753, no one could be a delegate who had not "strictly conformed to the prescribed limitation of the number of negro slaves in proportion to his white servants, who had not in his family at least one female instructed in the act of reeling silk, and who did not annually produce fifteen pounds of silk for every fifty acres of land owned by him."

The company retired with the happy satisfaction of having generally contributed towards the hilarity and gaiety of the evening.

Retaining his keen interest in the art of war, and desiring to inform himself about important military operations during the Revolution, Washington spent the early morning of the next day in inspecting the remaining traces of the lines constructed by the British for the defence of Savannah in 1779. As it fortunately chanced, General McIntosh had been second in command under General Lincoln at the time of the storming of the works; and gave the President a detached and lively account of the principal events of interest which happened during the siege and attack of the city.[1] The following unsatisfactory and accidentally ungrammatical entry is found in the President's diary for this day (Saturday, 14th):

A little after 6 o'clock, in Company with Genl. McIntosh, Genl. Wayne,[2] the Mayor and many others (principal Gentle-

[1] In a biography of General McIntosh we find: "Upon the occasion of President Washington's visit to Savannah in May, 1791, he was attended by General McIntosh when he inspected the lines constructed by the British in 1779 for the defence of Savannah, and the approaches and batteries then made by the Allied Army. Having himself participated in the siege and in the assault of the 9th of October, General McIntosh was able to convey to the President full information touching the whole affair. The earth mounds covering the slain, the lines of circumvallation, the sand parapets and gun chambers, had not then yielded to the influences of time and an encroaching population. The scars of the siege were still upon the bosom of the plain, and some of the houses within the limits of the city bore the marks of the lethal missiles which were then hurled. About him stood those who had passed through that baptism of fire. The President exhibited a deep interest in everything he then saw and heard."

[2] Anthony Wayne was born in East Town, Chester County, Pennsylvania, January 1, 1745. After serving as land surveyor and financial agent in Nova Scotia, he returned to Pennsylvania. He was a member of the Colonial House of Representatives, 1774–75. He was commissioned colo-

THE HARBOR OF SAVANNAH

men of the City,) I visited the City, and the attack & defence of it in the year 1779, under the combined forces of France and the United States, commanded by the Count de Estaing & Genl. Lincoln.[1] — To form an opinion of the attack at this distance of time, and the change which has taken place in the appearance of the ground by the cutting away of the woods, &c. is hardly to be done with justice to the subject; especially as there is remaining scarcely any of the defences.

Dined to day with a number of the Citizens (not less than 200) in an elegant Bower erected for the occasion on the Bank of the River below the Town. — In the evening there was a tolerable good display of fireworks.

On the preceding day, in the Council Chamber, the Aldermen of Savannah had drawn up and ratified an address to the President. Accordingly the officials of the City now waited in a body on the President — presumably about noon on Saturday — resplendent in all the bravery of their official insignia. The Marshal carried a white staff six and a half feet long, bearing the device "M.C.S."

nel of the Fourth Regiment, Pennsylvania troops, January 3, 1776; commissioned brigadier-general, February 21, 1777, and joined the army under General George Washington in New Jersey. He served brilliantly throughout the Revolution, his best-known achievement being the capture of Stony Point, for which he received the thanks of Congress and of the General Assembly of Pennsylvania. He received brevet rank of major-general, October 10, 1783. He removed to Georgia and settled on a tract of land donated him by that State as a recompense for his military service, and served in the Second Congress, as Representative from Georgia, March 4, 1791, to March 21, 1792. Nominated by Washington as major-general and General-in-Chief of the United States Army, he was confirmed April 3, 1792. Defeated the Indian tribes of the Northwest at the battle of Fallen Timbers, August 20, 1794. He is known as "Mad Anthony Wayne" for his unexpected success in perilous expeditions. Washington describes him as "more active and enterprising than judicious and cautious." He died in Presque Isle, Pennsylvania, December 15, 1796.

[1] Traces of these lines of defence are still visible in the rear of the town. For an account of their appearance as late as 1848, see Lossing.

in white letters on a red field; the Constable carried a blue staff of like proportions, bearing the name and number of his ward in white letters on a red field; and even the scavenger, if he were there — and what city official, especially the scavenger, would have been absent on such an occasion! — bore his staff of office, one foot long, black with each end red. The Mayor of the Corporation, Thomas Gibbons, delivered the following address to the President, in the presence of a respectful and interested audience:

Sir,

The Mayor and Aldermen of the City of Savannah do unanimously concur in presenting their most affectionate congratulations to you on your arrival in this city. Impressed with a just sense of your great and eminent services to America, permit us, the Representatives of the City, to assure you of the high opinion the citizens entertain of your elevated virtues.

We respect you as one of the richest and most valuable blessings divine goodness has bestowed on the People of these United States; your presence is an evidence of the watchful care you have for every part of the extended empire over which you preside. If we cannot, by external shew, demonstrate that respect for you which is in the power of the more wealthy of our sister states to display, yet none estimate your merits higher than the People of Georgia. The historic page bears record of our sufferings in the late Revolution, and the vestiges of war remain within view of our capital; and although peace was, in 1783, restored to America, yet Georgia continued to suffer under the destructive ravages of an Indian war, and it has been reserved for the efficacy of the present Government to give peace to our state.

May the blessings of the Government long continue under your administration, and may it please the Great Ruler of Events to grant you long residence on earth, and to length of days add the blessings of uninterrupted health, that the advantages of the present Government may be permanently established.

TH. GIBBONS, Mayor

COUNCIL CHAMBER, *May* 13, 1791.

The President in his answer complied with the formalities of the occasion:

GENTLEMEN,

Your affectionate congratulations on my arrival in this city, and the very favorable sentiments you express towards me, are received with gratitude, and thanked with sincerity. Estimating favors by the cordiality with which they are bestowed, I confess with real pleasure, my obligations to the Corporation of Savannah, and I can never cease to entertain a grateful sense of their goodness.

While the virtuous conduct of your citizens, whose patriotism braved all the hardships of the late war, engaged my esteem, the distress peculiar to the state of Georgia, after the peace, excited my deepest regret.

It was with singular satisfaction I perceived that the efficacy of the General Government could interpose effectual relief, and restore tranquillity to so deserving a Member of the Union. Your sentiments on this event are worthy of citizens, who, placing a due value on the blessings of peace, desire to maintain it on the immutable principles of justice and good faith.

May the harmony of your city be consequent on your administration, and may you individually be happy.[1]

G. WASHINGTON

[1] It is worthy of remark that Savannah's streets, "State," "Congress," "President," recall the events of the Revolution; and even more definitely the city wards which have the names; Washington, Greene, Warren, and Franklin. A quotation from a recent address by P. W. Meldrin, when Mayor of Savannah, epitomizes the city's romantic history: "Every spot is hallowed. Where the Vernon River flows by Beaulieu, the dashing d'Estaing landed to make his attack with the allied forces of Savannah. Hard by is Bethesda, 'House of Mercy,' where Jew, Protestant and Roman Catholic united in founding Georgia's noblest charity. There it was that

The Grand Lodge of Masons of Georgia, desirous of paying tribute to the illustrious brother on the occasion of his visit to the city, gathered at Brown's Coffee House on Saturday; and there proceeded in Masonic order to the house provided for the President, where the following address was delivered by George Houstoun, Grand Master of all the Masons in the State of Georgia:

SIR, and BROTHER,

The Grand Master, Officers, and Members of the Grand Lodge of Georgia, beg leave to congratulate you on your arrival in this city.

Whilst your exalted character claims the respect and deference of all men, they, from the benevolence of masonic principles, approach you with the familiar declaration of fraternal affection.

Happy indeed that Society, renowned for its antiquity, and pervading influence over the enlightened world, which, having ranked a FREDERIC at its head, can now boast of a WASHINGTON as a Brother — a Brother who is justly hailed the Redeemer of his Country, raised it to glory, and by his conduct in public and private life has evinced to Monarchs, that true majesty consists not in splendid royalty, but in intrinsic worth.

With these sentiments they rejoice at your presence in this state, and, in common with their fellow citizens, greet you thrice welcome, flattering themselves that your stay will be made agreeable.

Wesley sang his inspired songs and Whitefield with his eloquence thrilled the world. On the river is the grove where General Greene lived and died, and Whitney wrought from his fertile brain the wonderful invention which revolutionized commerce. Near at hand, almost sunk into oblivion, is the spring made historic by the daring of Jasper and Newton. There stands Savannah's pride, her Academy of Arts and Science. Over there is the home where Washington was entertained, and across the street are the guns which he captured at Yorktown. Here, at our very feet, Casimir Pulaski fell, charging at the head of his legion, while Jasper, rescuing the colors, yielded up his gallant life."

May the Great Architect of the Universe preserve you, whilst engaged in the work allotted you on earth, and long continue you the brightest pillar of our temple; and, when the supreme fiat shall summon you hence, they pray the Mighty I Am may take you into his holy keeping.

GEORGE HOUSTOUN, Grand Master of
All Masons in the State of Georgia.

GRAND LODGE IN SAVANNAH, 14*th May*, 1791.

The President neatly "covered the ground" in his very brief reply:

GENTLEMEN,

I am much obliged by your congratulations on my arrival in this city, and I am highly indebted to your favorable opinions.

Every circumstance concurs to render my stay in Savannah agreeable, and it is cause of regret to me that it must be so short.

My best wishes are offered for the welfare of the Fraternity and for your particular happiness.

G. WASHINGTON

The formal ceremonies being concluded, the Grand Master introduced to the President the Right Worshipful Past Grand Master, officers, and members.

On this day was presented to Washington the address of the German Congregation of Ebenezer — which is unique in that it is written in Latin. It follows below:

TO THE PRESIDENT OF THE UNITED STATES OF AMERICA.

Permittas, quaeso, Illustrissime Washington! ut devoti piique animi sensa TIBI declarem, cui contigerit insignis illa felicitas, TE Savannae adeundi, virum, tot tantisque factis illustrem. Profecto admiratus sum TUAM humanitatem et indulgentiam, qua me hominem ignotum excepisti, qui non ausus essem ad TE accedere nisi ab amico optimo certior factus essem, tristem abs TE discedere neminem. Georgia laetatur de

TE et Splendidissima praesentia, qua eam exhibarare dignatus es. Diu vivas o Washington! deliciae americani populi, tuumque nomen, et facta illustria vera posteritas celebrabit. Semper precabor Deum Optimum Maximum, qui TE praesidem harum civitatum constituit, ut omnibus rebus conatibusque Tuis propitius adsit. Accipe hanc tenuiorem epistolam, nullo ornatu commendabilem, eadem indulgentia, qua me excipere dignatus es. Anglice quidem scripturus eram si facultate pollerem eleganter scribendi, et ut dignum esse posset insignibus virtutibus et illustrissimis Factis TUIS. Peregrimes, in hanc provinciam missus sum benignissimam doctrinam Redemtoris nostri profitendi inter posteros colonorum Salisburgensium, quos inprimis quia curae meae concrediti sunt, cum omni gente germanica Georgiae Americanae Tuo potentissimo patrocinio magnopere comendo. Ego vero nunquam desinam ardentissimas preces mittere ad Deum benignissimum, pro totius populi Americani salute.

JOHN EARNST BERGMAN,
Minister of the German Congregation of Ebenezer
SAVANNAH d. 14. *May* 1791.

The events for the remainder of this day and evening, in which the President participated are thus excellently described in a contemporary print:

In the afternoon the President honored the Citizens with his company at a dinner prepared for him under a beautiful arbor, supported by three rows of pillars, entirely covered with laurel and bay leaves, so as to exhibit uniform green columns. The pillars were higher than the arbor, and ornamented above it by festoons, and connected below by arches covered in the same manner. The place on which it stood was judiciously chosen, presenting at once a view of the city and of the shipping in the harbor, with an extensive prospect of the river and rice lands both above and below the town. But the principal advantage which resulted from its situation and structure was the opportunity which it afforded to a great body of people to have a distinct and uninterrupted view of that object to which all eyes and hearts appeared to be attracted.

Georgia: Savannah

A company of nearly 200 citizens and strangers dined under it, and the satisfaction which each one enjoyed in paying this personal tribute to the merit of a man who is, if possible, more beloved for his goodness than admired for his greatness, produced a degree of convivial and harmonious mirth rarely experienced.

Every one beheld with delight in the person of our President the able General, the virtuous Patriot, the profound Politician; in a word, one of the most shining ornaments that ever dignified human nature.

The Artillery Company dined under another arbor erected at a small distance, and received merited applause for the great dexterity which they displayed in firing at each toast. Their fires were returned by Fort Wayne, and the ship Thomas Wilson, which was moored opposite to the arbor; her decorations through the day, and illumination at night, had a fine effect.

The following toasts were given:

1. The United States of America.
2. Prosperity to the Citizens of Savannah and its vicinity. (By the President.)
3. The Fair of America.
4. The Vice-President of the United States.
5. The memorable Era of Independence.
6. The Count d'Estaing.
7. The Memory of General Greene.
8. The Arts and Sciences.
9. The Memory of those brave Men who fell before the Lines of Savannah on the 9th of October, 1779.
10. The Friends to free and equal government throughout the globe.
11. All foreign Powers in Friendship with the United States.
12. May Religion and Philosophy always triumph over Superstition and Prejudice in America.
13. The present dexterous Corps of Artillery (The President's toast).

(After the President retired.)

THE PRESIDENT OF THE UNITED STATES.

The construction of the arbor, and the manner in which the entertainment was provided and conducted, did great honor to the gentlemen to whose direction the whole was committed.

In the evening there was a handsome exhibition of fireworks, and the amusements of this day of joy and festivity were concluded by a Concert.

The Chatham Artillery Company, which won such favor in the President's eyes during his stay in Savannah, was organized on May 1, 1786. On the 20th of June following it was called upon to pay the soldier's tribute to the memory of Major-General Nathanael Greene. This Revolutionary hero had settled at "Mulberry Grove" in 1783, and frequently visited Savannah. A sunstroke carried him off on June 19, 1786. At the front of the funeral procession was the Chatham Artillery firing minute guns and advancing; and at the grave it fired a salute of thirteen guns. Not long after the President's departure, this company received from the President the gift of the "Washington Guns," two six-pounder bronze fieldpieces. Upon one of the guns are inscribed the words: "Surrendered by the capitulation of York Town, October nineteenth, 1781. *Honi soit qui mal y pense.* — G. R." — with the imperial crown. It was cast in 1756, during the reign of George II. These guns, though long since lost to service, are prized as precious relics by the ancient artillery company. In this connection it may be mentioned that at the house of General Greene, near Savannah, his daughter in 1807 received the brass cannon, captured at Eutaw Springs, which Congress voted to her gallant father.

GENERAL JAMES JACKSON

Georgia: Savannah

The day after the departure of "General Washington," as he was usually called, the following card appeared in the public journals of Savannah:

General Jackson [1] requests Captain Else of the Artillery, and Montfort of the Volunteer Infantry, to accept his best thanks for their soldierly conduct at the reception, during the stay, and on the departure of the President. He likewise presents his thanks to the Commissioned and Non-Commissioned Officers and Privates of each Corps.

It is a pleasure to the General to announce to the Artillery the very general applause they received on Saturday, and, what ought to immortalize the corps, the approbation of their conduct, expressed in the warmest terms by the Commander in Chief of the United States. The General hopes that this character, so firmly established, will long continue them an ornament to the Militia, and an honor to the State of Georgia.

[1] James Jackson was born in Moreton-Hampstead, Devonshire, England, September 21, 1757. He removed to Georgia in 1772 and located in Savannah. He studied law just prior to the Revolution. He first served in 1776 as a private in the Volunteer Light Infantry of Savannah; was soon promoted to command of the company. He served throughout the Revolution, and participated in many engagements, notably Blackstocks and the Cowpens. He was appointed by the Legislature to the command of the Georgia Legion, and remained in command until the evacuation of Savannah, receiving the keys of the city from the British, July 12, 1782. After the Revolution he resumed the practice of law. On the organization of the State militia, he was appointed to the command of the Chatham Regiment; was later a brigadier of the State, and ultimately major-general of the First Division. He was a member of the first Constitutional Convention of Georgia, in 1777; clerk of the court, by election of the Provincial Congress, 1776–77. Member of the Georgia House of Representatives on various occasions, from 1781 to 1788. In 1788, at the age of thirty-one, he was elected governor of Georgia, but declined on the score of youth and inexperience. Elected to the First Congress (March 4, 1789–March 3, 1791); contested the election of Anthony Wayne in the Second Congress, and the seat was declared vacant by the House, March 21, 1792. Elected to the United States Senate and served from March 4, 1793, until his resignation in 1795. Was presidential elector in 1797; governor of Georgia, 1798–1801; again elected to the United States Senate, and served from March 4, 1801, until his death in Washington, D.C., March 16, 1806. His remains were interred in the Congressional Cemetery, Washington, D.C.

The Field Officers of the Chatham Regiment will be pleased to communicate this order, and to receive the General's highest commendations of their attention to the duties required of them.

JAS. JACKSON
Brigadier General first District

SAVANNAH, *May sixteenth*, 1791.

CHAPTER IX

THE SIXTH STAGE

Augusta, Georgia, and Columbia, South Carolina

THE graciousness and hospitality of the people of Savannah made a most pleasant impression upon the President. He was in no hurry to leave; and "took things easy" on Sunday. After attending morning service, he held quite a reception at his lodgings — as he records in the diary, "receiving a number of visits from the most respectable ladies of the place (as was the case yesterday)." The use of the adjective in this association is strange to modern ears, and provokes a smile. When he finally did make a late start, he had a splendid farewell retinue — being "Escorted beyond the limits of the City by most of the Gentlemen in it."

If Washington was pleased by his reception in Savannah, the people of Savannah were equally pleased — and probably more enthusiastic in expression than the dignified and impassive Washington. The following tribute to Washington after his departure appeared in the "Georgia Gazette" of Savannah and deserves quotation in full:

It is highly pleasing to a grateful and patriotic mind to reflect upon the happy consequences which will probably flow from the tour which the President is now performing. His admirable qualities has long since extended his fame to the utmost limits of civilization; but it is only by personal interviews that a just idea can be acquired of the amiableness of his temper and his engaging manners. The intelligent serenity of his countenance, the unaffected ease and dignity of his deportment, while they excite the most profound respect, naturally rivet the affections to him. As the most unlimited confidence is reposed in his prudence, abilities, and patriotism, this effect must have essential influence in giving energy to that government in the administration of which he has so considerable a part.

Once more Washington had the pleasure of dining with his sprightly and charming friend, Mrs. Greene. A glimpse of the life at "Mulberry Grove" is caught in a letter Mrs. Greene wrote to a friend, Miss Flagg:

If you expect to be an inhabitant of this country, you must not think to sit down with your netting pins; but on the contrary employ half your time at the toilet, one quarter to paying and receiving visits; the other quarter to scolding servants, with a hard thump every now and then over the head; or singing, dancing, reading, writing, or saying your prayers. The latter is here quite a phenomenon; but you need not tell how you employ your time.

An even more explicit description is given by General Greene shortly after his arrival there in 1785:

We found the house, situation, and out-buildings more convenient and pleasing than we expected. The prospect is delightful, and the house magnificent. We have a coach house and stables, a large out kitchen, and a poultry-house nearly fifty feet long, and twenty wide, parted for different kinds of poultry, with a pigeon-house on the top, which will contain not less than a thousand pigeons. Besides these, are several other buildings convenient for a family, and among the rest, a fine smoke-house. The garden is in ruins, but there are still a great variety of shrubs and flowers in it.[1]

[1] In another letter to his friend Ethan Clark, of Newport, Rhode Island, to whom the above letter is addressed, Greene says (April, 1786): "This is a busy time with us, and I can afford but a small portion of time to write.

GENERAL NATHANAEL GREENE

After a delightful sojourn here of a few hours, during which he dined with his charming hostess, the President set forth once more on the "open road," and after travelling fifteen miles lodged at "one Spencers." Washington's observations upon Savannah, and his brief record of the wholly uneventful two days (Monday and Tuesday) which followed, are copied below:

Savanna stands upon what may be called high ground for this Country — It is extremely sandy wch makes the walking very disagreeable; & the houses uncomfortable in warm & windy weather, as they are filled with dust whenever these happen. — The town on 3 sides is surrounded with cultivated Rice fields which have a rich and luxuriant appearance. On the 4th or backside it is a fine sand. — The harbour is said to be very good, & often filled with square rigged vessels, but there is a bar below over which not more than 12 feet water can be brot. except at sprg. tides. — The tide does not flow above or 12 or 14 miles above the City though the River is swelled by it more than double that distance. — Rice & Tobacco (the last of wch. is greatly increasing) are the principal Exports — Lumber & Indigo are also Exported, but the latter is on the decline, and it is supposed by Hemp & Cotton. — Ship timber, viz: live Oak & Cedar, is (and may be more so) valuable in the exptn.

We are planting. We have got upwards of sixty acres of corn planted, and expect to plant one hundred and thirty of rice. The garden is delightful. The fruit-trees and flowering shrubs form a pleasing variety. We have green peas almost fit to eat, as fine lettuce as ever you saw. The mocking birds surround us evening and morning. The weather is mild, and the vegetable kingdom is progressing to perfection. But it is a great deduction from the pleasure we should feel from the beauties and conveniences of the place, that we are obliged to leave it before we shall have tasted of several kinds of fruits. We have in the same orchard apples, pears, peaches, apricots, nectarines, plums of different kinds, figs, pomegranites, and oranges. And we have strawberries which measure three inches around. All these are clever, but the want of our friends to enjoy them with us renders them less interesting." Consult G. W. Greene: *Life of Nathanael Greene* (Houghton, Mifflin & Co., 1890).

Monday, 16th.

Breakfasted at Russells — 15 miles from Spencer's — dined at Garnets 19 further & lodged at Pierces 8 miles more, in all — 42 miles to day.

Tuesday, 17th.

Breakfasted at Spinner's 17 miles — dined at Lamberts 13 — and lodged at Waynesborough (wch. was coming 6 miles out of our way) 14, in all 43 miles — Waynesborough is a small place, but the Seat of the Court of Burkes County — 6 or 8 dwelling houses is all it contains; — an attempt is making (without much apparent effect) to establish an Academy at it as is the case also in all the Counties.

The preparations for Washington's reception by the citizens of Augusta are most succinctly exhibited in the orders issued from time to time, and published in the "Augusta Chronicle" of May 21st:

GOVERNMENT HOUSE
AUGUSTA, *April* 25, 1791

GENERAL ORDER.

Ambrose Gordon,[1] Esq. Major of the Richmond County regiment of militia, with not less than fourteen volunteers, are directed to hold themselves in readiness to march and escort the President of the United States to this place.

By order of the Commander in Chief.

Attest. J. MERIWETHER, Sec'y.

GOVERNMENT HOUSE
May 9, 1791

GENERAL ORDER.

Major Gordon is directed to march without delay with

[1] Colonel Ambrose Gordon, 1751–1804, soldier of the Revolution and officer of the Georgia State militia, was born in New Jersey, June 28, 1751. Removing to Georgia he settled in Washington County in 1784. His death occurred January 28, 1804, and the body rests in old St. Paul's churchyard at Augusta, Georgia.

the escort ordered the 25th April last, the nearest route to Savannah.

By order of the Commander in Chief.

Attest. J. MERIWETHER, Sec'y.

Tuesday, May 17, 1791.

Ordered,

That the State Officers, together with General Twiggs [1] and the sheriff of Richmond County, do assemble at the State-house to-morrow at 11 o'clock, A.M. from whence they are to proceed in the following order of procession to meet the President of the United States:

The sheriff of Richmond County — General Twiggs — The Secretary of the state — The Governor's Secretary — His Excellency the Governor — Judge Walton — Governor's Secretary — The Treasurer, The Solicitor General — The Attorney General, The Surveyor General, Clerk of the House of Representatives — Secretary of the Senate.

Ordered,

That the artillery take post at the old fort — and upon the President's approach to the town, to fire a salute of fifteen rounds.

Attest. J. MERIWETHER, S. E. D.

[1] General John Twiggs was born in one of the Northern States, Maryland, it is thought, June 5, 1750. Some time prior to the Revolution, he removed to Georgia accompanying John Emanuel, whose daughter Ruth he married. Settling in St. Paul's Parish (Richmond County), he at once identified himself with the Georgia patriots, among whom his genius for command soon made him an acknowledged leader. During the war he commanded an independent body of troops, and record is left of no braver or more efficient officer.

For his gallant services he was made Brigadier-General in 1781 and later given extensive tracts of land by the Georgia Legislature. He filled many important public offices, including several terms in the General Assembly; represented the State in treaty negotiations with the Indians at Augusta in 1803; and, having been raised to the rank of Major-General in 1792, was requested, as ranking militia officer, to take charge of the State Government in the interregnum of two months following the retirement of Governor Mathews from office. This, however, he modestly declined to do. He died March 29, 1816.

STATE HOUSE, AUGUSTA, *May* 18, 1791

The officers having assembled agreeably to the order of yesterday, at 11 o'clock set forward, accompanied by a numerous train of respectable citizens; at the distance of five miles from town, the President of the United States appeared in sight, when the procession halted, at which time he alighted from his coach, mounted his horse, and advanced with Major Jackson and the Federal Marshal; his excellency the Governor at the same time, attended by the Secretary of the State, moved forward, and after being announced, congratulated the President on his near approach to the residence of government; — this ceremony being ended, the procession was resumed, and the President conducted to the house provided for his reception.

Attest. W. URQUHART, S. E. D.

In his diary Washington made the following brief statement:

Breakfasted at Tulcher's 15 miles from Waynesborough; and within 4 miles of Augusta met the Govor. [Telfair],[1]

[1] Edward Telfair was born in 1735 on the farm of Town Head, Scotland. Educated at the grammar school of Kirkudbright, he emigrated to America at the age of twenty-three as the representative of a business house. He settled first in Virginia, next lived for a time in Halifax, North Carolina, and in 1766 settled in Savannah, Georgia. He was a member of committees in July, 1774, raised by the people of Georgia for assisting the other colonies in asserting American rights; delegate to the Provincial Congress of Georgia, January, 1775; assisted in seizing the powder in the public magazine in Savannah. In June, 1775, he was elected a member of the Council of Safety; and was a delegate to the Provincial Congress of Georgia, July, 1775. In 1778 he was chosen a delegate from Georgia to the Continental Congress, serving until January, 1783; reëlected in May, 1785, but did not serve. He was chosen Boundary Commissioner in 1783; and the same year assisted in negotiating treaties with the Indians. He was elected Governor of Georgia in 1786; and was a member of the Convention which ratified the Constitution of the United States. In 1789 he was again elected Governor of Georgia. He died in Savannah, September 19, 1807. He accumulated a considerable fortune, and the charitable bequests of his daughters are remembered with gratitude for their magnitude and liberal scope.

GEORGE WALTON

Judge Walton,[2] the Attorney Genl. & most of the principal Gentlemen of the place; by whom I was escorted into the Town, & recd. under a discharge of Artillery, — the distance I came to day was about 32 miles....

The road from Savanna to Augusta is, for the most part, through Pine barrens; but more uneven than I had been accustomed to since leavg. Petersburgh in Virginia, especially after riding about 30 miles from the City of that name; here & there indeed, a piece of Oak land is passed on this Road, but of small extent & by no means of the first quality.

The President was conducted by "the upper road"; and arriving at Augusta about one o'clock, accompanied by a numerous retinue, rode through lines of cheering spectators down Broad Street to the house prepared for his entertainment, Captain Howell's artillery all the while firing salutes. A feature of the parade was a detachment under the command of Major Ambrose Gordon, of the Augusta Volunteer Light Horse, who "cut a very superb appearance — their uniform being blue, faced with red and laced

[2] George Walton, born in Prince Edward County, Virginia, in 1749; he became an orphan at an early age. When twenty years old, he removed to Savannah, Georgia, and there entered upon the practice of law. He took an active part in the popular movements looking toward independence in 1774. He was elected a member of the Council of Safety, June 22, 1775; and acted as Secretary of the Provincial Congress which convened at Savannah, July 4, 1775. He drafted the famous address to the people of Georgia on the state of American affairs. Chosen as delegate to the Continental Congress by the Provincial Congress which assembled in Savannah, January 20, 1776, he continued as a member of the Continental Congress until October, 1781, save for an interval in 1779, when he filled the gubernatorial chair of Georgia. As colonel of the First Battalion of the First Regiment of Foot Militia, he was sorely wounded in the defence of Savannah, December, 1778. In January, 1783, he was elected Chief Justice of the State of Georgia. In 1787 he was appointed a delegate from the State of Georgia to the Federal Convention, but did not attend. In 1789 he was again elected Governor of Georgia. In 1795 and 1796 he represented Georgia in the Continental Congress. For fifteen years and until his death, February 2, 1804, he served as Judge of the Middle Circuit of Georgia.

with silver, their caps and other accoutrements equal to their uniforms, and the horses nearly of a colour and in good order."

Governor Telfair's family residence, "The Grove," near Augusta, was the scene of a large and brilliant dinner to the President at four o'clock in the afternoon of this day. Here were gathered many patriots who, like the Governor, during the Revolution

> On war's red touchstone
> Rang true metal.

After dinner, when stories and anecdotes regaled the over-grave President until he quite unbent, the following toasts were drunk:

1. The United States.
2. The State of Georgia. (The President's toast.)
3. The joyful occasion.
4. The Vice-President.
5. The 4th of July, 1776.
6. The 17th October, 1777.
7. 19th October, 1781.
8. The first of May.
9. The memory of General Greene.
10. The memory of those who bravely fell in defence of American Liberty.
11. Our Ministers at Foreign Courts.
12. Agriculture.
13. Commerce.
14. Arts and sciences.
15. Republican virtue.

Especial significance in the minds of the assembled guests attached to two of the toasts — the 17th October, 1777, when Burgoyne surrendered five thousand eight hundred men at Saratoga; and the 19th October, 1781 —

when the famous soldier, Lord Cornwallis, yielded to combined American and French forces under Washington at Yorktown and virtually brought to a close the bitter and protracted struggle for independence. Later the President drank tea with "many well dressed ladies" — an enthusiastic compliment as coming from Washington, who usually thought he had done his full duty by the fair sex when he called them "respectable." Mrs. Telfair gave a ball "to the Ladies" that evening at "The Grove," at which the President was present for a short time.

On Thursday morning the citizens of Augusta voted to the President, and forthwith presented to him the following address:

SIR,

Your journey to the southward being extended to the frontier of the Union affords a fresh proof of your indefatigable zeal in the service of your country, and an equal attention and regard to all the people of the United States. With these impressions the citizens of Augusta present their congratulations upon your arrival here in health, with the assurance that it will be their greatest pleasure, during your stay with them, to testify the sincere affection thay have for your person, their sense of obligations for your merits and services, and their entire confidence in you as the Chief Magistrate of their country. On your return, and at all times, their best wishes will accompany you, while they retain the hope that a life of virtue, benevolence, and patriotism, may be long preserved, for the benefit of the age, and example to posterity.

In the name of all the citizens,

GEORGE WALTON,
JOHN MEALS,
THOMAS CUMMING,
PETER CARNES,
SEABORN JONES.[1]

AUGUSTA, *May* 19, 1791.

[1]Thomas Cumming, first Intendant of the Town of Augusta, and first

To this simple and friendly address, the President replied as follows:

GENTLEMEN,

I receive your congratulations on my arrival in Augusta with great pleasure. I am much obliged by your assurances of regard, and thank you with unfeigned sincerity for the favorable sentiments you are pleased to express towards me.

Entreating you to be persuaded of my gratitude, I desire to assure you, that it will afford me the most sensible satisfaction to learn the progression of your prosperity. My best wishes for your happiness, collectively and individually, are sincerely offered.

G. WASHINGTON.

president of Georgia's oldest bank, the Bank of Augusta, chartered December 6, 1810, was born May 30, 1765, and died March 6, 1834, in Augusta, Georgia, where he lies buried. He was a man of outstanding prominence and broad interests. For many years he was a trustee of Richmond County Academy and was one of the commissioners appointed in 1791 to examine into the condition of the State Treasury. His oldest son, William Cumming, was a gallant soldier of the War of 1812, holding the rank of Colonel in the United States Army.

Peter Johnston Carnes, one of the delegation of five Augusta citizens, presenting President Washington on his visit to Georgia in 1791 a welcome address printed on parchment, was a man of prominence and ability. A member from Jefferson County to the Constitutional Convention of 1798, he was the author of the clause prohibiting the further importation of slaves into the State. During the years 1799–1804 Peter Carnes and George Walton served as Solicitor-General and Judge, respectively, of the Middle Circuit of Georgia.

Seaborn Jones, Revolutionary patriot, was born in Halifax County, North Carolina, in 1758. He was one of seven sons, and, after the death of their father, the family moved to Georgia, settling in what was later Burke County, just prior to the Revolution in which all seven of the brothers served. Following the war, Seaborn Jones, then a man of prominence in his section, filled with distinction a number of high public offices, being the first Speaker of the Georgia House of Representatives under the Constitution of 1789; one of Georgia's four presidential electors of 1793; a member in the General Assembly in 1787, 1789, and 1790, and Intendant or Mayor of Augusta, Georgia, for several years. He was a pew-holder in old St. Paul's Church, and a trustee of the Richmond County Academy. His death occurred about 1823 and the body lies buried in St. Paul's churchyard.

HOUSE OF DR. E. E. MURPHY, AUGUSTA, GEORGIA
Where Washington was entertained at a public banquet, May 18, 1791

Augusta and Columbia

At half-past ten o'clock on the morning of this day the Augusta Volunteer Light Horse encamped on the bank of the river. After pitching their tents and finishing their pickets, they

completed a very handsome grove, which looked as if the beautiful hand of nature had exerted herself on this joyous occasion, and seconded their efforts in honor to the saviour and friend of his country. About 3 o'clock, they paraded to receive the illustrious President of the United States of America — during the discharge of a salute from the artillery, the horses stood extremely well. When the President passed, the officers saluted; and as soon as he was seated and the firing over, they sat down to an elegant dinner, provided by themselves, on the occasion, and drank the following toasts:

1. The President of the United States of America; may he return safe and in health to his favorite seat.
2. The Vice-President of the United States of America.
3. The Congress of the United States.
4. Louis the XVI and the patriots of France.
5. The memorable era of Independence.
6. The Governor of Georgia.
7. The fair sex of Georgia.
8. Population and industry.
9. The friends of freedom.
10. Salutary laws and well supported.
11. The memory of those brave heroes who fell in defence of their country's independence.
12. May we never want a heart or a hand to support the Federal Government.
13. Improvements and extension to the navigation and commerce of Georgia.
14. May unanimity and virtue ever be the characteristic of Americans.
15. May merit ever be the only foundation of distinctions among freemen.

They made a handsome figure vying with each other in adroitness and soldier-like behaviour. They spent the remainder of the evening together with that conviviality, hilarity and harmony, due to the joyous event for which they had been embodied.

The frankness of the narrator is delightful: the connotation of "conviviality, hilarity and harmony" leaves nothing to be desired.

At half-past four o'clock that afternoon the President partook of an "elegant dinner" provided by popular subscription at the Court-House, which was attended by Governor Telfair and a large number of citizens. After dinner the usual number of toasts were drunk — conspicuous among which was the last: to North Carolina and Rhode Island, the hesitant sisters.

1. The United States.
2. The State of Georgia, and prosperity to Augusta. (*By the President.*)
3. The Vice-President and Congress.
4. Louis XVI and the other Allies of the Union.
5. The National Assembly of France.
6. The memory of General Greene and those who fell in defence of our country.
7. The Marquis de la Fayette.
8. The defenders of the rights of human nature throughout the world.
9. Agriculture, manufactures, and commerce.
10. The arts and science.
11. The arms of defence.
12. The important 4th of July, 1776.
13. May the old age of America flourish in the liberty of its youth.
14. The perfection of the Federal Constitution.
15. Prosperity to our two new admitted Sister States.

In the evening the President, as he says, with comical spelling, "went to an Assembly . . . at the Accadamy," there being present between "60 & 70 well dressed ladies" (evidently the Augusta ladies had fine taste in the art of costume, to impress "the General"), the "largest number of Ladies," according to the "Augusta Chronicle," "ever assembled at this place." The following morning, records the President in his diary, "Viewed the Ruins, or rather small Remns. of the Works which had been erected by the British during the War and taken by the Americans. — Also the falls, which are about 2 miles above the Town;—and the Town itself." Although he doesn't mention it in his diary, the President, as fully attested by the "Augusta Chronicle," "honored the examination of the students at the Academy with his presence." The Richmond Academy is an ancient institution, with an honorable history. On July 31, 1783, the Legislature of Georgia passed a law for the establishment of a "Seminary of Learning." The building first used as a schoolhouse in 1785 was located below the bridge on Bay Street, between Elbert and Lincoln Streets. "From 1780 to 1786, while Savannah [the Seat of State Government] was occupied by the enemy, Augusta was declared the temporary capital of the State; and there being no public buildings in Augusta suitable for the purpose, those of the Academy were used as the State House, and the State and Federal Courts were held there." [1] The records of the Academy show that, at the

[1] *History of Augusta, Georgia.* By C. C. Jones, Jr., and Salem Dutcher. (Syracuse, New York, 1890.) Under an act of 1780, a lot on Broad Street was reserved "for houses of public seminary and schools." A new board of commissioners — namely, William Glascock, George Walton, Joseph Pannel, Andrew Burns, and Samuel Jack — somewhat later was empowered to sell certain lots, the proceeds to be used to establish and maintain a

examination in 1789, to Edward (Edmund?) Bacon, who excelled in general learning, was presented a gold medal of the value of an eagle, with a device thereon indicative of the occasion, and that "of the girls of the Academy" Sally Parish excelled, and to her was awarded a volume of Thomson's "Seasons." On the occasion of the President's visit, Master Edmund Bacon was chosen as the orator of the day. Addressing himself directly to Washington, he delivered the following specimen of the poetic art of that day and locality:

In ages past, we see a splendid train
Of heroes shine, in panegyric's strain —
Historic pens have varnished o'er their crime,
And prais'd, in them, the vices of the time:
To conquer nations; millions to devour;
To reign in all the wantonness of power;
To follow glory; to acquire a name;
Their cause ambition, and their objective fame.
'Tis ours to boast a hero great and good;
With courage and benevolence endued.
Superior genius you, whose breast can feel
No other motives but your country's weal.
Superior firmness with such virtues arm'd;
Your people loving, by your people lov'd.
Let not th' expressions of our love offend
Our Saviour, father, citizen and friend.
Deny us not the pleasure thus t' impart,
Without disguise, the feelings of the heart.
Thou friend of science, liberty, and laws,
Forever active in thy country's cause;
We are thy children — let thy fancy trace,
In us, the congregated, rising race,

seminary. This is the origin of the Richmond Academy. By its charter its trustees were *ex-officiis* commissioners of the town. The first master of the Academy was William Rogers, of Maryland.

Augusta and Columbia

Adopted, ere we drew the vital air,
And snatch'd from slavery by thy watchful care.
Heirs of that freedom, by that valor won;
May we ne'er mar the work by thee begun!
As we've been taught to glow at thy renown,
So we'll transmit by bright example down.
Each future babe shall learn to lisp thy name;
To love thy worth and emulate thy fame.
Whene'er the powers of infant reason dawn,
Full in his view thy portrait shall be drawn.
Hence on his mind these truths will be impress'd;
That virtue can be only truly blest.
Though power may glare in all the pomp of state;
That virtue only can be truly great.
Though vanity may bask in flattery's rays;
That virtue only meets with honest praise;
That virtue only claims our whole esteem;
That virtue only reigns with power supreme.
In our full hearts, what grateful raptures rise!
When o'er past scenes, our active fancy flies:
We hail the day, you took the glorious field,
And made the doughty British Lion yield!
Then, though the sceptre waited on your word,
For calm retirement, you resign'd the sword.
You scorn'd the glory power usurp'd imparts;
You scorned to reign but in a people's heart.
Again we see you bless Potomack's shore,
Resolv'd to leave sweet Vernon's shades no more.
Delightful seat! by our fond choice design'd,
T' enjoy, in peace, your self approving mind.
Again your country's call obey'd.
With fond regret, you left your fav'rite shore,
To feel the weight of public cares once more.
Hail joyous day! what acclamations rung!
Joy fill'd each eye, and rapture mov'd each tongue,
At your instalment! — never monarch wore
So bright, so rich a diadem before.
No more let sparkling dross ambitions move;

Your diadem, is — universal love.
But hold — this theme is painful to your ear;
Though lightly touch'd, by gratitude sincere —
Indulge our joys, forgive our forward zeal;
Let your own heart imagine what we feel!
What various transports in our bosoms glow,
Swell the full heart, and at the eyes o'er flow!!
Almighty God! Since virtue is thy ear;
O hear a nation's universal prayer!
May all the joys, this transient scene can know,
Full on his heart, in gentle currents flow! —
May all the joys, benevolence inspires,
Pursue him still when he from time retires!
May this one joy, forever crown the whole;
And with immortal rapture fill his soul!
May he, from heaven's sublime, eternal scenes,
See future millions happy through his means!!!
And let mankind this serious truth confess;
None ere was prais'd so much, — none ever flatter'd less.

In a contemporary print it is solemnly recorded of young Bacon's address to the President, that it was delivered "with such distinctness of articulation; such propriety of pauses and emphasies; and in a manner so truly pathetic, as to keep that illustrious hero and a numerous collection of gentlemen in tears almost the whole time the little orator was speaking." Such a poem, even to-day, might well move any one to tears. Homage to the sensibility of our ancestors![1]

[1] At the centennial celebration of Richmond Academy on June 29, 1893, the orator of the day, the Honorable William H. Fleming, said among other things: "In 1791 the academy was signally known by the presence of General Washington. I gather from the statements of the chronicles there the distinguished visitor intended to depart on the twentieth of the month, but was prevailed upon to remain another day by two inducements that were offered him. One was the examination of the pupils of the Richmond Academy; and the other was a ball to be given by Mrs. Telfair. Now which of

At the State House this day (20th) was done the following Address of the Executive of the State of Georgia, which was then presented to the President:

My warmest congratulations on your arrival at the residence of government in this state, are presented with a peculiar pleasure, as well as a feeling sensibility; and I am persuaded that these emotions are perfectly congenial with those of my fellow citizens.

After the gratification felt from your presence among them, they will naturally contemplate the many unavoidable inconveniences arising in so arduous and extensive a tour with the most solicitous anxiety not less impressed, my cordial wishes shall accompany you through every stage on your return to the seat of the Government of the United States.

Long may you remain to fill the exalted station of Chief Magistrate of the American republics, as the just reward of that patriotism which marked every act of your life, whilst engaged in the arduous struggles of a long and complicated war, gave tone to the liberties of your country, immortalized your name throughout the nations of the world, and created an unbounded confidence in your virtue, with the strongest attachment to your person and family, in the minds of American citizens.

EDWARD TELFAIR.

STATE-HOUSE, AUGUSTA,
May 20, 1791.

these two inducements offered him affected most strongly his heart and head, the recitation and the speeches or the music and the dance, is unfortunately shrouded in mystery. But in the absence of proof to the contrary, I think we are excusable for claiming that it was his interest in learning, and his appreciation of the importance of this institution that caused the chief magistrate of the Union and the foremost man of the age to alter his high purpose and linger in our midst another day. This explanation appears the more probable from the fact that we have no information as to whom, among the fair maids and matrons at the ball, the 'Father of his Country' led in the frolicksome reel or clasped in the palpitating waltz. While, on the other hand, we are reliably informed that he was present at the examination of the Academy Students, and, in the language of the Chronicle, 'expressed himself handsomely of their performance.'"

To which the President of the United States was pleased to make the following answer:

SIR,

Obeying the impulse of a heart felt gratitude, I express with particular pleasure my sense of the obligations which your Excellency's goodness and the kind regards of your citizens, have conferred upon me.

I shall always retain the most pleasing remembrance of the polite and hospitable attentions, which I have received in my tour through Georgia, and during my stay at the residence of your government.

The manner in which your Excellency is pleased to recognize my public services, and to regard my private felicity, excites my sensibility, and claims my grateful acknowledgment.

You will do justice to the sentiments which influence my wishes, by believing that they are sincerely preferred for your personal happiness, and the prosperity of the state in which you preside.

That afternoon, with a "select party," the President, as he states in his diary,

Dined at a private dinner with Govr. Telfair today; and gave him dispatches for the Spanish Govr. of East Florida, respecting the Countenance given by that Government. to the fugitive Slaves of the Union — wch. dispatches were to be forwarded to Mr. Seagrove, Collector of St. Mary's, who was requested to be the bearer of them, and instructed to make arrangements for the prevention of these evils and, if possible, for the restoration of the property — especially of those slaves wch. had gone off since the orders of the Spanish Court, to discountenance this practice of recg. them.

On Saturday morning, about six o'clock, the President made his departure from Augusta; and as he crossed the Savannah River by the bridge he received the "salute of

Major Gordon's horse and Captain Howell's artillery." At the entrance to the bridge His Excellency the Governor, and the Federal and State officers, paid their compliments and bade the President farewell. Says a writer in the "Augusta Chronicle":

Much commendation is due to the officers and men of the two corps who were in service upon this occasion, for their attention and adroitness, and particularly to that of the horse which went as far as Savannah, and arrived in a short time to a perfection of discipline and order.

We are happy upon the present occasion to announce to our readers, that during his stay here, the President gave repeated demonstrations of the most entire satisfaction; and that all orders of men appeared anxious to pay respect to the person and character of this illustrious and good man.

Washington in his diary has recorded his impression of the falls of the river, two miles above Augusta, and of the town itself:

These falls (as they are called) are nothing more than rapids. — They are passable in their present state by boats with skilful hands, but may at a very small expence be improved, by removing a few rocks only, to streighten the passage. — Above them there is good boat navigation for many miles; by which the produce may be, & in some measure is, transported. — At this place, i. e. the falls, the good lands begin; & encrease in quality to the westward & No.ward. — All below them, except the Interval lands on the Rivers and Rice Swamps which extend from them, the whole Country is a Pine barren. — The town of Augusta is well laid out with wide & spacious Streets. — It stands on a large area of a perfect plain but it is not yet thickly built tho' surprizingly so for the time; for in 1783 there were not more than half a dozen dwelling houses; now there are not less than........ containing about............Souls of which about........

are blacks. — It bids fair to be a large Town being at the head of the *present* navigation, & a fine Country back of it for support, which is settling very fast by Tobacco planters. — The culture of which article is encreasing very fast, and bids fair to be the principal export from the State; from this part of it, it certainly will be so.

Augusta, though it covers more ground than Savanna, does not contain as many Inhabitants the latter having by the late census between 14 & 1500 whites and about 800 blacks.[1]

A final memento of Washington's visit to Augusta is the following set of orders which appeared in the "Augusta Chronicle," May 21, 1791:

GENERAL ORDER.

The Commander in Chief is particularly gratified with the military appearance and discipline of the volunteer troop of horse, under the command of Major Gordon, as well as with the promptitude with which they have executed the duties assigned them, during the distinguished and honorable service in which they have been engaged, and presents his thanks to Major Gordon and through him to each individual in his corps.

Attest. J. MERIWETHER, Sec.

GOVERNMENT HOUSE, AUGUSTA.

AFTER ORDERS

The escort under the command of Major Gordon is hereby discharged.

By order of the commander in chief.

Attest. J. MERIWETHER, Sec.

[1] In 1791, as we learn from the *Memorial History of Augusta, Georgia*, Augusta is said to have contained two hundred and fifty houses and a population of eleven hundred. The public buildings consisted of a church, a court-house, and an academy wherein between eighty and ninety pupils were instructed, a stone jail, a government house for the accommodation of the Governor and the State officials, and three warehouses capable of stor-

GENERAL WADE HAMPTON

Augusta and Columbia

The citizens of Columbia were fully apprized of the coming of Washington; and on Monday, 18th, a committee from Columbia consisting of four prominent citizens — Colonel Taylor, Colonel Wade Hampton, and Mr. Lythgoe, all of Columbia, and Mr. Jameson, of Granby,[1] set out from Columbia for Augusta, for the purpose of accompanying the President to Columbia. They arrived in time to escort the President out of Augusta at six o'clock on Saturday, 21st. The President records for the remainder of that day: "Dined at a house [2] about 20

ing ten thousand hogsheads of tobacco. In that year over six thousand hogsheads of tobacco were there inspected.

[1] Colonel Thomas Taylor, who is presumably referred to here, was probably born in Virginia. He and his brother James were among the first settlers on the east side of the Congaree River; and were the most influential men of the community. At the opening of the Revolution, Captain James Taylor raised a company at Camden, and Thomas Taylor was commissioned Colonel of the regiment. Both he and his brother were captured at Fishing Creek, but succeeded in effecting their escape while on the march to Camden under guard of a detachment of Tarleton's dragoons. (Consult Johnson's *Traditions* for many incidents connected with Colonel Taylor's army experiences.)

Wade Hampton was born in South Carolina in 1754; received a good schooling and devoted himself to agriculture; was active in pre-Revolutionary movements; served under Marion and Sumter; was elected to the Fourth Congress (March 4, 1795, to March 3, 1797); reëlected to the Eighth Congress (March 4, 1803, to March 3, 1805); presidential elector on the Jefferson and Burr ticket in 1801; Colonel in the United States Army in 1808; was appointed brigadier-general in February, 1809, and major-general March 2, 1813; served in the War of 1812 and resigned April 6, 1814; was reputed the wealthiest planter in the United States and the owner of three thousand slaves in 1830; died in Columbia, South Carolina, February 4, 1835.

Of Mr. Lythgoe, nothing is known save that he was a prominent citizen of Columbia.

Mr. Jameson was probably the Mayor of Granby.

[2] In his *History of Edgefield County*, John A. Chapman says the house here mentioned by Washington was the "Pine House," or "Piney Woods House." "If I am not mistaken," he says, "it has been in the ownership of the Bettis family ever since a period anterior to the Revolutionary War."

miles from Augusta and lodged at one Odem, about 20 miles farther." Says a contemporary print:

On the 22d general Winn,[1] and several other respectable gentlemen, rode out to meet him, and about sun set, arrived at Granby, proceeding immediately to the ferry on the Congaree river, leading from Granby, to Columbia; the banks of the river at that place were lined with the neighbouring inhabitants, who anxiously waited for the president's arrival. He was attended from the ferry by a number of gentlemen, on horseback, and when advanced near to the state house, the light horse under command of captain Kershaw, completely accoutred, formed on the left, near the edge of the woods, and saluted him with much respect; he was then conducted to a house comodiously prepared for his reception, where a few gentlemen, and the officers of the troop were introduced.

Washington records that he passed the first falls in the Congaree, just above the village of Granby, in a "flat bottomed boat at a Rope ferry"; and that he travelled forty-eight miles that day, breakfasting at a point twenty-one miles from Augusta. "The whole road from Augusta to

[1] Richard Winn was born in Eastern Virginia about 1750; received a limited schooling; removed to Georgia; entered the Continental service early in the Revolutionary War, and in 1775 was a lieutenant of South Carolina rangers, participating in the battle on Sullivan's Island. He was then placed in command of Fort McIntosh, Georgia, promoted to the rank of colonel, and later commanded the militia in Fairfield District, South Carolina; was wounded at the battle of Hanging Rock; was actively engaged during the remainder of the war. After the war he succeeded General William Henderson in the command of the Fairfield militia, with the rank first of brigadier-general, and then major-general, of militia. His home was on the hill where now stands the residence of ex-Senator Thomas H. Ketchin, opposite the hill on which is Mount Zion Academy, established by the Mount "Sion" Society in 1777, to which in 1785 General Winn gave one hundred acres of land. He was a member of the General Assembly which met at Jacksonborough, January 18, 1782; was elected to Congress, serving March 4, 1793, to March 3, 1797, twice alternating with General Thomas Sumter; was reëlected to Congress, serving from March 4, 1801, to March 3, 1813. In 1813 he removed to the eastern part of the country, dying there in the same year.

Columbia," he adds, "is a pine barren of the worst sort, being hilly as well as poor. This circumstance added to the distance, length of the stages, want of water and heat of the day, foundered one of my horses very badly."

Ever since 1718, when a trading-post called Fort Congarees had been established on the west bank of the river, the site of Columbia had been more or less frequented; and throughout the century down to the Revolution the early records contain references to the Congarees, the Fort at the Falls, Fort Granby, and Friday's Ferry. Fort Granby, a dwelling fortified by the British, was one of a chain of military posts from Camden to Charleston. This post was captured by Colonel Lee, of the famous partisan "Legion," in May, 1781. In time, the many natural advantages of the site, says August Kohn, pointed to the inevitable development here of a great inland centre. By an act ratified March 22, 1786, it was voted by the South Carolina Assembly to remove the seat of government from Charleston to a site at Friday's Ferry. It is interesting to recall that the two names considered for the new capital were Washington and Columbia — the latter winning by a vote of eleven to seven. In four years a village had sprung up there — the wooden houses, painted gray or yellow according to the taste of the inhabitants, giving, as Michaux remarks (1807), a "very agreeable appearance." The State House — "surrounded with lofty forests which afford a grateful shade and give the scenery a rural and charming cast" — stood on an eminence directly in the centre of the township; and although not fully completed in 1790, accommodated the Constitutional Convention of that year.[1]

On Monday, 23d, the President held a huge reception at noon — to accommodate the very large number of gentlemen of Columbia, Granby, Winnsborough, Camden, Statesburgh, Bellville, Orangeburgh, and their vicinity who had assembled to pay him their respects. After this fatiguing ceremony was over, the President was conducted to the Assembly Room of the Representatives in the State House, where were assembled "sixty ladies who upon his entering the room arose and made an elegant appearance, to whom he was individually introduced. The ladies were then led by the gentlemen (there being present 153) to the Senate Room, where they sat down together in a well-conceived arrangement to a farmer's dinner, where plenty abounded, and from the satisfaction visibly expressed on each countenance it is but just to conclude, that concord and true hilarity presided."

Memorable among the toasts were: one to the National Assembly, expressing sympathy for the French Revolution on the part of South Carolinians, so many of whom emigrated from France; one to the memory of Justice Henry Pendleton,[2] through whose vigorous efforts the

[1] The commissioners, named in the act ratified March 22, 1786, who were authorized to "lay off six hundred and fifty acres of land near Friday's Ferry, on the Congaree River, on the plain of the hill whereon James and Thomas Taylor resided," were: Commodore Alexander Gillon, Judge Henry Pendleton, General Richard Winn, Colonel Richard Hampton, and Colonel Thomas Taylor.

[2] Henry Pendleton was born in Virginia. He was elected Judge of the Courts of Law of South Carolina, April 17, 1776. He was captured in the Revolution by a party of British, and afterwards exchanged, and became

STATE HOUSE, COLUMBIA, SOUTH CAROLINA, IN 1794

capital of South Carolina had been removed from Charleston to Columbia; one to Miss Assumption, who had been equally courted and flouted; and — most extraordinary and comical of all — one likening Washington to a gorgeous flower! To what a pitch of fatuous adulation our ancestors did go! There was never a time when Washington was more truly admired than he is to-day. And surely that is because we understand him better, and see in him a more human figure. A full list of the toasts given after the dinner follows:

1. The United States.
2. (By the President.) The State of South-Carolina.
3. The National Assembly of France — a happy termination to their manly revolution.
4. The federal legislature — may their virtues and abilities be as much admired abroad, as they are respected at home.
5. The 23d of May, 1788.
6. A speedy establishment of the central federal city.
7. May our mild laws, and the happy administration of them, render America an asylum for the oppressed.
8. The late American army — may their meritorious conduct serve as an example for future armies.
9. The memory of General Greene, and all who with equal virtue and alacrity espoused our glorious cause.
10. The memory of Justice Pendleton — may the independent firmness of his principles ever be endearing to the friends of Columbia.

an aide of General Nathanael Greene. "He bore the orders of his gallant chief in the battle of Eutaw." With Justices Burke and Grimké, he was appointed Commissioner to form a complete and accurate digest of the State laws; was a member of the Convention of the People of South Carolina which assembled at the Custom House, Charleston, in May, 1788. He lived in Greenville District; and the house he occupied was situated on or near Golden Grove Creek. He died in 1788.

11. Sufficient means and speedy measures for opening the inland navigation of America.
12. The farmers, manufacturers and merchants of America — may their well directed exertions reward their industry.
13. America's best infant — Miss Assumption and her sponsors.
14. Increase to our exports, and decrease to our imports.
15. An increase of well established seminaries of learning.

After the President had retired, a toast to him — enthusiastically drunk — was couched in this strange, botanical form:

The magnificent Aloe of America.[1]

Our ancestors beyond peradventure of a doubt knew how to "say it with flowers"!

At eight o'clock that evening, the President returned to the Assembly Room, where a grand ball was held which

[1] I am indebted to Mr. Paul C. Standley, Assistant Curator, Division of Plants, Smithsonian Institution, for the following statement in answer to my inquiry:

"The title of 'The Magnificent Aloe of America' applied to George Washington doubtless has reference to the well-known century plant (of the genus *Agave*) which is often referred to in the earlier botanical works as American Aloe, although the plant has no very close relationship with the Old-World plant to which that name properly belongs. The century plant consists of a large cluster of heavy dagger-shaped leaves whose margins are furnished with short hocked spines. From the centre of the mass of leaves rises a flower stalk, sometimes twenty feet high or more, which branches above like a candelabrum and bears masses of yellow flowers. There is a popular belief that this plant blooms only after having attained the age of one hundred years — hence the common name. It is scarcely necessary to state that this belief is incorrect, for in the wild state the plants produce their flowers at a much earlier age. Century plants are of imposing appearance and are a conspicuous feature of the landscape where they occur."

It was presumably the popular view of the century plant as the handsomest and most majestic in appearance of American plants which prompted the singular toast to George Washington.

lasted until eleven o'clock. "We cannot better attribute the regret which arose at the separation of this company," says a contemporary print, "than the happiness conferred by the presence of the ladies at dinner, the gentlemen vying with each other to repay by every agreeable attention and respect the ladies acceptance of their invitation." Thus was effected, in a most charming way, a neat balancing of social accounts.

It was not in accordance with the President's itinerary to remain in Columbia later than the 23d; but, as he says in his diary for the 24th, "the condition of my foundered horse obliged me to remain at this place, contrary to my intentions, this day also." As he walked through this "wilderness of pines" — down State Street, considerably "overrun with bushes," with a pleasing glimpse here and there of a cultivated spot of a few acres — and made inquiries of the "Gentlemen of the Town" who had accompanied him, he came to certain conclusions which he thus set down in his diary for that day:

Columbia is laid out upon a large scale; but, in my opinion, had better been placed on the River below the falls. — It is now an uncleared wood, with very few houses in it, and those all wooden ones — The State House (which is also of wood) is a large and commodious building, but unfinished — The Town is on dry, but cannot be called high ground, and though surrounded by Piney & sandy land is, itself, good — The State House is near two miles from the River, at the confluence of the Broad River & Saluda. — From Granby the River is navigable for Craft which will, when the River is a little swelled, carry 3000 bushels of grain — when at its usual height less, and always some. The River from hence to the Wateree below which it takes the name of the Santee is very crooked;[1] it being, according to the computed distance near 400 miles — Columbia from Charleston is 130 miles.[2]

This day, the President dined "in private" with a few gentlemen — probably at the home of Commodore Alexander Gillon.[3] At the request of the gentlemen present, Commodore Gillon delivered the following address to the President:

Sir,

The citizens of Columbia, Granby, and the vicinity, offer their professions of respect and affection for your attentive visit.

Could the expression of our sentiments add lustre to the

[1] At Buck's Head Neck, near Fort Motte, just above the juncture of the Congaree and Wateree (which form the Santee), the Congaree makes a sweep of eight miles and approaches itself to within the distance of a quarter of a mile. (B. J. L.)

[2] The town records of Columbia were burned along with the city during Sherman's occupation. They probably contained allusions to Washington's visit, and in particular some entry regarding the house engaged for Washington's entertainment. I have been unable to ascertain where Washington lodged during his sojourn in Columbia. It is not unlikely that he had his headquarters at Rives's Tavern.

[3] Alexander Gillon, born in Rotterdam, Holland, in 1741, lived for a time in England. In 1765 he emigrated to Charles Town; and there, July 6, 1766, was married to Mary Splatt, widow of William Cripps. In addition to other real estate, he owned a tract of 5500 acres on the Congaree River known as "Gillon's Retreat." He took part in various naval enterprises in the early years of the Revolution, notably the capture of two British vessels blocking the harbor of Charles Town in 1778. He was appointed Commodore in the South Carolina navy early in 1778. In the *Indien*, leased from the Chevalier Luxembourg, and renamed the *South Carolina*, he made a number of valuable prizes in 1781. The following year he commanded the fleet of fifty-nine vessels which captured the Bahama Islands. He served for several terms as member of the House of Representatives of South Carolina; also was chosen Lieutenant-Governor in 1783, but declined to serve. He was elected to Congress in 1784; also served in Congress in 1793–94. He was a member of the South Carolina Constitutional Convention. He was married, a second time, February 10, 1789, to Ann, daughter of Rev. Dr. Purcell, of St. Michael's Parish, Charleston. He died at "Gillon's Retreat" on the Congaree, October 6, 1794.

COMMODORE ALEXANDER GILLON

justly merited eulogy of an admiring world we would recount with pleasing recollection the eventful scenes of glory in which you have borne so conspicuous a part; but as no idea of gratitude or praise can transcend your merit, so has no term of approbation been omitted to express it; it is then but left for us to declare, that our hearts cheerfully adopt those plaudits of praise which have resounded from every quarter of our grateful continent.

And since the duties of your important station call you from us, go, America's best friend, leaving us to implore our eternal guardian to bestow on you every felicity he admits on earth, and, when it shall please him to summon you from us, that he enfold you, as that which in perfection nearest approached those selected by him, to waft you to his celestial abode.

(Signed) by request,

A. GILLON.

The President's reply is the briefest on record for the trip — although doubtless adequate to the occasion:

GENTLEMEN,

I am much obliged by your professions of respect and affection, and I am truly grateful for your kind regard and good wishes.

Replying to them with sincere acknowledgment, I desire to assure you, that I shall always remember with pleasure your polite attentions.

G. WASHINGTON.

CHAPTER X

THE SEVENTH STAGE

Camden, South Carolina, and Charlotte, North Carolina

ON the morning of the 25th, accompanied by the troop of Light Horse under Captain Kershaw, Washington made his customary early start (four o'clock) for an unusually tedious day's journey — as the foundered horse had to be led slowly along. The following observations Washington entered in his diary:

> Breakfasted at an indifferent house 22 miles from the town,[1] (the first we came to) and reached Camden about two o'clock, 14 miles further.........The Road from Columbia to Camden, excepting a mile or two at each place, goes over the most miserable pine barren I ever saw, being quite a white sand, & very hilly. — On the Wateree within a mile & half of which the town stands the lands are very good,— they Culture Corn, Tobacco & Indigo. — Vessels carrying 50 or 60 Hhds. of Tobo. come up to the Ferry at this place at which there is a Tobacco Warehouse.[2]

At the Wateree, which was reached about noon, there was an exceptionally large concourse of people including almost the entire population of Camden. Loud and long were the cheers of the multitude; and the throng quickly joined Washington's train as it moved on into Camden. A

[1] Columbia.

[2] In his Journal (May 6, 1791) William Loughton Smith describes Camden as "a pretty town of about seventy houses and some very good dwellings." Writing to his wife from Camden (May 10, 1790) James Iredell says: "This really is a very pretty town — a fine, high, healthy situation — and many very handsome houses in it."

halt was made at the public square of the town, the time being about two o'clock; and Colonel Joseph Kershaw,[1] the Intendant of the town, speaking in behalf of the local committee, delivered the following address, which is conspicuous for its high tribute to Baron de Kalb:

SIR: Impressed with every sentiment of friendship, esteem and gratitude which can actuate the human heart, and amid the congratulations and voluntary homage of freemen and fellow-citizens that accompany your progress in the Southern States, the citizens of Camden and its vicinity, in whose country the ravages and distresses of war were once as severely and painfully felt, as the blessings of peace and good government are now gratefully cherished, yielding to the universal sentiment, but more to the impulse of our own hearts, beg leave to express the satisfaction and happiness we feel, at seeing among us our great deliverer — the venerated chief, who heretofore under the standard of liberty, defended the invaded rights of America, and led her troops with success through all the doubtful changes of a perilous war; now our first civil magistrate, under whose administration we forget our dangers and perilous past, and rest in the perfect enjoyment of those invaluable rights secured to us by his labours.

[1] Joseph Kershaw, first heard of in South Carolina as clerk in the store of James Laurens & Co., Charleston (1756); removed to Pine Tree Hill (Camden) about 1758, as agent of the commercial firm of Ancrum, Lance, and Loocock. Within a few years he was engaged in many industries, principally flour-milling; was leading man in the district at the outbreak of the Revolution. He was a delegate to the Congress of the Province of South Carolina, which assembled at Charleston, January 11, 1775; elected by the Congress in June, 1775, a member of the Committee of Continental Association; member of the first Legislative Council, 1776; served in the Revolution with the rank of colonel, commanding the regiment of militia from Camden District; built powder magazine for the State in 1777 at the cost of £9000; captured at Camden by the British in 1780, loaded with irons, and later banished to British Honduras. He removed to Bermuda, and remained there in exile for fifteen months, until exchanged near the end of the war. He was married about 1763 to Sarah Mathis, Quakeress. He was regarded as the "Father of Camden" and a leading patriot of his day. Died December 28, 1791.

We congratulate you, Sir, on your return thus far; and we hail your arrival in this town with a welcome, though less splendid, yet not less sincere, than what you have anywhere received.

And now, Sir, permit us to bring to your recollection that noble foreigner, the Baron deKalb, whose dust, with that of many other brave officers, is entombed on the plains of Camden; to him we owe this grateful mention, who, despising ease and inaction, when the liberties of his fellow-creatures (however distant) were threatened, entered the lists in our late contest, and fell bravely fighting for the rights of mankind.

May Almighty God long preserve a life so beloved, and make the future as happy as the past has been illustrious; and at the close of a life rendered thus illustrious, may you greet on the happy shores of blissful immortality, the kindred spirits of those heroes and patriots, who have in all past ages been distinguished as the guardians of liberty and the fathers of their country.

Signed by order of the inhabitants of Camden and its vicinity:

Joseph Kershaw
John Chesnut [1]
William Lang [2]
Isaac DuBose [3]
Adam F. Brisbane [4]
James Kershaw [5]
Joseph Brevard [6]
Isaac Alexander [7]
Samuel Boykin [8]
D. Starke.[9]

---

[1] John Chesnut, son of James Chesnut, was born in the Shenandoah Valley, Virginia, June 18, 1743. His father and uncle, James and Benjamin, originally came from Ireland, settling in Pennsylvania in 1688. After his father's death, John moved south with his mother and family, finally settling at Knight's Mill near Camden, South Carolina, then called Pine Tree. He began as clerk in the grocery store of Joseph Kershaw, and before he was twenty-one he became a member of the firm. In 1770 he was married to Sarah Cantey, born in the Wateree, February 15, 1753. Entered service in the Revolution as Paymaster with the rank of Captain, being

And it is noteworthy that, in his reply, Washington pays

attached to the Third Regiment. Served in South Carolina and Georgia, being present in various engagements. When Charleston was evacuated, he was taken prisoner and paroled. By order of Lord Rawdon, he was imprisoned and chained to the floor, for refusing to fight his own countrymen. In 1775 he was sent to the First Provincial Congress of South Carolina. In 1788 he was a member of the convention of the people to frame the constitution. He was one of the first Trustees of the South Carolina College, founded in 1802. He served also as member of the State House and Senate. He died in April, 1818.

He was described by Miss Harriet Pinckney as "one of the handsomest men of his day."

[2] William Lang, born near Wakefield, in Yorkshire, England, February 16, 1746; emigrated to the colony of South Carolina in 1770, settling at Camden; became one of the prominent citizens of the town. In 1775 he was married to Sally Wyley. He was a supporter of the American cause during the Revolution; a member of the commission for extending the boundaries of Camden in 1798. He died in 1815.

[3] Isaac Dubose was the son of John Dubose, of an old Huguenot family, who had settled, about the middle of the eighteenth century, on Lynches River, in the Old Cheraws; served with distinction in the Revolution as lieutenant in the Second Regiment of Foot, organized in 1775; removed from Chesterfield County to Camden, shortly after the Revolution; was held in high esteem by the people; a member of the Constitutional Convention (1790), Intendant of Camden (1792), and member of the Legislature in 1796, 1800, and 1806. He was twice married: to a Serrée (or a Dutarque), and second, in 1797, to Catherine Dubose, of Camden. His daughter, Mary, was thrice married, her second husband being Richard Lloyd Champion, son of Richard Champion. He died in 1816.

[4] Adam Fowler Brisbane was born in Charleston in 1754; was married to Mary Camber, of Georgia, at the age of twenty-one; removed to Camden as early as 1780; member of the Legislature from the Camden District in 1780; member of the Constitutional Convention of South Carolina in 1790; first President of the Camden Orphan Society, 1787; and appointed one of the first Judges of the County Court of Kershaw in 1791. His residence, furnished, was placed at the disposal of Washington on his visit to Camden in 1791. He died in 1797.

[5] James Kershaw, son of Joseph and Sarah (Mathis) Kershaw, was born in 1764; educated in England; was twice married: first (1798) to Sarah English, second (1813) to Mrs. Lydia Ann Vaughan; leader in the social life of Camden, as evidenced by his diary.

[6] Joseph Brevard was born in Iredell County, North Carolina, July 19, 1766; entered the Revolutionary service as a mere boy. In 1782, at the age of sixteen, he was commissioned as lieutenant in the North Carolina line, filling this position until the end of the war; settled in Camden immediately

due heed to the popular feeling — which was his own — regarding that martyr of the Revolution, DeKalb:

GENTLEMEN: The acknowledgments, which your respectful and affectionate address demand, I offer to you with unfeigned sincerity. I receive your congratulations with pleasure, and estimating your welcome of me to Camden by a conviction of its cordiality, I render those thanks to your

---

after the Revolution; elected sheriff of Camden District in 1789; appointed Commissioner in Equity for Northern District of South Carolina, October 14, 1791. He was married to Rebecca, daughter of Colonel Eli Kershaw, March 17, 1793. He became distinguished as a lawyer. In December, 1801, he was elected one of the Judges of the highest State Court; wrote three volumes of *Law Reports*, also *Digest of Statute Law* to 1814; resigned judgeship in December, 1815; elected to Congress in 1818, and served one term. He died at Camden, October 11, 1821.

[7] Isaac Alexander, son of Abraham Alexander of Charlotte, North Carolina, who presided over the Mecklenburg Convention of 1775; graduated from Princeton College in 1772, the classmate of James Madison and Aaron Burr; practised medicine in Charlotte and served for one year as first president of Queen's Museum; removed to Camden, about 1784, where for nearly thirty years he was a leading physician and citizen; served as a surgeon in the American army during the Revolution; and attended Baron De Kalb in his mortal illness; Representative in the South Carolina Legislature in 1786, was Intendant of Camden in 1794, and one of the first Trustees of the South Carolina College. He was married: first, to Margaret, daughter of Dr. William Brisbane, of Charleston; second, to Sarah, sister of Phineas Thornton. He died in 1812.

[8] Samuel Boykin, son of William Boykin and his wife, née Bryant. Tall and massive, he acted as a leader in the early "Regulation" activities in South Carolina; served as a delegate to the Provincial Congress of South Carolina in 1775, and was elected a member of the Committee of Continental Association from Saxe Gotha. At the defence of Charleston in midsummer, 1775, he was captain of a company of Catawba Indians in the successful defence of Sullivan's Island. He was active as a partisan throughout the Revolution under Taylor and Sumter. He was married to Elizabeth Brown, by whom he had four children. He was severely injured by some ruffian wagoners, whom he, with the aid of some friends, soon after severely chastised, and died from the effects of these injuries in December, 1791.

[9] Douglas Starke was a planter by profession; served in the Revolution; was present at the fall of Charleston in 1780; was a Justice of the Peace at Camden in 1787; was a representative citizen of Camden.

polite and hospitable attentions to which they are so justly entitled.

Your grateful remembrance of that excellent friend and gallant officer, the Baron de Kalb, does honor to the goodness of your hearts; with your regrets I mingle mine for his loss, and to your praise I join the tribute of my esteem for his memory.

May you largely participate the national advantages, and may your past sufferings and dangers, endured and braved in the cause of freedom, be long contrasted with your future safety and happiness.

G. Washington.

The President was now conducted by the reception committee to the house "especially prepared for him," which, if tradition be correct, was the residence of Mrs. Brisbane.[1] The President dined late "with a number of Ladies & Gentlemen at a public dinner," he says; which took place, it is believed, at the home of Colonel John Chesnut.[2] In the "Chesnut Family Chronicle," written by Sally Chesnut at the dictation of her father, James Chesnut, appears the statement: "In 1791 Washington in making his tour through the South stopped in Camden, and was the guest of Col. John Chesnut. After returning home he sent him a plow accompanied by the following letter . . ." Clearly the public dinner followed by a reception and ball, was held at the house of Col. John Chesnut. Follows the letter above mentioned:

[1] On this site, near the southeast corner of Fair and York Streets, now stands the Brasington house.

[2] This house, a large frame building, is still standing on the northwest corner of King and Fair Streets. It is identified on the testimony of Miss Mary Kershaw, who told her nephew, Judge Kershaw, that she had once attended a reception to General Washington in that house.

MOUNT VERNON *June* 26 1791

SIR

In conformity to my promise, when I saw you in Camden, I have selected one of my drill plows, which will be sent to Norfolk, whence it will be forwarded to Charleston, directed to you, and addressed to the care of General Pinckney.

The original intention of the drill plough, on the principle of that which is sent to you, was to plant the grain or seed in rows, at equal distances — the distance to be determined by the space at which the holes were made from each other — their number for corn was only four. But in sowing gran and some other kinds of grain in drills the holes were increased to the number now in the barrel.

The application of this plough to the planting of indigo will, in my opinion, be productive of dispatch, regularity, and an abridgment of labour.

The continuity in which the indigo seed is sown, in the same row, will require an additional number of holes — the proportioning of which, and their size, in order that the seed may issue in proper and equal quantity, may occasion some waste at first — but the loss of seed in determining them will be no object, compared with the advantages, when the just size and number of the holes are ascertained.

You will perceive that the plough which is sent, is drawn by a swingle tree — but they may likewise be made with shafts, the barrels may be extended to six feet, or to such length as to answer for any number of rows, that may be thought necessary, compartitioned as to prevent an accumulation of the seed at either end. You will have occasion to prefix a ploughshare to each row of holes, and proportion your force of horses or oxen to the draft.

The footstock to which the truck wheel is fixed, and which may be raised or depressed, is intended to regulate the depth of the plough's insertion into the ground.

The band which crosses the barrel in a certain direction, was placed, when the grain was to be deposited at equal distances, to prevent its emission at more holes than one — in sowing the indigo seed it will not be wanted.

The harrow will be proportioned to the plough or ploughs,

ROBERT FIELD'S ENGRAVING OF WASHINGTON
After a painting by Walter Robertson

and so constructed as effectually to cover the seed, without adding more than is unavoidable to the weight.

I hope you will sufficiently comprehend the principles of this plough to render its adoption highly useful to the planting interest of South Carolina.

Should the experiment so eventuate, my agency therein will be most agreeably rewarded.

I am sir

Your most obedient servant

G WASHINGTON—

In a contemporary print it is stated that the Chief Magistrate sought an introduction to each of the ladies, and that "every one took delight in contemplating this dignified personage, whose presence inspired and animated every social and convivial breast."[1] There seems some reason to believe that the "breasts" were more than usually "convivial"—as the ladies withdrew after the third toast, and the President withdrew about midnight. An unusually large number of toasts—seventeen in all—were drunk, as below; and as an evidence of how little pride the people had yet developed in the Confederation, it is to be noted that the words United States have not yet attained to the dignity of capitals when printed in the contemporary newspapers. Once again lively gratitude is expressed to the "brave Baron de Kalb"; and here, as elsewhere throughout the Southern States, the name of Nathanael Greene is seen to be held in grateful remembrance for his splendid military achievements.

Follow the toasts:

1. The united states of America. May they rival in the

[1] Charleston *City Gazette and Daily Advertiser*, June 6, 1791.

arts and sciences, as they have already equalled in arms and excelled in the mild arts of peace and government, the polished and enlightened nations of Europe.

2. The Congress. May wisdom inspire, virtue direct, and unanimity inform, their councils.
3. (By the President.) The Governor and state of South Carolina.
4. Louis the 16th and the French Nation, the noble and generous allies of America. May a true spirit of freedom, tempered with moderation and generous politeness, prevail in the constitutional reform.
5. The Vice-President of the united states. May he long bless his country with the ability and integrity that has hitherto characterized him.
6. The memory of General Greene. May his name inspire us with gratitude so long as his military achievements excite our applause.
7. The memory of the brave Baron deKalb. May every generous American mix the tributary tear of grateful remembrance with the dust that covers over his grave.
8. General Lincoln. May a generous country never forget his steady virtue, patriotism and services.
9. The memory of the brave martyrs in the cause of American liberty. May their names ever be grateful to our memories; and may their fates animate posterity with the love of freedom and their country.
10. The brave seamen of America, who fought and died in the glorious cause.
11. The agricultural and commercial interests of the united states. May they advance hand in hand, and reciprocally support each other.
12. The manufactories of the united states. May they rapidly improve; and may fashion favor their growth.
13. The fair of America. May wisdom with modesty, beauty with prudence, and every virtuous attraction, always distinguish them:
14. True religion, unmixed with hypocricy and intoleration; but distinguished for charity and benevolence.

15. (By the President.) The town of Camden, and prosperity to it.

(And, after the President retired:)

16. The President of the united states.
17. Lady Washington.

The following morning (26th), the President rode on horseback to the tomb of DeKalb,[1] where he reverently paused for a few moments in respect for the fallen hero (to-day he would have laid a wreath upon the grave); and afterwards made a tour of inspection of the works and redoubts erected by the British.[2] He then resumed his journey, his destination being Charlotte in North Carolina. At the site of the battle of Gum Swamp, he "very affectionately" bade adieu to his Camden friends who had attended him thus far upon his journey. In response to their urgent invitation to remain longer in their midst, he explained that he had already been several days longer on his tour than he had intended and that public business demanded his immediate return. His diary for this day is as follows:

After viewing the british works about Camden I set out for Charlotte — on my way — two miles from Town — I examined the ground on wch. Genl. Greene & Lord Rawdown had their action.[3] — The ground had but just been taken by the former — was well chosen — but he not well established in it before he was attacked; which by capturing a Videt was, in some measure by surprise — Six miles further on I came to the ground where Genl. Gates & Lord Cornwallis had their

[1] Now the old Presbyterian Cemetery.

[2] Compare *Historic Camden*, by Kirkland and Kennedy (Columbia, 1905), footnote, pp. 312–13.

[3] On Hobkirk's Hill, April 25, 1781.

Engagement wch. terminated so unfavourably for the former.[1] — As this was a night meeting of both Armies on their March & altogether unexpected each formed on the ground they met without any advantage in it on either side it being level & open. — Had Genl. Gates been ½ a mile further advanced, an impenetrable Swamp would have prevented the attack which was made on him by the British Army, and afforded him time to have formed his own plans; but having no information of Lord Cornwallis's designs, and perhaps not being apprised of this advantage it was not seized by him.

Camden is a small place with appearances of some new buildings. — It was much injured by the British whilst in their possession.[2]

After halting at one Sutton's 14 m. from Camden I lodged at James Ingrams 12 miles father.

A memorable incident is associated with Washington's journey through South Carolina. At Camden was living that Richard Champion, Englishman, who in the early days of the Revolution had kept Robert Morris, his business correspondent, informed of the actions of the British Government. Champion was active in local English politics, and nominated Burke for Parliament at the famous election in 1774. In the spring of 1782, Champion was appointed by Burke, then paymaster-general, as his deputy, a post which he held until the collapse of the Ministry in 1784. Champion started his famous china factory

[1] On the north side of Sanders's Creek, August 16, 1780. The two generals were approaching each other in the night, along a road filled with deep sand; and neither of them had any knowledge of the fact, until their advanced guards came in contact. The battle occurred early in the morning. (B. J. L.)

[2] Lord Rawdon, the British commander there, alarmed for the safety of his forts in the lower country, set fire to Camden on the 10th of May, 1781, and retreated down the Santee. (B. J. L.)

at Bristol in the year of the passage of the Stamp Act. The china factory was not a financial success, and was abandoned by Champion during the Revolution. In 1784, Champion removed to Camden, South Carolina, where he resided with his brother-in-law, Caleb Lloyd, who had been stamp distributor.

During Washington's tour through South Carolina, Champion wrote the following letter, hitherto unpublished, which accompanied a letter, book, and parcel all intended for Washington:

Mr Champion presents his Compliments to Major Jackson, and requests the favour of him to present the Letter, Book and parcel which accompanies this, to the President. Mr Champion has taken the Liberty to intreat the Honour of the President's acceptance of a Book, and a Manuscript enclosed. And he will trespass on the Indulgence of Major Jackson to beg him to procure the President's acceptance of the Parcel. It contains two Reliefs in a very fine Porcelain, exquisitely wrought round with flowers. The one of Dr Franklin, the other taken from a Relief, (a good likeness, as he was informed of the President when young,) which Mr Champion directed a Statuary to make. But in the likeness Mr Champion finds himself disappointed. He therefore merely presents it as a Curiosity, made from a beautiful native Porcelain, which is to be found in America. Mr Champion took a similar Liberty during the War, in sending these Reliefs to the President, by way of Paris, but he never knew whether they arrived safe. These were finished, the ornaments having been enamelled with gold, which he laments is not the Case with these. But being two which he had by him, he brought them out England with him, and through forgetfulness or accident omitted it.

Mr Champion begs Major Jackson will pardon the Trouble he has given him, and will do him the Honour to accept one of the Considerations himself, which accompanies the other.

M[r] Champion meant to have trespassed further upon Major Jackson's Indulgence in requesting to know whether the President had a Levee, but he finds that his stay will be short, and therefore is unwilling to break in upon the hour before Dinner, as the President must necessarily be fatigued, but will hope at that time to have the Honour of being presented to him.

[Endorsed]: From
M[r] Champion
at Camden.[1]

The plaque, of pure white porcelain, referred to in this letter, is now in the National Art Gallery at Washington, and is herewith reproduced with the courteous permission of the owner, Mr. W. G. Peter. It is thus described by the late Charles Henry Hart: "The portrait is evidently after Peale's picture of 1777. Above the medallion are the emblems of the revolted colonies, liberty cap, and rattlesnake, crowned by a coronet with thirteen points, for the thirteen original states, each point capped with a star. Beneath the emblem is the shield of the Washington arms, and around it the flags of the Congress are festooned. When we remember that this was made in England by an Englishman during the heat of the war, his daring and friendliness must elicit our homage and our admiration."[2] Hart says that the greatest work of Champion's china factory at Bristol, England, was "the tea-service he made and presented to Mrs. Burke in commemoration of her husband's return as member for Bristol."

Richard Champion was a warm friend of the Colonies,

[1] In Washington Papers, vol. 298, p. 40055, Library of Congress.
[2] See "Original Portraits of Washington," by C. H. Hart, *Century Magazine*, vol. 43.

THE RICHARD CHAMPION PLAQUE OF WASHINGTON
PRESENTED TO WASHINGTON IN 1791

and a great admirer of Washington and Franklin. In a remarkable letter to Ralph Izard from Bristol, July 16, 1777, Champion says: "May you then — when we cease to be one people — enjoy that happiness, which was formerly our common lot — and practising the Virtues which have characterized an Englishman — may you continue the race of Heroes to which — well as I love my country — I must almost confess — England itself has lost its claim." [1] In the very year of Washington's Southern tour, Champion died (October 7, 1791). His only granddaughter was married to the only son of Chancellor De Saussure of South Carolina. The "Work," which accompanied the letter and plaque was Champion's own pamphlet — probably the pamphlet on "America" issued in 1784. The letter, hitherto unpublished, is herewith reproduced in full:

To the President of the United States
Sir

Although your Fellow Citizens felt the full force of the invigorating Hand which first secured to them their Liberty and their Peace, and which has since, by its wise Administration, supported their Rank amidst the Nations of the Earth, there still remained, amongst many of them, an unsatisfied Desire, an anxious Wish to behold the face of their Benefactor, to whom, as the first and best Instrument of a merciful Providence, they are indebted for these Blessings. It was an Event which seemed necessary to the Consummation of their Happiness. They have now obtained the Gratification of their Wishes. For this auspicious Day has brought with it its full Accomplishment.

Amidst the Congratulations which surround you on this happy occasion, suffer me, Sir, a Sharer in the Distress, a par-

[1] *Correspondence of Ralph Izard.* (Francis and Co. 1844.)

taker in the Joys of my Country, to pay my humble Tribute of affectionate Duty and respectful Acknowledgment.

United, Sir, to this Country by Blood, by Affinity, and by an early and zealous Attachment to Liberty, the most active Exertions within the Compass of my small Power and Ability, and upon the purest principles, was made by me during the War; in the earlier part of it to promote Reconciliation, in the latter Stage, Peace. It was equally Patriotism both in England and America (yet few in England felt the force of this Duty) to oppose Attempts alike tyrannce [tyrannous] and unjust, unpolitic and absurd, upon the success or failure of which depended the Ruin or Preservation of their Liberty.

The Attempt failed, and the Sovereignty of the United States was acknowledged. This awful Separation of a great Empire, whose united Efforts had equalled the most powerful Exertions of antient or modern Times, made a deep Impression upon the Minds of those, who conceived at least the possibility of converting the antient Affection of Fellow Citizens into the Attachment of faithful Allies. Under this Impression a Work was offered by me to the Public, with a View to point out the true Interests of a People, who had too long unhappily forsaken them. But the offering was fruitless. Our Separation appeared to be confirmed. Yet the Distance preserved by Great Britain was not without its Utility to this Country. It demonstrated to us, that from her own Exertions, America should derive her Strength. Of this Work, I beg, Sir, the Honour of your Acceptance. I have since published another, which is in some Measure a Continuation, but unfortunately I have no Copy.

Many Years have now elapsed since I became a Citizen of this State. A Period, almost wholly spent in Retirement devoted to literary Pursuits. The Manuscript which accompanies this, and of which I likewise beg, Sir, your Acceptance, contains some cursory Reflections upon the Country, which you now honour with your Presence. It is a mere sketch, written upon a temporary occasion, never published and is intended for a large work; of which I have many Materials, and which a very perfect knowledge of the Court of Great

Britain, during the reign of its present Monarch, has afforded me.

Vanity is said to be, probably with Truth, the ruling Passion of an Author. But, Sir, Vanity on this Occasion almost ceases to be a foible. Affection, Duty, Veneration, and every Incitement which can warm the Heart of a Man in private Life, at the Sight of his Benefactor, must operate in the highest and most powerful Degree at the Sight of the Benefactor of Millions. The Widow, Sir, will throw in her Mite. And even the feeble Voice of an humble Individual will be heard, when, amidst a whole People, he turns to you, Sir, who, under Providence, was our greatest Benefactor; when in imploring for you all manner of Happiness and Prosperity, and in that Prayer is included the Happiness and Prosperity of the United States, he joins the universal Cry in saluting you, the Father of your Country.

History, Sir, is sparing of Characters in which the Virtues of public and of private Life, conspicuously shewn in the various and trying Occasions which you have experienced, have been so fully proved, and so strikingly exerted. You was drawn, Sir, from the privacy of Retirement by Nations who, differing in Principles and discordant in manners, were unanimous in their Call upon you. The Integrity of your Principles, the Mildness of your Manners, converted their Austerity or their Licentiousness into union of Sentiment, and Liberality of Opinion. And when in an unequal and unexpected Contest, you were devoid of every other Resource, than those which you drew from the greatness of your Abilities, the firmness of your Mind, unappalled in Danger, and prepared for Events, your Caution and Prudence secured our Safety, your Activity and Valour established our Independence.

Yet, Sir, whilst the Plaudits of a well-earned Triumph were sounding in your Ears, you lost not the Relish of Retirement, of those solid Satisfactions which your Integrity and your Patriotism had so justly and dearly purchased. Such however was the Situation of your Fellow Citizens, that your Absence from the Administration was incompatible with their Safety. They were constrained, Sir, to do violence to their Feelings, in requesting of you the Sacrifice of the sweets of Retirement; in which at an advanced Period of Life, we can alone be said to live. But the Prosperity of your Country, the fate of future Millions depended upon your Compliance. And you hesitated not, even at the Greatness of this Sacrifice. You, Sir, cheerfully obeyed the Call of your fellow Citizens, and assumed the Administration.

And now, Sir, tried as you have been in the most critical Situations—in Adversity, whose rugged Brow has only served to illustrate your Virtues, in Prosperity whose swelling sails have not disturbed the Serenity of your Mind, in the Administration of Government, which has proved a Source of Blessing to your Country, what more have we to ask of the most high God, than a Continuance of the Happiness which we enjoy under your Government. And that, when full of Days and full of Honour, it shall please his Providence to remove you into the Regions of Eternity, you may leave the People of these United States, which first formed under your Auspices, and now nurtured by your Care, are rising into a great and powerful Nation, happy in themselves, and happy in the Remembrance of those Virtues, to which they owe these Blessings. In the Remembrance of those Actions which will be faithfully recorded by Posterity, for the Benefit and Instruction of the future Ages of the World. It is for them, Sir, that your Labours have been employed, and by them your Actions will be approved.

I have the Honour to be with every grateful Sentiment of Esteem, Respect, and Attachment,

Sir
Your much obliged, faithful,
and most obedient Servant
RICHARD CHAMPION

ROCKY BRANCH
May 24th 1791
[Edorsed in G. W.'s hand:]
From
Richd Champion Esqr 24th May 1791[1]

[1] Letters to Washington, Library of Congress. It may be that the "work" which Champion presented to Washington along with this letter

Washington's diary for Friday (27th) is as follows:

Left Ingrams about 4 o'clock, and breakfasting at one Barr's 18 miles distant lodged at Majr. Crawford's 8 miles farther — About 2 miles from this place I came to the Corner where the No. Carolina line comes to the Rd. — from whence the Road is the boundary for 12 miles more. — At Majr. Crawford's I was met by some of the chiefs of the Catawba nation who seemed to be under apprehension that some attempts were making, or would be made to deprive them of part of the 40,000 Acres wch. was secured to them by Treaty and wch. is bounded by this Road.[1]

The following brief comment on the land through which Washington passed appears in the diary for Saturday, 28th:

It was not, until I had got near Barrs that I had quit the Piney & Sandy lands — nor until I had got to Crawfords before the lands took quite a different complexion — here they began to assume a very rich look.

At the boundary line, Washington was met by a party of the Mecklenburg Horse — but, says Washington,

was his *Comparative Reflections on the past and present Political, Commercial and Civil State of Great Britain, with some Thoughts concerning Emigration*, published anonymously on the eve of his departure for America in 1784. A second edition, published in 1787, bore Champion's name as author. Compare *Historic Camden*, by Kirkland and Kennedy (Columbia, S.C., 1905), pp. 362–66.

[1] The Catawba (Kadapau) were found living about where we have always known them as early as 1567. The small remnant may still be found on Catawba River, about on the border of North Carolina and South Carolina. Save for their alliance with the hostil Yamasi in 1715, they were uniformly friendly to the English and afterwards to their successors, the Americans. Through warfare with other Indian tribes and through disease which was prevalent among them, they were reduced by the end of the eighteenth century to but a pitiful remnant. In 1763 they had confirmed to them a reservation of fifteen miles square, on both sides of the Catawba River, within the present York and Lancaster Counties, South Carolina. Consult *The Siouan Tribes of the West*, by James Mooney; and *Indians of North Carolina* (Washington, 1915).

"these being near their homes, I dismissed them." Moreover, according to the account of Dr. Charles Caldwell,[1] an incident which Washington mentions in his diary, he was met at the boundary line between North and South Carolina by thirteen young men from the Salisbury Military Company, one to represent each of the original thirteen colonies. Caldwell's is the fullest account extant of personal incidents connected with Washington's time, other than Washington's diary; and is given below in full. Caldwell, who was vain and eccentric, evidently regarded the whole occasion as one deserving elaborate description; and in spite of the egoism displayed, the recital has a peculiar interest:

One reminiscence more, connected with Salisbury, shall close the history of myself in the South; at least, in that particular part of the South. It was during my residence in that place, that I had first an opportunity of seeing and approaching the person of General Washington, and the gratification of being noticed by him. The circumstances of the case were as follows:—

Some years after his first election to the chief magistracy

[1] Charles Caldwell, according to his own statement, was born "in Orange, now Caldwell County, on Moon's Creek, a small branch of Dan River, about twenty miles south of the southern border of Virginia," on May 14, 1772. While still a young man, Caldwell was appointed Professor of Natural History in the University of Pennsylvania. About 1819 he removed to the West and became head of the medical department of Transylvania University, Lexington, Kentucky. Later (1837) he founded the Louisville Medical Institute, in which he occupied the chairs of the Institutes of Medicine, Medical Jurisprudence, and Chemical Medicine. A man of distinction, though strangely eccentric and vain, Caldwell was widely acquainted with eminent scientists and distinguished public characters in England and Europe as well as in the United States. He died in Louisville, Kentucky, on July 9, 1853. At the time he wrote, he claimed that his autobiography covered the longest period of time (almost eighty years) ever covered by any autobiography.

of the Union, the General made the tour of the Southern States; to all of which, Virginia excepted, he was personally a stranger. In his journey to the South, he travelled by the eastern and low-country route; but, on his return, journeying in North Carolina, by the western and hill-country route, he passed through Salisbury.

On learning that such was the course he purposed to pursue, the youth of note in the place, high-toned in feelings of State pride and patriotism, and not disinclined to military pomp and show (I being one of them), met in a body, as if by an instinctive impulse, on the call of another young man and myself, organized themselves into a company of light dragoons, and elected, as their captain, a gallant and gentlemanly officer, and a splendid swordsman, who, in our revolutionary war, had distinguished himself as standard-bearer in one of the corps of Lee's legion of horse. The leading and most highly prized object of the company was to meet General Washington, at the confines of South and North Carolina and escort him, as a guard of honor, through about two-thirds, breadth, of the latter State.

When our company was organized and fully equipped, we rode as fine and richly caparisoned horses, wore as costly and splendid uniforms, and made as brilliant an appearance as any cavalry company of the same size (fifty-five, officers and privates), which the General had ever reviewed. Of this fact (no doubt the most highly-prized one that could have been communicated to us) we were kindly and courteously assured by himself. My rank in the company was that of a standard-bearer.

Instead of the whole command proceeding in a body to meet the President (such was Washington at the time), a detachment of thirteen privates (one for each State) was dispatched to meet him at the southern boundary of North Carolina (a distance of about seventy or eighty miles), welcome him to the State by a salutatory address, and escort him to within about fifteen miles of Salisbury, where the whole company was encamped to receive him.

Of this detachment, chosen by lot (for no private was willing to yield to another the eagerly-sought honor and gratification of belonging to it), I was, with the highly-prized approbation of my comrades, appointed to the command. And never was man more proud of an appointment. I would not have exchanged my post for that of Governor of the Commonwealth. I was to receive the President, at the head of my escort, and deliver to him, in person, the intended address of welcome into my native State. And my supposed fitness for a very creditable discharge of that duty (for, as heretofore mentioned, I was accounted an excellent speaker), had contributed not a little toward my appointment to the office.

In a short time my address was mentally composed, and committed, not indeed to paper, but to my memory; and I often repeated it, silently, when in company, but audibly, when alone; thinking of but little else, either by day or by night, except; the strict discipline and soldier-like appearance of my little band.

At length, flushed with high spirits and bounding hearts, we were in full march toward the boundary line of the State.

From the time of our advance within ten miles of the place of our destination, I kept, in my front, three videttes, distant a mile from each other — the nearest of them being a mile from the head of my little column — to convey to me half-hourly intelligence respecting the approach of the President, who was understood to travel alternately in his carriage and on horseback. At length one of my *look-outs* returned, at full speed, with information that a travelling carriage had been seen by him, and was then about a mile and a half in his rear. Instantly, everything was in complete preparation for the coming event. Had an enemy been advancing on us, or we on him, our excitement could not have been more intense. Our column was compact, our steeds reined up to their mettle, but held in check; each man, his cap and plume duly adjusted, seated firmly and horseman-like in his saddle, and our swords drawn and in rest, the sheen of their blades as bright and dazzling as the beams of a southern sun could render it.

In this order we advanced slowly, until a light coach made its appearance in our front, and became the object of every eye of our party. The day being warm, the windows of it were open, and my first glance into its interior plainly told me that Washington was not there. But his secretary was; and he informed me that the General was on horseback, a short distance in his rear. Proceeding onward, the movement of a few minutes brought us in full view of Washington, on the summit of a hill, seated on a magnificent milk-white charger, a present to him by Frederick of Prussia, near the close of the revolutionary war. Nor is it deemed an inadmissible deviation from my narrative to add that that present was accompanied by another, from the same royal personage, still more highly complimentary and honorary — an exquisitely finished and richly ornamented dress-sword, inscribed, in gold letters, "From the *oldest* to the *greatest* general of the age." When a courtier, of supple knee and oily tongue, ventured to differ from Frederick in relation to the sentiment expressed by this inscription, and even presumed virtually to contradict him, by saying: "Sire, permit your subject to believe that you are yourself the greatest general of the age;" the monarch replied: "No, I am not; Washington surpasses me. I conquered *with means;* he has conquered *without them.*"

The circumstances of my first view of the great American were as well calculated to render the sight imposing, not to say romantically picturesque and impressive, as any that the most inventive and apt imagination could have devised. The day (the hour being about 11 A. M.) was uncommonly brilliant and beautiful, even as the product of a southern climate. The sky was slightly azure, its arch unusually lofty and expanded, and not a cloud interposed to detract from its radiance. I was ascending a hill of sufficient elevation to shorten materially the distance to the horizon, which rested on its top; and the road leading up it was lined, on each side, by ancient forest-trees, in their rich apparel of summer foliage.

In the midst of this landscape, already abundantly attractive and exciting, just as I had advanced about half-way up the hill, the President turned its summit, and began to descend. The steps of his charger were measured and proud, as if the noble animal was conscious of the character and standing of his rider. On the bright canvas of the heavens behind them, the horseman and horse formed a superb and glorious picture. As the figure advanced, in the symmetry and grace of an equestrian statue of the highest order, it reminded me of Brahma's descent from the skies. True, the charger did not, in his pride and buoyancy, "paw the bright clouds, and gallop in the storm;" but he trod with unusual majesty on the face of the hill.

As I approached the President, an awe came over me, such as I had never before experienced. And its effect on me was as deeply mortifying, as it was unprecedented. Never had I previously quailed before anything earthly. But I was now unmanned. Not only did I forget my oft-repeated address, but I became positively unable to articulate a word. My imagination had placed me, if not in the immediate presence of a god of its own creating, in that of a man so far above the rank of ordinary mortals, as to be approximated to that of the gods of fable. Having advanced, therefore, to within a becoming distance from him, I received him, in silence, with the salute of my sword. I could do no more; I became actually giddy; for an instant my vision grew indistinct; and, though unsurpassed as a rider, I felt unsteady in my seat, and almost ready to fall from my horse, under the shock of my failure, a shock trebly strengthened and embittered by its occurrence at the head of the band I commanded, and under the eye of the man I almost adored. My employment of the term "adored" is neither unpremeditated nor inadvertent. It is deliberate and earnest. For, were alleged in disfavor of me, that I actually idolized the illustrious personage then before me, I could hardly appeal to my conscience for the incorrectness of the charge.

Quick to perceive my embarrassment, and equally inclined and prompt to relieve it, Washington returned my salute with marked courtesy, and, speaking kindly, paused for a moment, and then desired that we might proceed, I riding abreast of him, on his left, and the privates of my escort falling in double file into the rear. This opportune measure set me more at my ease; but still I did not venture to open my lips, until my silence rendered me seriously apprehensive that the President would deem me wholly incompetent to the complimentary duty on which I had been dispatched. And that thought produced in me a fresh embitterment. But many minutes had not elapsed when my condition and prospects began to brighten.

Fortunately, I possessed an intimate and accurate acquaintance with the people and localities of the tract of country through which we were to journey, as well as with its general and special history, both remote and recent. And it had been the theatre of several memorable enterprises and scenes of battle and blood, during the revolutionary war. Most of the conflicts had occurred between Whigs and Tories; but some of them between the troops under General Greene and Lord Cornwallis. And respecting each and all of them, I had learned so much from my revolutionary father and brothers, who had been engaged in several of them, that my familiarity with them was almost as minute and vivid as if I had been an actor in them myself. But, before speaking of them, I held it to be a duty, which I owed to myself, to apprise General Washington of the cause of my failure, on first approaching him, to tender to him the salutation to which he was entitled, and which I had intended.

As soon, therefore, as I had recovered the complete command of my mind and my tongue, I frankly, and, now, with no lack of readiness and fluency, communicated to him the cause of my previous silence. I told him that I had been dispatched by my commanding officer, with the escort which I led, to meet and salute him, with a becoming welcome, to the State of my nativity. My mortifying failure to discharge that duty I entreated him to attribute to the deep and irresistible embarrassment I had experienced on my first approach to him. This explanation was closed by an assurance, under a manifestation of feeling which must have been obvious to him, that his presence had for a short time so completely overawed me, as to deprive me entirely of the power of utterance; and that it had been hence impossible for me to greet him with any other salutation than that of my sword; which, I added (perhaps too ostentatiously, and, therefore, improperly), I would have been proud to have wielded, under his command, in the late war, had I not been too young.

Giving me a look, if not of *approval*, certainly of neither dissatisfaction nor rebuke —

"Pray, sir," said he, "have you lived long in this part of the country?"

"Ever since my childhood, sir."

"You are then, I presume, pretty well acquainted with it."

"Perfectly, sir; I am familiar with every hill, and stream, and celebrated spot it contains."

"During the late war, if my information be correct, the inhabitants were true to the cause of their country, and brave in its defence."

"Your information *is* correct, sir. They were, almost to a man, true-hearted Whigs and patriots, and as gallant soldiers as ever drew swords or pointed rifles in behalf of freedom. In Mecklenburg County, where we now are, and in Rowan, which lies before us, a Tory did not dare to show his face — if he were known to be a Tory. It was in a small town, through which we shall pass, that Lord Cornwallis lay encamped, when he swore that he had never before been in such a d-n-d nest of Whigs — for that he could not, in the surrounding country, procure a chicken or a pig for his table, or a gallon of oats for his horse, but by purchasing it with the blood of his soldiers, who went in quest of it."

"Pray, what is the name of that town?"

"Charlotte, sir, the county town of Mecklenburg, and the place where independence was declared about a year before its declaration by Congress; and *my father* was one of the Whigs who were concerned in the glorious transaction. We shall arrive at Charlotte to-morrow morning," I continued, "where you will be enthusiastically received, by five hundred at least — perhaps twice the number, of the most respectable inhabitants of the country; a large portion of whom served, in some capacity, in the revolutionary war — several of them, I believe, as officers and privates, under your own command.

ENGRAVING BY BARTHELEMY JOSEPH FULEVAN ROGER

After the medallion painted by the Marquise de Bréhan in New York, 1789

When I passed through the town yesterday morning, a large number of them had already assembled, and the crowd was rapidly increasing. And they are exceedingly provident. Convinced that they cannot all be supplied in the town, with either food or lodging, many of them have brought with them large and well-covered farm-wagons, for their bed-chambers, and enough of substantial food, already cooked, for a week's subsistence. Others again have already erected, and are still erecting, for their temporary residence, in the midst of a beautiful and celebrated grove (where a victory was gained, by a company of militia riflemen, over a party of Tarleton's dragoons), the very tents under which they slept as soldiers, in the service of their country. And they are about as obstinate and noisy a set of gentlemen as I have ever met, or ever wish to meet again — especially when in a hurry. I was obliged, much against my will, to hold a long parley with them, yesterday morning, when I wished to be in motion to meet you, lest you might anticipate me in reaching the boundary line of the State."

The General was evidently pleased with my narrative, and so diverted by the increased freedom and ease of my manner (for I was now perfectly myself), that though he did not actually smile (for he very rarely smiled), he seemed at times, as I fancied, more inclined to a little merriment than to maintain unchanged his habitually grave and dignified aspect.

Reference was then made to several events of note, which had occurred in the southern revolutionary war. And respecting one of them, in particular, of great brilliancy, and no little moment, I was astonished to find that I was much better informed than Washington himself. To such an extent was this true, that he appeared to be even more astonished than I was. Indeed, from some of the expressions used by him, I was at first apprehensive that he was incredulous of my story. This induced me to speak with more energy and positiveness than I had previously employed, and to specify a few of the most striking and memorable events of the affair. I allude to the battle at Ramsauer's Mill, in which about three hundred Whigs, then fresh from their homes, and who had never before been in a field of battle, attacked and defeated, with great slaughter, in a selected and fortified position, twelve hundred Tories, and made six hundred of them prisoners.

The reason why I was better informed than Washington respecting this gallant and sanguinary action, is plain and satisfactory. It had been fought in an obscure and rather frontier situation, in the South, by two bodies of militia, and had never been fully recorded in print. To Washington, therefore, no opportunity to read an account of it had been presented; a formal dispatch respecting it had not been forwarded to him, because it had no immediate connection with the regular army; and the sphere of his operations being in the North, little or no correct intelligence in relation to it had been communicated to him through any other channel.

But very different had been my opportunity to acquire information with regard to that action. With a large number of the Whigs engaged in it, my father and brothers were acquainted at the time; and with not a few of them I myself became acquainted, as a youth, at a subsequent period. Nor was this all. One of my brothers had himself been deeply concerned in the battle, having led into it about sixty of the most disciplined and expert riflemen in the country.

From my early boyhood, therefore, I had been familiar with the details of the "Battle of Ramsauer's Mill," having heard them recited scores of times, in the form of a fireside and exciting story.

I need hardly remark that, by the indulgent attention with which the President honored my narratives and representations, and the kind and complimentary replies he occasionally made to me, I was highly gratified. He at length inquired of me whether he might expect to meet at Charlotte any of the leading members of the convention which prepared and passed the Mecklenburg Declaration of Independence, and especially whether my father would be there. I replied that my father was dead, and that Dr. Brevard, the author of the Declaration was also dead; that, of the members of the convention still living, I knew personally but two — Adam Alexander, who had been president of the body, and John McKnitt

Alexander, his brother, who had been its Secretary; that they were far advanced in life, and lived at some distance from Charlotte, but that I felt confident their ever-green spirit of patriotism, united to their strong desire to see him, would bring them there, should they be able to travel.

On the evening of that day, having arrived at the headquarters of the troop to which I belonged, I surrendered my place to my superiors in rank, and received from Washington, in their presence, a compliment — peculiarly gratifying to me, as well on account of the manner of its bestowal as of its own import — on what he was pleased to pronounce my "honorable and exemplary deportment as an officer, and the interesting and valuable information I had imparted to him respecting the country and its inhabitants" through which I had escorted him.[1]

On Saturday, 28th, Washington left Crawford's at four o'clock in the morning, and after travelling eighteen miles, reached Harrison's.[2] After a brief rest, Washington drove thirteen miles farther; reaching Charlotte before three o'clock. "On this eventful Saturday," we are told, "crowds of people on foot, on horseback, and the better order of peasantry in vehicles, came to the little village of Charlotte to catch a glimpse of Washington. It was the first and only time that many of them had seen the tall and dignified form of the man who will always be marked as the greatest American. The streets and adjoining roads were lined with men, women and children for hours before his arrival, for it was not as a certainty known when he

[1] *Autobiography of Charles Caldwell, M.D.* With a Preface, Notes, and Appendix, by Harriot W. Warner. (Philadelphia: Lippincott, Grambo, and Co., 1855. Pp. 88–96.)

[2] Harrison's was about three miles below the present Pineville. It disappeared after Pineville built up.

would reach Charlotte."[1] At the outskirts of the town, it would appear, Washington was met by a group of principal citizens of the little hamlet, headed by the Revolutionary soldier and patriot, General Thomas Polk. At the opening of the War of Independence, Polk was Colonel of the militia of Mecklenburg, and even earlier, he had been an active leader in agitating for separation from Great Britain. During the spring of 1775, a number of meetings were held at the academy in Charlotte, known as Queen's Museum or College, looking toward independence. "Tom Polk," says Richard Cogdell in a letter (June 18, 1775) to Richard Caswell, afterwards Governor of North Carolina, "is raising a pretty spirit in the back country" — referring to the passage of a series of drastic resolutions at Charlotte, May 31, 1775, virtually asserting independence of Great Britain and setting up a government in its place for the people of Mecklenburg County. This is believed by many people to have followed a meeting of May 20th preceding, at which a declaration of independence was read. Colonel Thomas Polk is known to have read some famous declaration or series of resolutions — either on May 20th or 31st — from the steps of the court-house door in Charlotte. His son-in-law, Ephraim Brevard, was the secretary of the meeting which, on May 31st, drafted the famous resolutions printed in many contemporary newspapers.[2]

As Washington, Polk, and party rode through the streets

[1] "Washington in Charlotte," by George R. Prowell, in *Charlotte Daily Observer*, January 9, 1898.

[2] Compare Archibald Henderson: *The Mecklenburg Declaration of Independence and the Revolution in North Carolina in 1775* (privately printed,

of the little hamlet,[1] lined with the sturdy yeomanry of Mecklenburg, their wives, and children, who greeted the President with many a hearty cheer, they passed through what is now Independence Square, where stood the old court-house, poised high above the ground on six tall pillars. "From the steps of the court house over there, sir," General Polk no doubt remarked to Washington, "I had the honor of reading what we Mecklenburgers regard as the first overt assertion of freedom from British rule promulgated on this continent." And he perhaps added with a laugh: "The people were so enthusiastic that they threw up their hats in all directions, and some of them fell on the roof of the court house."

The President's party soon reached the handsome colonial residence of General Polk, which had been used by Cornwallis in 1780 as headquarters.[2] Here Washington found, as he says, a "Table prepared for the purpose,"—

1916); and "The Mecklenburg Declaration of Independence," in *Mississippi Valley Historical Review*, vol. v, no. 2 (September, 1918). The Mecklenburg Resolves of May 31, 1775, were printed in *The North Carolina Gazette* of June 16, 1775, a copy of which was enclosed in the letter of Richard Cogdell mentioned above.

[1] Washington in his diary calls it a "trifling place." In 1800 it contained only 65 free persons and 59 slaves. In his diary (May 6, 1791), William Loughton Smith, of South Carolina, says: "Near Charlotte are some finely cultivated fields. This place does not deserve the name of a town, it consists only of a wretched Court House, and a few dwellings falling to decay. There is a good tavern kept by Mason, where, however, I paid the dearest bill on the road."

[2] This house stood back of the northeast corner of the present Jordan's Drug Store. On October 11, 1780, General Polk wrote as follows from "Camp, Yadkin River," to the North Carolina Board of War: "I have the pleasure to inform you that on Saturday last the noted Colonel Ferguson, with 150 men, fell on King's Mountain; 800 taken prisoners, with 150 stand of arms. Cleveland and Campbell commanded. Glorious affair. In a few days doubt not we shall be in Charlotte, and I will take possession of my

evidently out in the yard, picnic style — to which a small party invited by General Polk sat down with Washington, Jackson, and Polk, which probably included Adam Alexander, John McKnitt Alexander, Robert Irwin, Nathaniel Alexander, afterwards Governor of North Carolina, General Joseph Graham, and his brother, General George Graham. Although no contemporary newspaper containing a description of the visit to Charlotte has come to light, it is scarcely to be doubted that, as was the uniform custom of the day, toasts were proposed and drunk. And what more likely than for Washington, turning to his hosts, to propose a toast to "The new Prosperity of this Town and Country, whose people were foremost in the demand for independence"? Of one thing we may be sure: that the table revolved about the events of the Revolution — of Greene and Cornwallis, of Davie and Sumner, of the battle of Charlotte and the affair at McIntire's farm, of King's Mountain and Ramseur's Mill — local engagements and battles in which certain of the guests had behaved with distinguished gallantry. Conversation turned, too, to the subject of Queen's Museum, the Fanueil Hall of western North Carolina, which Washington perhaps visited — for he says in his diary concerning Charlotte: "The Court-house of Mecklenburg is held in it — There is a school (called a College) in it at which, at times there has been 50 or 60 boys." Here General Polk's son-in-law, Ephraim

house and *his* lordship take the woods." In his *Men and Times of the Revolution*, Elkanah Watson says of a visit to Charlotte in 1785: "I carried letters to the courteous General Polk, and remained two days at his residence in the delightful society of his charming family."

Brevard, who is said to have drafted the Resolves of May 31st, had served as a tutor; and here, a few years before Washington's visit, that great Carolinian, Andrew Jackson, acquired a smattering of learning. General Thomas Polk was a trustee of this little college — first as Queen's Museum and afterwards when its name was changed to Liberty Hall.[1]

After the open-air dinner at General Polk's, which was followed by a reception, the President and Major Jackson were escorted to Cook's Inn, a two-story building kept by one Captain Cook. "In those days," said Dr. George Graham in a lecture on the historic localities of Mecklenburg County, "gentlemen wore their hair long, plaited in a cue and powdered, and a box of powder always formed a place in their dressing case. On this occasion the President, after making his toilet, neglected to replace the box in his valise, and it became the property of Mrs. Cook, who amused herself with powdering the heads of the girls and young ladies who rushed to the inn after the departure of the great hero to hear the news, remarking to each one as she applied the puff: 'Now you can always remember that you have had the distinction of having your hair powdered from General Washington's box.'"[2]

[1] Consult "The Story of Queen's College or Liberty Hall in the Province of North Carolina," by Marshall De Lancey Haywood in *North Carolina Booklet* (1912).

[2] Elizabeth Kennedy, daughter of James Kennedy, a prosperous merchant who lived where the Central Hotel was afterward located, was one of the party thus honored, and afterward related the incident. Cook's Inn was on the site of Query's Store, which was standing in 1893; hereon now stands the Selwyn Hotel. Dr. Graham's lecture was published in the *Charlotte Observer*, December 25, 1893.

CHAPTER XI

THE EIGHTH STAGE

North Carolina: Salisbury and Salem

WASHINGTON'S punctuality on his long journey through the Southern States, says Custis, "astonished every one. The trumpet call of the cavalry had scarcely ceased its echoes when a vidette would be seen coming in at full speed, and the cry resound far and wide, 'He's coming!' Scarcely would the artillery-men unlimber the cannon, when the order would be given, 'Light your matches, the white chariot is in full view!'

"Revolutionary veterans hurried from all directions once more to greet their beloved chief. They called it marching to headquarters; and as the dear glorious old fellows would overtake their neighbors and friends, they would say, 'Push on, my boys, if you wish to see him; for we, who ought to know, can assure you that he is never behind time, but always punctual to the moment.'

"It was thus that Washington performed his memorable tour . . . everywhere received with heartfelt homage that the love, veneration, and gratitude of a whole people could bestow; and there is no doubt yet living a gray head who can tell of the time when he gallantly rode to some village or inn on the long-remembered route to hail the arrival of the white chariot, and join in the joyous welcome to the Father of his Country." [1]

[1] G. W. P. Custis: *Recollections and Private Memoirs of Washington* (New York, 1860).

On the morning of the 29th of April, Washington was waited upon by the Honorable John Steele, Representative in Congress from the Salisbury District, who, as Washington records in his diary, "was so polite as to come all the way to Charlotte to meet me." Five years later he was appointed by Washington Comptroller of the United States Treasury, a post he held under Washington, Adams, and Jefferson; and he was offered the post of Secretary of the Treasury as successor to Oliver Wolcott, which he declined. "North Carolina has produced few individuals," says David L. Swain in writing of Steele, "whose public services offer more interesting topics for history and biography."[1] Steele, courtly, handsome, and bland, was very congenial with Washington. Doubtless their conversation touched as much on scientific agriculture — for Steele like Washington was a farmer who used methods much in advance of the day — as on the political questions of the hour. This day was a quiet Sunday—Washington leaving Charlotte at seven o'clock and dining at "Col. Smith's 15 miles off." This was Colonel, afterwards General, John Smith, who was said to be a captain in the first regiment of Revolutionary troops organized in the colony of North Carolina. Here, "in this secluded and lonely spot, a daily requiem is sung by the murmuring winds and carolling birds. . . . On an eminence to the right, after entering the place, is seen the family burying ground, filled and surrounded with a group of trees, out of the centre of which

[1] Consult Archibald Henderson: "John Steele," in *North Carolina Booklet*, vol. XVIII, nos. 3 and 4 (1919).

rises two Lombardy poplars, shooting their natural spires towards the sky."[1] On this quiet Sunday, Washington and his party were hospitably received and entertained by Colonel Smith and his wife, *née* Sarah Taylor Alexander. Mrs. Smith, a lineal descendant of the Earl of Stirling, was the widow of Colonel Moses Alexander, sometime head of the Mecklenburg militia.[2]

Leaving Colonel Smith's on Sunday afternoon, the President arrived in time for supper at the home of Major Martin Phifer (Pfeiffer),[3] "Red Hill," in Cabarrus County, near Buffalo Creek, three miles west of the present Concord. The house stood on a prominent eminence overlooking for many miles the surrounding country. Major Phifer was a great hunter, and kept his table well supplied

[1] Consult "Visit to the Homestead of Col. Moses Alexander," by Mrs. H. M. Irwin, in *The Southern Home*, May 7, 1880. A copy of this article was furnished me by Colonel F. Brevard McDowell, of Charlotte, North Carolina.

[2] In the family burying-ground of this country estate, now known as the "Morehead Place," in Cabarrus County, lie buried Major Robert W. Smith, the General's only son, a very wealthy man, who was painted by Rembrandt Peale; William Lee Alexander, son of Mrs. Smith by her first marriage, educated at Princeton and a distinguished lawyer; and his wife, Elizabeth, a daughter of Judge Richard Henderson, famous jurist-pioneer and President of the Transylvania Company.

[3] Martin Phifer (2), son of Martin (1) and Margaret (Blackwelder) Phifer, was born at "Coldwater," Cabarrus County, North Carolina, March 25, 1756. The Phifers were from Berne, Switzerland, and of German origin, descending from the Knights of Pfeiffersburg. Martin (1) and John Phifer, father and uncle respectively of Martin Phifer (2), came to America in 1739; and one year later settled in Cabarrus (now Mecklenburg) County, North Carolina. Martin (2) served with gallantry in the Revolution. He was Captain of an "Independent Company of Light Horse," and participated in various engagements, notably Wright's Mill and Germantown. According to tradition he was with Washington at Valley Forge. At one time he commanded a regiment of North Carolina State Militia, with the rank of colonel. In 1778 he was married to Elizabeth Locke. He died at "The Black Jacks," November 12, 1837.

with deer and other game. "He was six feet in height, of great strength and vigor. His complexion was ruddy and bright, animated and inviting. His hair he always wore brushed back, and in middle life, as it was turning gray, with his firm step, large and well built form, he was a fine specimen of a man — the handsomest man in all that part of the country. . . . When Washington made his tour South, he was the private guest of Martin for one night and part of the day. His wife, Elizabeth, made great preparation for the great man's coming, and was sorely disappointed when she found her distinguished guest so simple in his diet." [1] Major Phifer served in the Revolution, and for a time had his headquarters at Philadelphia.

Washington made an unusually early start on Monday, 30th — "at 4 o'clock I was out from Major Fifers" — being accompanied by General Steele; and after going about ten miles was met by a party of horse from Rowan County at the dividing line between Mecklenburg and Rowan. This was the party to which, presumably, young Charles Caldwell and his twelve companions were attached; it consisted of fifty-five in all, under the command of Captain John Beard, who had served in the Revolution. As Washington and his cavalcade neared the home of Richard Brandon, Esq. — at what is known as the old "Stockton Place," about six miles southwest of Salisbury — he bade the cavalcade stop and rode forward alone to

[1] *Genealogy and History of the Phifer Family*, by Charles H. Phifer (Charlotte, 1910). Mrs. Phifer, *née* Elizabeth Locke, came of a distinguished family of noble descent. Major Phifer was said to be at one time the largest landowner in North Carolina.

the door of the farmhouse. Somewhat fatigued from his early start and exertions of the journey — for Washington was about sixty — and anticipating the ordeal of a long public reception at Salisbury, Washington determined upon a little rest and refreshment. At the door, in answer to his knock, appeared the rosy-cheeked, bright-eyed Betsy Brandon of some twelve summers. In reply to the stranger's inquiry if he might have a cup of coffee and some light refreshment, she answered that there was no one at home.

"I am all alone," explained little Betsy, plaintively. "Everybody has gone to see General Washington but me. And oh! I do so wish I could see him!"

"Well," replied the benign-looking stranger, who quickly won little Betsy's confidence, "I think we can arrange that. Let's make a bargain. If you'll make me a cup of coffee, I'll promise you a sight of General Washington."

The bargain was immediately closed, the cup of coffee quickly prepared by the excited Betsy, and even more quickly drunk by the tired traveller.

"Now," demanded Betsy, eager in her excitement and all unsuspicious, "you must keep your promise and show me General Washington."

Imagine her astonishment, not unmixed with dismay, when the mild-mannered stranger, with a grave and genial smile, replied:

"General Washington is now before you." [1]

[1] "George Washington's Tour through North Carolina," by Archibald Henderson, in the *Charlotte Observer*, January 14, 1912.

MONTFORT STOKES

At the county line, the President and his cavalcade were met by the Rowan Light Horse Company, "completely equipped and uniformed," under the command of Captain Montfort Stokes, the intimate friend of Andrew Jackson.[1] About five miles from Salisbury, the President was met by a "large number of the most respectable gentlemen of the town and country," headed by Judge Spruce Macay, the Mayor of the Corporation of Salisbury, and including, no doubt, such distinguished citizens as the Honorable Maxwell Chambers, Dr. Charles Harris, Captain Lewis Beard, General Matthew Locke, the Honorable William Lee Alexander, and Dr. Samuel Eusebius McCorkle. Washington was doubtless impressed by the striking resemblance to Thomas Jefferson of the eminent Dr. McCorkle, graduate of Nassau Hall, and head of the famous Zion–Parnassus School — delightful union of Hebraism and Hellenism — the first (1785) normal school for teachers established in the United States. In this group was the Mayor's brother-in-law, a young man who afterward became a great criminal lawyer and the friend of John Marshall, Archibald Henderson. From this hour dated his admiration amounting to adulation of Washington. He would not permit other men — "ordinary mortals" — to be classed in the same category or mentioned in the same breath with Washington.[2] The Hon-

[1] Montfort Stokes was born in Lunenburg County, Virginia, March 12, 1762; died at Fort Gibson, Arkansas, November 4, 1842. See footnote, *post*.

[2] Consult "A Federalist of the Old School," in the *North Carolina Booklet*, vol. XVII, nos. 1 and 2 (1917).

orable Spruce Macay, the Mayor of the Corporation, was a distinguished jurist, and a famous teacher of the law. Under him studied the brilliant partisan leader, General William Richardson Davie, afterwards Governor of North Carolina and "father of the University," and the reckless, hare-brained son of old Waxhaw, cock-fighter, horse-racer, Andrew Jackson. Macay was married to Frances, daughter of Judge Richard Henderson, in 1785. He travelled the western circuit which carried him to the outposts of civilization in Tennessee, where he proved a terror to the horse-stealer and other criminals of the border.

"At the skirt of the town," we read in a contemporary print, "he [Washington] was saluted by about forty boys in uniform, who had chosen officers, and arranged themselves for that purpose" — each boy wearing in his hat a bucktail as a symbol of independence. This incident was "very pleasing to the President," who described it as "the nicest thing he had seen." [1] At the court-house he was saluted by the artillery company as he passed, and about eight o'clock when it was announced that he had entered his lodgings, the brass six-pound pieces were discharged fifteen times. A vast crowd from the town and the sur-

[1] "Visit of General Washington to Salisbury, N.C.," by Rev. A. W. Mangum, *The University Monthly*, vol. IV, no. 6 (1884). Cf. also Rev. Jethro, Rumple's *Rowan County* (1881). Dr. Mangum, afterwards Professor of Philosophy at the University of North Carolina, collected historical materials concerning Rowan County many years before Dr. Rumple began his investigations. Some of these historical papers, written in entertaining style, were published in magazines and in newspapers; others still remain in manuscript.

rounding country for miles around gathered at the court-house in the public square and gave him an enthusiastic greeting with fervent cheers upon his arrival, as he rode majestically on horseback through the throng; and during the course of the day he "frequently gave the people opportunity of seeing him." He then had breakfast at the tavern or hotel of Captain Edward Yarborough, on East Main Street.[1] During the forenoon he was "waited upon by the Hon. Mr. Steele, the Hon. Judge Macay, and Max. Chambers, Esq. magistrate of police, with a number of other gentlemen," who presented him with the following address:

SIR,

We have the honour to signify to you the joy which your presence, after a tedious journey, affords to the inhabitants of this place. Words are wanting to express the gratitude we owe to heaven for continuing your life, on which our national glory and domestic tranquility, even at this day, seem suspended. Situated at a remote distance from the seat of government, deriving no advantage from the establishment of post roads, and destitute of regular information, we are sometimes at a loss to form proper opinions of national measures; but we nevertheless boast, that we have been and still are zealously attached to order, and effective government. And having been ranked with those who suffered in the late war, we pledge ourselves to be amongst the foremost to maintain and perpetuate the federal government. That your life,

[1] Edward Yarborough, appointed by the North Carolina Provincial Congress, May 8, 1776, ensign in Captain Jacob Turner's company of Foot, Third Regiment, American Army; commissioned first lieutenant, Third Regiment, April 16, 1777; received commission as captain on May 10, 1779; completed his military service on January 1, 1783; was original member of the North Carolina Society of the Cincinnati, organized at Hillsborough, with General Jethro Sumner, of Warren County as President, and the Reverend Adam Boyd, brigade chaplain, of Wilmington, as Secretary.

justly dear to the people of this country, a life precious, an ornament to human nature, and a blessing to the United States of America, may long be preserved, is the fervent and unanimous prayer of the people of this village.

SPRUCE MACAY
MAX: CHAMBERS
JNO. STEELE
M. STOKES
CHAS. HARRIS
L. BEARD.[1]

[1] Spruce Macay, of Scotch ancestry, was the son of James Macay of the "Jersey Settlement," prominent citizen, influential in councils of Church of England in St. Luke's Parish, and Clerk of the Committee of Safety for Rowan County during the early years of the Revolution. Spruce Macay was educated at the famous "log college" of Dr. David Caldwell. He was a member of the North Carolina Assembly for the Borough of Salisbury (1784), and member of the North Carolina Council of State (1781–82–83). In 1782 he was elected Judge of the Court of Oyer and Terminer for Mongan District, and rode the western circuit. Elected Judge of the Superior Court by the North Carolina Legislature in 1790, he served in this position until his death in 1808. He was married twice: to Frances, sister of Archibald Henderson, Esq., on May 27, 1785; and to Elizabeth Haynes, December 30, 1794. He was an able jurist, and enjoyed great popularity throughout the State. He lies buried beside his first wife at the Jersey Meeting-House, Rowan County.

Maxwell Chambers, a native of Pennsylvania, was born in 1742 and settled in Rowan County as early as 1764. He was Treasurer of the Committee of Safety for Rowan County (1775–76). After the Revolution he lived at "Spring Hill," near Salisbury. He was a leading merchant of the town, a man of wealth, member of the House of Commons from Salisbury (1779, 1789, 1790), and member for Rowan County in the State Convention of 1789, which ratified the Constitution of the United States. Lord Cornwallis used his house as headquarters in 1781. "His life," says General John Steele, "was a continued series of virtuous and charitable actions." He died in 1809.

John Steele, son of William and Elizabeth (Maxwell) Steele, was born in Salisbury, November 16, 1764; studied under the famous divine, Dr. James Hall, graduate of Nassau Hall, at "Clio's Nursery." As a lad he served in the Continental Army. After the Revolution he became a merchant and planter; prominent in local affairs, represented the Borough of Salisbury in the State Conventions of 1788 and 1789; member of Congress, 1789–93; Comptroller of the United States Treasury (1796–1802) under Washington, Adams, and Jefferson. He was offered by Adams the post of Secretary of

GENERAL JOHN STEELE

JUDGE SPRUCE MACAY

In reply, the President followed the formula which he used for most occasions — advocacy of the good policy

the Treasury, which he declined; Commissioner to treat with Indians, 1798; Commissioner on North Carolina–South Carolina boundary line (1805–08; 1812–13); Commissioner on North Carolina–Georgia boundary line (1807); member of the North Carolina Legislature 1806, 1811–13, of which he was sometime Speaker; elected for another term on August 14, 1815, the day of his death. He was married to Mary Nesfield, February 9, 1783.

Montfort Stokes, the son of David and Sarah (Montfort) Stokes, was said to descend from Simon de Montfort. He became a seaman, and eventually served in the United States Navy under Commodore Decatur. Captured during the War of 1812, he experienced intense sufferings aboard a prison ship. For many years he lived at Salisbury, where he was clerk of the Superior Court. He was chosen principal clerk of the State Senate; and later declined the post of United States Senator, to which office he had been elected. Elected in 1815, he served in the United States Senate from December 4, 1816, until March 3, 1823; member of the State Senate in 1826, State House of Representatives in 1829–30; Governor of North Carolina (1830–31), resigning that office to accept from his old friend, Andrew Jackson, the position of Indian Agent in Arkansas. He superintended the removal of the Indians west of the Mississippi River and continued to reside in Arkansas until his death.

Charles Harris, son of Charles Harris and Elizabeth Baker, was a noted physician of his day. The Harris family, originally of Wiltshire, England, emigrated to America from Ayrshire, Scotland, whither they had removed from Wiltshire, in the latter part of the seventeenth century. The elder Charles Harris settled about 1751 at Rocky River in Anson, afterwards Cabarrus, County. His son, Dr. Charles Harris, resided at "Favoni" in Cabarrus County, part of the original Harris estate. It was here that Dr. Charles Harris conducted what was probably the first medical school in North Carolina. His brother Samuel was a graduate of Princeton (tutor 1788–89), as was also his nephew, Charles Wilson Harris, who was one of the faculty of the University of North Carolina in its opening years. Dr. Charles Harris was twice married — first to Sara Harris, second to Lydia Houston Brevard. Although not a resident of Salisbury, he signed the address to Washington, as a leading man of that section, who was often in Salisbury at the home of his nephew, Robert Harris. Another strong reason for his being a signatory to this address is that his own half-brother, Major Thomas Harris, a valiant officer of the Continental Army, had fought under Washington himself at Monmouth and Trenton. Consult "The Harris Letters," edited by Professor H. M. Wagstaff (*James Sprunt Historical Publications*, vol. XIV, no. 1), University of North Carolina; and Dr. K. P. Battle: *History of the University of North Carolina.*

Lewis Beard, son of John Lewis Beard, one of the first settlers of Salis-

of supporting the Federal Government and passing wise laws.

GENTLEMEN:

Your expressions of satisfaction on my arrival in Salisbury, are received with pleasure, and thanked with sincerity. The interest which you are pleased to take in my personal welfare, excites a sensibility proportioned to your goodness. While I make the most grateful acknowledgement for that goodness, allow me to observe that your own determination, co-operating with that of your fellow-citizens throughout the union, to maintain and perpetuate the federal government, affords a better assurance of order and effective government, with their concomitants private and public prosperity, than the best meant endeavors of any individual could give. Our national glory, and our domestic tranquility, can never be tarnished or disturbed, while they are guarded by wise laws founded in public virtue. Among the measures which an enlightened and patriotic legislature will pursue to preserve them, I doubt not the means of diffusing useful information will be duly considered. My best wishes for the prosperity of your village, and for your individual happiness are sincerely offered.

After these ceremonies were concluded, the gentlemen of the town conducted the President to Hughes's Hotel,[1] where an elegant dinner was served. "On his way to dinner he passed through great crowds of people who had collected for the purpose of seeing their illustrious and

bury, was a leading citizen of Salisbury. At the cost of thirty thousand dollars he erected a magnificent bridge over the Yadkin. His estate on the Yadkin was known in after years as the "Bridge Place." He represented the Borough of Salisbury in the House of Commons (1791, 1792), and the County of Rowan in the State Senate in 1793. He married Susan, the daughter of one of Salisbury's first settlers, a prominent attorney, John Dunn, Esq.

[1] This house, which was to the east of the public square and nearly opposite the entrance of Meroney's Hall, was standing in 1881.

revered Chief Magistrate. He bowed respectfully to the people and passing the artillery company he was again saluted with a discharge of the pieces, followed by three cheers — 'Long live the President! Long live the President! Long live the President!'" As the President passed through the public square, a worthy old citizen, Richard Walton, an emigrant from Great Britain who had met King George, approached the President and, seizing his hand, earnestly exclaimed: "I have shaken hands with one king and you are the second" — which reveals the pitch of adulation to which Washington had been elevated in the public consciousness.

At dinner it is recorded that the President was "chearful" and that he "appeared highly pleased with the appearance of the upper country." In his diary he records: "The lands between Charlotte & Salisbury are very fine, of a reddish cast and well timbered, with but very little underwood — Between these two places are the first meadows I have seen on the Road since I left Virga. & here also we appear to be getting into a Wheat Country."

After dinner fifteen toasts were given — a discharge of artillery accompanying every toast:

1. The Government of the United States.
2. The Governor and State of North Carolina. (By the President.)
3. The constitutional liberty of the people.
4. The committee of Congress who reported the declaration of Independence.
5. May Congress take effectual measures to disseminate political knowledge.

6. May Congress take early and effectual measures to disseminate political knowledge.
7. May harmony subsist between federal and state governments.
8. The agriculture, manufactures and commerce of the United States.
9. The European powers in alliance with the United States.
10. May the French revolution terminate favorably to liberty.
11. May the services of General Greene be remembered with gratitude by the people of the southern states.
12. May reason, and not the sword, terminate all national differences.
13. May the officers in every department have a sacred regard to national justice.
14. The friends of religion, morality, and useful knowledge. (Here the President retired — and the next toast was)
15. GEORGE WASHINGTON — *Long may he live.*

It was said that the whole was "conducted with decorum; and festivity and joy were seen on every face." At the banquet, many Colonial and Revolutionary incidents were narrated by the gentlemen of the town, led by that attractive Irishman, Albert Torrence,[1] who kept the famous tavern on the Yadkin which the British denominated "Tarrant's."

We may be sure that Washington was made aware of Salisbury's pride in the great explorer and Indian fighter, Daniel Boone, whom the organization known as Richard

[1] Albert Torrence, born 1752, was of Irish birth. He settled in Rowan County shortly before the Revolution, building a home on the heights, later known as "The Heights of Gowerie," overlooking the Yadkin River, on the opposite side of which was the historic "Jersey Settlement." It was from this height that Cornwallis cannonaded the forces of General Nathanael Greene in the latter's retreat through North Carolina in 1781. The Torrence home was a centre of culture and refinement. Albert Torrence died in 1825.

PICTURES OF KING GEORGE AND QUEEN CHARLOTTE WHICH HUNG ON THE WALLS OF STEEL'S TAVERN
SALISBURY, NORTH CAROLINA

(See reverse)

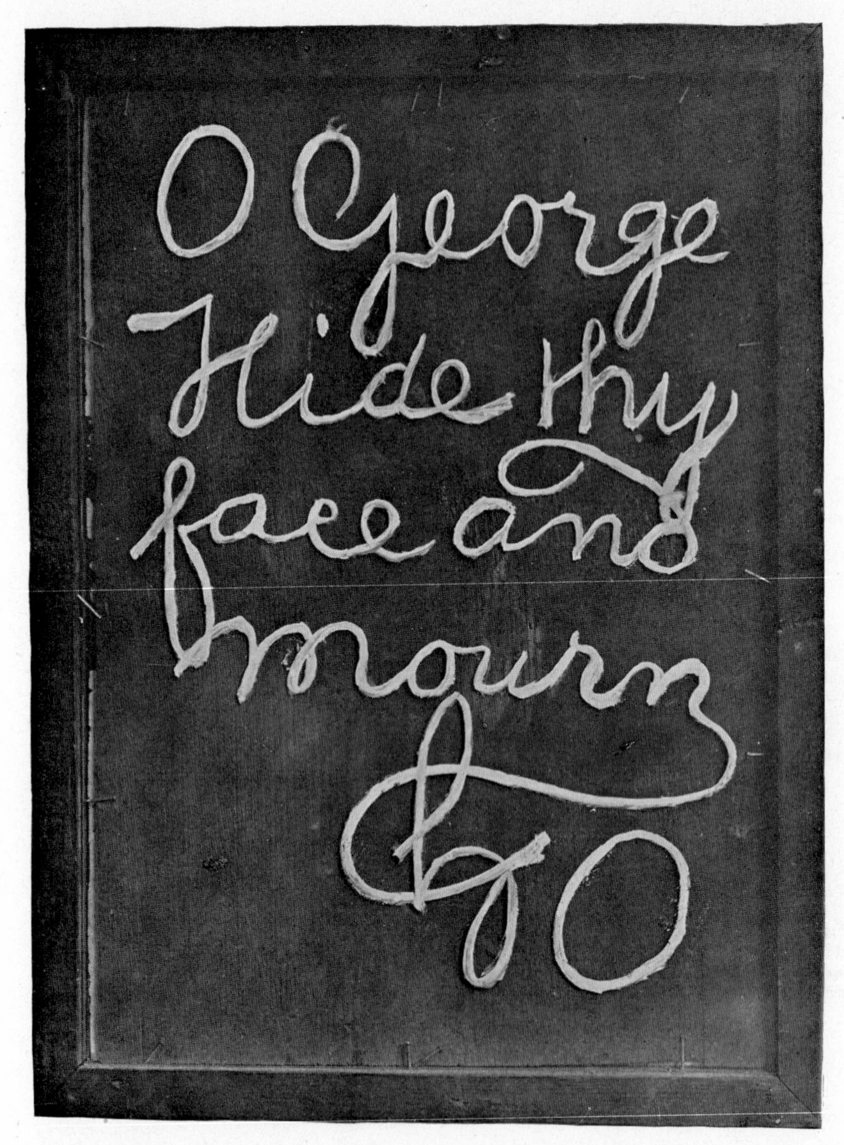

INSCRIPTION WRITTEN BY NATHANAEL GREENE ON BACK OF PICTURE OF KING GEORGE

Henderson and Company had despatched on a great tour of exploration through Kentucky in 1769. The occupation of the town in succession by Lord Cornwallis and General Greene was no doubt vividly described to Washington, in particular the incident of Greene in utter dejection arriving at Steel's Tavern in February, 1781, and Mrs. Steel's impulsive gift to him of her savings for years, two small bags of specie. The President was given the opportunity to visit Steel's Tavern, only a few steps from Hughes's Hotel, and to see the picture of George III, on the back of which Greene, in his delight over Mrs. Steel's gift, wrote with a coal taken from the fireplace: "O George! Hide Thy Face and Mourn." And doubtless the President participated heartily in the applause which greeted the toast; "May the services of General Greene be remembered with gratitude by the people of the Southern States!" [1]

During the afternoon Washington drank tea at Hughes's

[1] The pictures of King George and Queen Charlotte, the back of the former bearing the defiant challenge of Greene, are still preserved, and are herewith reproduced. They are beautiful colored prints, and were brought to Mrs. Steel from England by her brother, Dr. Maxwell, long before the Revolution. Mrs. Steel, the mother of General John Steele (who added the final letter), died shortly after Washington's arrival. General Steele had the greatest affection for Washington, but he loved his wife, who was a Miss Mary Nesfield, even more. On one occasion (January 31, 1793), he wrote her from Philadelphia: "I dined to-day at the President's in a very large company of ladies and gentlemen . . . Without you, I feel like Captain O'Blunder 'Alone in the throng' . . . The President to-day asked me to drink a glass of wine with him. This is considered here a great honor, it may be so; but I would have been more gratified in drinking a glass with my own dear Polly." In connection with General Greene's visit to Salisbury consult Archibald Henderson: "Elizabeth Maxwell Steel," in *North Carolina Booklet*, vol. XII, no. 2 (1912).

Hotel with about twenty ladies who had been assembled for the occasion; Mrs. Steele, Mrs. McCorkle, Mrs. Macay, Mrs. Torrence, Mrs. Chambers, Miss Elizabeth Henderson, Miss Sally Alexander, Miss Mary Faust, Mrs. Lewis Beard, Mrs. Giles, Mrs. Kelly, and others whom tradition has ignored. After this "interesting ceremony," as Washington would call it, he returned to Yarborough's Hotel; but the people besieged the place and clamored for another sight of the President, for a speech. Washington came forth in response to the clamors of the excited throng; and, standing upon the steps of Yarborough's Hotel in the light of the setting sun and shading his face from its rays with his handkerchief, he said with eloquent and touching simplicity: "You see before you only an old gray-haired man."

A reliable historian states: "That night there was a grand ball given to the President at Hughes's Hotel attended by the prominent gentlemen and ladies of Salisbury. . . . How far the 'Father of his Country' participated in the amusements and festivities of the occasion, tradition saith not." [1] We do know that the town was il-

[1] Rev. Jethro Rumple, in *History of Rowan County*. He adds: "There is still in the county a relic of this ball — a brown satin dress, worn by Mrs. Lewis Beard — the daughter of John Dunn, Jr. It is in the possession of Mrs. Mary Locke, granddaughter of Col. Moses A. Locke, and great granddaughter of the lady who wore it." The Reverend A. W. Mangum, who collected his materials long before Rumple studied the question, makes no mention of a ball, in a manuscript account of Washington's visit to Salisbury, preserved in the archives of the University of North Carolina. No mention of it is made in the full contemporary account of the doings of the day, sent to Mr. Fenno, editor of the *Gazette of the United States*, with a note bearing the initials "A. T.," which probably identifies the writer as Albert Torrence. No doubt at Salisbury, as afterwards at Georgetown and

luminated, that night, with a "real North Carolina effulgence" — with lamps, doubtless of a primitive style, and burning tar-barrels, which gave the effect of a Dantean Hades. And to add to the illusion, the pieces of artillery on the square continued at intervals to roar their salutes of belching smoke and flame. What excitement! What a day for this loyal historical town! To think that the literal minded Washington, in speaking of place and people, could say in his diary only this — which was all quite true: "Salisbury is but a small place altho' it is the County town, and the district Court is held in it; — nor does it appear to be much on the increase, — there is about three hundred souls in it and tradesmen of different kinds." At least we know that the day Washington reached Salisbury he "foundered another of his (my) horses" — an important historical incident which is herewith conscientiously recorded. There is balm for Salisburians in the record of the Reverend A. W. Mangum, who thus concludes his manuscript account of Washington's visit: "The people of Salisbury of every class were impressed with the plainness of his apparel and his affable manners. He was dressed in plain homespun and was courteous and pleasant to all. He expressed himself more pleased with the plain, frank, earnest welcome of Salisbury than the gaudy and fantastic reception at Charleston." [1]

elsewhere on the trip, there was dancing — called a "ball" — following the "Tea Party." In "The Harris Letters" (*Sprunt Historical Publications*, vol. XIV, no. 1, University of North Carolina), Professor H. M. Wagstaff states that a ball was given at Albert Torrence's in honor of Washington.

[1] A poem, "Salisbury Town," by Charles Benton Canady, contains this stanza:

The next morning Washington set off at four o'clock, being escorted as far as the Yadkin River by the gentlemen who dined with him and the company of cavalry. At Long's Ferry he made a short address to the military company, under the command of Captain John Beard, and "took leave of the other gentlemen in the most polite and affectionate manner." Washington's account in his diary for Tuesday, May 31st, is as follows:

> Left Salisbury about 4 o'clock; at 5 miles crossed the Yadkin, the principal stream of the Peedee, and breakfasted on the No. Bank, (while my Carriages & horses were crossing) at a Mr. Young's fed my horses 10 miles farther, at one Reeds — and about 3 o'clock (after another halt) arrived at Salem, one of the Moravian towns 20 miles farther — In all 35 from Salisbury.
>
> The road between Salisbury & Salem passes over very little good land, and much that is different [indifferent?]; being a good deal mixed with Pine, but not sand.
>
> Salem is a small but neat village; & like all the rest of the Moravian settlements, is governed by an excellent police — having within itself all kinds of artizans — The number of Souls does not exceed 200.[1]

If from less spacious scenes we glance
At those adventurous days now gone,
Their hardships, brightened with romance
Hallow the soil we stand upon.
Here Boone released his restless soul
To hew a pathway to the west,
Cornwallis here, with Greene his goal,
Spurred northward in his eager quest,
And Jackson, merry Andrew then
Read here his Blackstone and his Coke,
And Washington, our chief of men
Came down to greet the Southern folk.

[1] In this same year William Loughton Smith, Senator from South Carolina, visited Salem, and makes the following entry in his diary: "Between 200 and 300 persons of this Sect here assembled live in brotherly love and

To the Inhabitants of the Town of Salisbury

Gentlemen,

Your expressions of satisfaction on my arrival in Salisbury are received with pleasure, and thanked with sincerity.

The interest, which you are pleased to take in my personal welfare, excites a sensibility proportioned to your goodness —— While I make the most grateful acknowledgement for that goodness, allow me to observe that your own determination, co-operating with that of your fellow-citizens, throughout the Union, to maintain and to perpetuate the federal-government, affords a better assurance of order and effective govern-ment, with their concomitants, private and public prosperity, than the best meant endeavors of any individual could give.

Our national glory, and our domestic tranquillity, can never be tarnished or disturbed, while they are guarded by wise laws, founded in public virtue.——

Among the measures which an enlightened and patriotic Legislature will pursue to prepare them, I doubt not the means of diffusing useful information will be duly considered.

My best wishes for the prosperity of your Village, and for your individual happiness are sincerely offered.

G^o Washington.

Salisbury and Salem

Washington's choice of Salem as one of the points on his route may have been dictated by the condition of the roads. But doubtless Washington desired to indicate his friendliness — the attitude of parental benevolence suited to a father of his country — toward a people who had proven by their deeds the sincerity of their neutrality, and their extraordinary ability to live in peace and amity with their neighbors, red as well as white. The Moravians were highly gratified to have the President visit their settlement; and showed him the utmost hospitality. Albert Torrence says that Washington was "received at the bridge by the people of the place, and conducted into town with a complete band of music playing before him. On his arrival the bells rung, and the church organ played almost the whole of the night." An interesting description of the doings of this day as contained in the "Salem Diary" for 1791, is as follows:

set a laudable example of industry. . . . Every man follows some occupation; every woman is engaged in some feminine work; a tanner, shoemaker, potter, saddler, tinner, brewer, distiller, etc. is here seen at work; from their labors they not only supply themselves but the country all around them. The first view of the town is romantic, just as it breaks upon you through the woods; it is pleasantly seated on a rising ground and is surrounded by beautiful meadows, well-cultivated fields, and shady woods. The antique appearance of the houses, built in the German style, and the trees among which they are placed have a singular and pleasing effect; the whole resembles a beautiful village, and forms a pastoral scene. . . . Mr. Bagge, one of the brethren and a respectable old gentleman, who keeps a store here . . . very politely conducted me to the single men's house, and to all the different trades. I found every one hard at work; such a scene of industry, perhaps, exists no where in so small a place. The brewery and distillery are considerable; the beer is very good, and a cordial made out of the whiskey excellent. Water brought from the adjacent rivulets is collected in large pipes and conveyed to all the houses. . . ." Cf. *Journal of William Loughton Smith. 1790–1791.* Edited by Albert Matthews. (Cambridge: The

May 31. At the end of this month the congregation of Salem had the pleasure of welcoming the President of the United States, George Washington, on his return journey from the southern states. We had already heard that he would return to Virginia by way of our town. This afternoon we heard that this morning he left Salisbury, 35 miles from here, so the Brn. Marshall, Koehler, and Benzien rode out a bit to meet him, and as he approached the town several melodies were played, partly by trumpets and french horns, partly by trombones. He was accompanied only by his secretary, Major Jackson, and the necessary servants. On alighting from the carriage he greeted the by-standers in friendly fashion, and was particularly pleasant to the children gathered there. Then he conversed on various subjects with the Brethren who conducted him to the room prepared for him. At first he said that he must go on the next morning, but when he learned that the Governor of our State would like to meet him here the following day he said he would rest here one day. He told our musicians that he would enjoy some music with his evening meal, and was served with it.[1]

The inn where Washington was entertained as the guest of the community is still standing — known to-day as the Old Salem Hotel.[2]

University Press.) From the *Proceedings of the Massachusetts Historical Society*, October, 1917.

[1] The original diary is in German; this translation has been courteously supplied me by Miss Adelaide L. Fries, Secretary of the Wachovia Historical Society, Winston-Salem, North Carolina. Frederick William Marshall was prominent in the founding of Salem. Bishop John Daniel Koehler was the pastor for Salem. The Reverend Christian Louis Benzien was one of the leading men of the community for years before and after Washington's visit. For details of the settlement, consult *History of Wachovia in North Carolina*, by J. H. Clewell (New York, 1902). The "Records of the Moravians of North Carolina," under the editorship of Miss Fries, are now being published by the North Carolina Historical Commission.

[2] The Salem Tavern, as it was called in the olden time, stands on the west side of Main Street, between West Street and Washington Avenue. When the present owners, a group of Moravian men, purchased the building, they took a frame section to the north about as large as the brick por-

The President of Salem Academy and College, boosting the building of great hotels and lamenting the general lack of progress, recently remarked at a banquet that, on visiting the room in Salem in which Washington slept, he was reverently told that it hadn't been touched since 1791. This, aside: — "And it looked it!"

At this time the Governor of North Carolina was Alexander Martin,[1] graduate of the College of New Jersey, who had removed from New Jersey to North Carolina about 1760. Martin had served during the Revolution under

tion. The part, built of brick, is the original historical building. Upon its walls is a tablet, placed there by the Daughters of the American Revolution, bearing the following inscription: "The Old Salem Tavern. Site selected 1768. First Building burned January 31st, 1784. Present Building erected 1784. President Washington entertained May 31st, 1791."

[1] Alexander Martin, born at Lebanon, New Jersey, about 1738, was the son of Hugh and Jane Martin. Hugh Martin emigrated from County Tyrone, Ireland, in 1721 and settled in Hunterdon County, New Jersey. Alexander Martin was graduated from Nassau Hall, September 29, 1756. He settled in Rowan County, North Carolina, about 1760; and after studying law, was active in its practice, often presiding over the District Court at Salisbury. In 1772 he removed to Guilford Court House. Member of the Colonial Assembly from Guilford County, 1774–1775. Appointed Lieutenant-Colonel of Second North Carolina Regiment, Continental Line, September 1, 1775; and promoted to colonelcy of same regiment, April 10, 1776, which he held until November 2, 1777, when he resigned. Participated in the Battle of Brandywine, September 11, 1775, and the Battle of Germantown, October 4, 1779. State Senator from Guilford County, 1778–1782, 1785, 1787–88; Speaker of the Senate, 1780, 1781, 1782. Acting-Governor of North Carolina, 1781–82; Governor, 1782–85, 1789–92. Chairman North Carolina Board of War, 1780–81. Elected to Congress from North Carolina, December 17, 1786; and on January 7, 1787, as delegate to the Constitutional Convention in Philadelphia. Elected to the United States Senate, serving from March 4, 1793, to March 3, 1799. Removed to his plantation "Danbury" in Rockingham County, 1789. President Board of Trustees, University of North Carolina, 1792–93. Received degree of LL.D. from the College of New Jersey in 1793. Member State Senate from Rockingham County, 1804, 1805. Died at "Danbury," November 2, 1807.

Washington, who presented to him a pair of silver cups at the time of his retirement from the service. During Washington's entire second term, Martin was Senator from North Carolina. He was a delegate from North Carolina to the Federal Convention at Philadelphia to frame the Constitution of the United States. A Federalist of the Washington type, he was capable, energetic, and conciliatory — winning popular favor to such an extent that he was six times Governor of North Carolina. He had a fine plantation on the Dan River in Rockingham County; and also a home at Martinsville (Guilford), where he entertained Washington on June 2d and 3d.

As illustrative of the attachment to Washington of Governor Martin and of the people of North Carolina, the following incident deserves record. On June 26, 1790, Governor Alexander Martin and the Council of State of North Carolina, in session at the Rockingham Springs, drew up the following letter which was transmitted to George Washington:

To the President of the United States.
Sir,

The governor and council of the State of North-Carolina embrace the earliest opportunity afforded them since the accession of this state to the constitution, and the completion of the union by all the states, of congratulating you upon this most auspicious event, by which all causes of future dissention among the states will be obviated — the impost, that great branch of revenue and support of public credit, collected with more facility, and our finances more properly arranged.

We congratulate ourselves with equal sincerity on beholding you, sir, in the highest departments which your virtues

SALEM TAVERN, NORTH CAROLINA

SALEM TAVERN TABLET

merited, and to which your country unanimously and gratefully appointed you.

The importance of your situation receives additional dignity by the veneration your country possesses for your character, and from a confidence that every power vested in you by the constitution, will be exerted for the happiness and prosperity of your country, by giving efficacy to such a system as will ensure and conciliate the public mind — a confidence felt by all — by none more powerfully than the citizens of this state.

We have just received the happy information of your recovery from a disorder which threatened your life; a life we may truly say as necessary as dear to us. With grateful hearts we return thanks to the great disposer of events for this beneficent mark of his attention in preserving you. May it long be shewn in continuing you among us, and when the awful day comes which is to separate you from us, may you receive the reward of those virtues which he only can bestow.

ALEXANDER MARTIN.
WYATT HAWKINS, President.

Done in council unanimously, at the Rockingham Springs, June 26, 1790.
By order
THOMAS HENDERSON, C. C.

To the above the President returned the following answer:

TO THE GOVERNOR AND COUNCIL OF THE STATE OF NORTH-CAROLINA.

GENTLEMEN,

I entreat you to be persuaded that nothing could have been more agreeable to me, than the proofs contained in your affectionate address of the friendly sentiments entertained by you for my person, as well as for the government which I have been appointed by my countrymen to administer. And I reciprocate, with heartfelt satisfaction, your congratulations on the completion of the union of all the states; an event, in my judgment, pregnant with more salutary consequences, than can easily be expressed or conceived

It will ever be my first wish and most strenuous endeavour, to justify, so far as may be in my power, the confidence which my fellow-citizens have thought proper to repose in me, by exerting every power vested in the President of the United States by the constitution, for the happiness and prosperity of our country; and by giving efficacy to such a system as will ensure the general welfare, and conciliate the public mind.

I desire, gentlemen, to make acceptable to you my acknowledgments for the kind concern you take in the restoration of my health and preservation of my life; and in the retribution I may receive after the conclusion of this mortal existence. May you, and the state in whose government you have the principal agency, be also the peculiar care of divine providence.

G. WASHINGTON

UNITED STATES, *August* 26, 1790.

The following is the entry in Washington's diary, under June 1st:

Having received information that Governor Martin was on his way to meet me; and would be at Salem this evening, I resolved to await his arrival at this place instead of halting a day at Guilford as I had intended;

Spent the forenoon in visiting the Shops of the different Tradesmen. The houses of accomodation for the single men & Sisters of the Fraternity — & their place of worship. — Invited six of their principal people to dine with me — and in the evening went to hear them sing, & perform on a variety of instruments Church music.

In the Afternoon Governor Martin as was expected (with his Secretary) arrived.

The Moravians in North Carolina have always been famous for their love of music, and for their communal cultivation of it both vocally and instrumentally. In their Moravian Museum at Salem is still preserved an ancient tune book which contains the music of a tune much the same as "My Country, 'tis of thee," which is entitled "God Save Great Washington." This tune was doubtless played by the trombonists who went to greet Washington upon his arrival — and perhaps again later, during his evening meal. In the same Museum is shown the old spinet upon which a young lady played for Washington's delectation. At the conclusion of her recital, she naturally expected that the great man, who had been standing near by, would compliment her upon her skill as an executant and upon her sympathetic touch. Her heart was all a-flutter as he drew near; but we must endeavor to imagine her disappointment and vexation when Washington, who had noted a wart on her hand, gave her a formula for taking it off. *Il ne manquait que ça!*

An account of the events of the day, much more interesting and graphic than Washington's, is found in the "Salem Diary," here set down in full:

June 1, the President and Major Jackson, accompanied by several Brethren, took a look at the workshops, Choir Houses, and other institutions of our town, and he expressed his pleasure with various things especially the water-works and its use. As a testimony of the loyal attitude of the Brethren in Wachovia toward the Government of these states an address was prepared, and the President set a time for its presentation. Therefore at two o'clock several Brethren brought it, and after Dr. Marshall had read it, according to custom, and had presented it, the President, in the same manner, presented his answer, couched in favorable terms, both papers being inserted in this Diary. Six Brethren were then invited to dine with him, and during the meal there was again music. Many people came from the neighborhood and from our other congregations to see the President, he being such a prominent figure in this land, and gladly gave them an opportunity to fulfil their desire. Toward evening the Governor of this State, Mr. Alexander Martin, arrived from his plantation some forty miles from here on Dan River. He, the President, and Major Jackson attended a song service that evening, the singing being interspersed with instrumental selections, and they expressed their pleasure in it. At the close of the day the wind instruments were heard sweetly beside the Tavern. During the day Major Jackson inquired concerning the principles of our congregation, and was much pleased at being presented with a copy of the Brethren's History, and of the Idea Fidei Fratrum.[1]

June 2, at four o'clock in the morning the entire company departed, the Brn. Marshall and Benzein accompanying them across the boundaries of Wachovia.

The address mentioned in this account breathes a spirit of great piety, voices sincere appreciation of the President's courtesy in visiting the Moravian Town, as it was commonly called, and avows a truly patriotic allegiance to the United States. The President's reply, with entire fitness, gives approval to the fundamental principles of good citizenship which characterize the Moravian Brotherhood. The address and reply, which are recorded in the "Salem Diary," are reproduced below in full:

To the President of the United States:

Happy in sharing the honor of a visit from the illustrious President of the Union to the Southern States, the Brethren of Wachovia humbly beg leave, upon this joyful occasion, to express their highest esteem, duty, and affection for the great patriot of this country.

Deeply impressed as we are with gratitude to the great au-

[1] According to information supplied me by Miss Adelaide L. Fries, Curator of the Wachovia Historical Society, Winston-Salem, North Carolina, the "Brethren's History" was doubtless the work of Cranz (Barby, 1771, first edition, 2000 copies; second edition, 1772). The copy presented to

SALEM GEMEINHAUS

FREDERICK WILLIAM MARSHALL

thor of our being for his unbounded mercies, we cannot but particularly acknowledge his gracious providence over the

---

Major Jackson was probably Latrobe's English translation, — the title-page reading as follows:

The
Ancient and Modern
HISTORY
of the
BRETHREN
or
A Succinct Narrative
of the
Protestant Church
of the
United Brethren,
or
Unitas Fratrum,
In the remoter Ages, and particularly in the present Century:
written in German
By David Cranz,
Author of the History of Greenland;
Now translated into English, with Emendations;
and published, with some additional Notes,
By Benjamin La Trobe.

I have considered the days of old, the years of ancient times.
Ps. lxxvii, 5.

London:
Printed by W. and A. Strahan;
And sold by J. Robson, in Bond Street; T. Cadell, in the Strand;
C. Dilly in the Poultry; and at the Settlements and
Chapels of the Congregations of the Brethren.
MDCCLXXX.

The *Idea Fidei Fratrum* was written by Bishop August Gottlieb Spangenberg, and printed (1779) at Barby, Saxony, in the Printing Office of the Unity. In 1796 it was translated into English by Benjamin La Trobe, under the title *An Exposition of Christian Doctrine, as taught in the Protestant Church of the United Brethren, or Unitas Fratrum.* This work was also translated and published in Danish, Swedish, Dutch, and French.

temporal and political prosperity of the country, in the peace, and wherein none can take a warmer interest than ourselves, in particular when we consider that the same Lord who preserved your precious person in so many ways has made you in a conspicuous manner an instrument in his hands to forward that happy constitution, together with these improvements whereby our United States begin to flourish, over which you preside with the applause of a thankful nation.

Whenever, therefore, we solicit the protection of the Father of Mercies over this favored country, we cannot but fervently implore his kindness for your preservation, which is so intimately connected therewith.

May this gracious Lord vouchsafe to prolong your valuable life as a further blessing, and an ornament of the constitution, that by your worthy example the regard for religion be increased, and the improvements of civil society encouraged.

The settlements of the United Brethren, though small, will always make it their study to contribute as much as in them lies to the peace and improvement of the United States, and all the particular parts they live in, joining their ardent prayers to the best wishes of this whole continent that your personal as well as domestic happiness may abound, and a series of successes may crown your labours for the prosperity of our times and an example to future ages, until the glorious reward of a faithful servant shall be your portion.

Signed, in behalf of the United Brethren in Wachovia,

FREDERICK WILLIAM MARSHALL,
JOHN DANIEL KOEHLER,
CHRISTIAN LEWIS BENZIEN.

SALEM, *the* 1*st of June*, 1791.

The President was pleased to return the following answer:

TO THE UNITED BRETHREN OF WACHOVIA:

GENTLEMEN:

I am greatly indebted to your respectable and affectionate expression of personal regard, and I am not less obliged by the patriotic sentiment contained in your address.

From a society whose governing principles are industry and love of order, much may be expected toward the improvement and prosperity of the country in which their settlements are formed, and experience authorizes the belief that much will be obtained.

Thanking you with grateful sincerity for your prayers in my behalf, I desire to assure you of my best wishes for your social and individual happiness.

G. WASHINGTON.

A word from the young Charles Caldwell, who seemed to glory in the rôle of guide to the President — apparently since it gave him such an unrivalled opportunity to display his own knowledge — will present some of the events of these days, as viewed from the peculiar angle of that very self-conscious young man:

During Washington's stay in Salisbury, I was much around his person, in the capacity of junior master of ceremony, and when the General left Salisbury, on his way to the north, I again, at the head of a new and larger escort, attended him to Guildford Courthouse, the celebrated battle-ground of Greene and Cornwallis, a distance, as well as I now remember, of about sixty miles. Having there conducted him over the field of action of the two armies, according to the best information I could collect respecting its localities and limits, we returned to the Court-house, where, conformably to my orders, I reluctantly took leave of him — he, to proceed on his journey to the then seat of government, and I to retrace my route to the South. Nor, highly flattered as I had been by his notice of me, and even by occasional marks of his apparent partiality toward me, and sincerely attached as I had become to his person, was the act of leave-taking, on my part, without much more emotion than I believed I should experience.

Having paid to him, at the head of my little squadron, the farewell ceremony, in military style, and being about to issue the command to move forward, Washington beckoned me to approach him. Having eagerly advanced to within a suitable distance, he bowed in his saddle, and extended to me his hand. That act, accompanied, as I fancied it to be, by an appearance, in his countenance, of marks of feeling, again completely unmanned and silenced me. As, on first meeting him, I was able to greet him only with my sword, I could now bid him a personal farewell in no other way than by the pressure of his hand; and, observing my emotion, my eyes once more swimming in tears, he returned the pressure, and addressed to me a few words, thanking me courteously for my devoted attention, and what he was pleased to call my numerous services to him, and hoping to see me during the prosecution of my studies in Philadelphia, to which place I had apprised him of my intention to repair, he again pressed my hand, and was forthwith in motion.

For a moment, I fancied my behavior to have been so unsoldier-like, that I almost hesitated to assume my station at the head of my escort; but, casting a look toward it, as it stood motionless in column, I perceived several of its members, some years older than myself, and noted for their firmness, wiping the moisture from their eyes, as I had just done from mine, and that sight did much to reconcile me to myself. It convinced me that the scene I had just passed through had been a moving one; and that, when affection is awakened, it is not unmanly for even a soldier to weep. I therefore replaced myself at their head, and led my comrades back to Salisbury.[1]

Washington gives the following account of the events of Thursday, 2d:

In company with the Govr I set out by 4 Oclock for Guilford — Breakfasted at one Dobsons at the distance of eleven Miles from Salem and dined at Guilford 16 Miles further, where there was a considerable gathering of people who had

[1] There seems to be some discrepancy between Caldwell's account and the events as recorded contemporaneously. The military escort from Salisbury left Washington at Long's Ferry, on May 31st, and returned to Salisbury, presumably accompanied by young Caldwell. Caldwell perhaps headed, or at least was one of, the party of light horse which met Washington near Guilford on June 2d.

SALEM BROTHERS' HOUSE

SALEM SISTERS' HOUSE

received notice of my intention to be there to day & came to satisfy their curiosity.[1]

On my way I examined the ground on which the Action between General Greene and Lord Cornwallis commenced—and after dinner rode over that where their lines were formed and the scene closed in the retreat of the American forces—The first line of which was advantageously drawn up, and had the Troops done their duty properly, the British must have been sorely galded in yr advance, if not defeated.—

The lands between Salem and Guilford are, in places, very fine; but upon the whole can not be called more than middling—some being very bad.—

On my approach to this place (Guilford) I was met by a party of light horse which I prevailed on the Governor to dismiss, and to countermand his orders for others to attend me through the State.[2]

An interesting side-light upon an important incident of the day is a description of a conversation with Washington which Thomas Jefferson records:

In conversation with the President to-day, and speaking about General Greene, he said that he and General Greene had always differed in opinion about the manner of using Militia. Greene always placed them in his front: himself was of opinion, they should always be used as a reserve to improve

[1] On the way, it seems, about eleven o'clock in the morning, Washington stopped for a drink of water at the home of Levi Buckingham, who lived about a mile northeast of Colfax Station, between Friendship and Kernersville, in Guilford County. Trivial as the incident is, it means something to the neighborhood; and the spring from which he drank is still pointed out. Little Sarah Buckingham (afterward Mrs. Jessup), then about nine years old, went down to the spring with her father; and often afterwards spoke particularly of Washington's firm tread and of his manifest enjoyment of simple country life. For this information I am indebted to Mr. John T. Brittain, of Asheboro, North Carolina.

[2] We are reminded here of William Blount's jocular remark in the letter to J. G. Blount, *ante:* "I have given this to Gov. Martin so that you may shortly expect to hear of pompous orders for equiping and training the Cavalry."

any advantage, for which purpose they were the *finest fellows* in the world. He said he was on the ground of the battle of Guilford, with a person who was in the action, and who explained the whole of it to him. That General Greene's front was behind a fence at the edge of a large field, through which the enemy were obliged to pass to get at them; and that in their passage through this they must have been torn all to pieces, if troops had been posted there who would have stood their ground; and that the retreat from that position was through a thicket perfectly secure. Instead of this, he posted the North Carolina militia there, who only gave one fire and fell back, so that the whole benefit of their position was lost. He thinks that the regulars, with their field pieces, would have hardly let a single man get through that field.[1]

[1] *Anas*, June 7, 1793. In his able work, "North Carolina, 1780–'81," David Schenck shows by a wealth of evidence that "the North Carolina militia were, by the *personal order* of General Greene, directly instructed *to fire twice*, and assured that he required no more of them." Compare chapter vii of that work, pp. 293–387.

CHAPTER XII

THE NINTH STAGE

The Return to Mount Vernon

FROM the public standpoint, Washington's Southern tour was concluded at Guilford Court-House, North Carolina. The remainder of the trip is just — going home. Washington's diary for this period is valuable as containing general observations upon the country, the people, and the tour, and is here set down without commentary.

Friday — 3^{d}

Took my leave of the Govern^{r} whose intention was to have attended me to the line, but for my request that he would not; and about 4 Oclock proceeded on my journey. — Breakfasted at troublesome Ironworks (called 15, but which is at least, 17 Miles from Guilford partly in Rain and from my information or for want of it was obliged to travel 12 Miles further than I intended today — to one Gatewoods within two miles of Dix' ferry over the Dan at least 30 Miles from the Ironworks. — The Lands over which I passed this day were of various qualities and as I approached the Dan, were a good deal covered with pine. —

In conversing with the Governor on the State of Politics in N^{o} Carolina I learnt with pleasure that opposition to the Genl Government, & the discontent of the people were subsiding fast — and that he should, so soon as he had received the Laws which he had written to the Secretary of State for, issue his proclamation requiring all Officers & Members of the Governm^{t} to take the Oaths prescribed by Law. — He seems to condemn the Speculaters in Lands and the purchases from the State of Georgia, & thinks as every sensible &

disinterested man must that schemes of that sort must involve the Country in trouble — perhaps in blood

Saturday 4th.[1]

Left Mr. Gatewoods about half after Six oclock — and between his house & the Ferry passed the line which divides the States of Virginia and No. Carolina & dining at one Wilsons[2] 16 Miles from the Ferry, lodged at Hallifax old Town.. — The Road from Dix' ferry to Wilson's, passes over very hilly (& for the most part) indifferent land, being a good deal mixed with pine though it is said here that pine when mixed with Oak, & more especially with hiccory is not indicative of a poor Soil. From Wilson's to Hallifax old town the Soil is good, & of a reddish cast.

Having this day passed the line of No. Carolina and of course finished my tour thro' the three Southernmost states a

[1] The following interesting entries are found in the manuscript diary of Richard N. Venable, at the time practising law in Pittsylvania County, Virginia. He was own brother to Abraham B. Venable, who served in Congress from March 4, 1791, to March 3, 1799; served in the United States Senate from December 7, 1803, to June 7, 1804, when he resigned. He perished at the burning of the theatre in Richmond, Virginia, December 26, 1811. The entries in Richard N. Venable's manuscript diary (1791–92) which pertain to Washington follow below:

Sat. 4th June 1791. Peytonsburg, Pittsylvania County. Gen'l Washington came in the evening — stayed at tavern — set out next morning before sunrise. . . .

Monday 6th. Charlotte Court (Charlotte County, Virginia). Great anxiety in the people to see Gen'l Washington. Strange is the impulse which is felt by almost every breast to see the face of a great good man — sensation better felt than expressed. In evening [I] came to Prince Edward C. H.

Tuesday 7th June. Gen'l Washington arrived at Prince Edward Court House, all crowding the way where they expect him to pass, anxious to see the Saviour of their Country and object of their love.

Mr. Venable was doubtless subject to the "strange impulse" of which he speaks, as he seems to have followed the President for several days. For these excerpts I am indebted to Mr. A. J. Morrison, Hampton Sidney, Virginia.

[2] The name in the original manuscript may possibly be "Wisom." In his sketch, "Washington's Journey through North Carolina in 1791," Richard G. Walzer, Esq., Lexington, North Carolina, states that the person here referred to is Nathanael Wilson, his great-great-grandfather.

general description of them may be comprised in the few following words. —

From the Seaboard to the falls of the Rivers which water the extensive region the lands, except the Swamps, on the Rivers, and the lesser streams which empty into them; & the interval lands higher up the Rivers is with but few exceptions neither more nor less than a continued pine barren very thinly inhabited. — The part next the Seaboard, for many Miles, is a dead level badly watered. — That above it is hilly & not much better wat.d but if possible less valuable on account of its hilliness and because they are more inconvenient to Market supposing them as capable as the lands below of producing Beef, Porke, Tar, pitch, & turpentine. — The land above the falls of the several Rivers from information, and as far as my own observation has extended, is of a very superior kind from these being of a greasy red, with large oaks, intermixed with hiccory Chesnut &c.a yielding producing, Corn Tob.o Wheat, Hemp & other articles in great abundance & are generally thickly inhabited comparatively speaking with those below

In the lower Country (near the Seaboard) in the States of S.o Carolina & Georgia, Rice, as far up as the low swamps extend is almost the sole article that is raised for Market; — Some of the planters of which grow as much Corn, as, with the Sweet Potatoes, support their people; — The middle Country — that is between the Rice lands and the fall of the Rivers & a little above them, is cultivated chiefly in Corn & Indigo — and the upper Country in Tobacco, Corn, Hemp & in some degree the smaller grains

It is nearly the same in N.o Carolina, with this difference however that, as not much rice is planted there, especially in the Northern parts of the State, Corn, some Indigo, with Naval Stores & Porke, are substituted in its place, but as Ind.o is on the decline Hemp, Cotton &c.a are coming in its place. The Inland navigations of the Rivers of these three States may be improved (according to the ideas I have formed of the matter) to a very extensive degree — to great & useful purposes — and at a very moderate expence compared with the vast utility of the measure; inasmuch as the falls in all of them are trifling and their length great; (quite to the Mount^{ns}) penetrating the Country in all directions by their lateral branches and in their present State except at the falls wch. as has been observed before are trifling except that of the Peedee navigable for vessels carrying sev^{l}. Hhd^{s}. of Tob^{o}. or other Articles in proportion.

The prices at which these Rice lands in the lower parts of the St[ate] are held is very great — those of y^{m} wch. have been improved com^{d} from 20 to 30 Sterl^{g}. — £50 has been given for some — and from £10 to 14 is the price of it in its rude state. — The Pine barrens adjoining these sell from one to two dollars pr Acre according to circumstances. — The interval Lands on the River below the falls, & above the Rice Swamps also command a good price but not equal to the ab^{e}. & the pine barrens less than those below — The lands of the upper Country sell from 4 to 6 or 7 dollars according to the quality and circumstances thereof.

In the upper parts of N^{o} Car^{a} Wheat is pretty much grown & the Farmers seem disposed to try Hemp but the Land Carriage is a considerable drawback having between 2 & 300 Miles to carry their produce either to Ch^{s}. Town, Petersburgh or Wilmington wch are their three great Marts though of late Fayettesville receives a g^{d}. deal of the bulky articles & they are water borne from thence to Wilmington.

Excepting the Towns (and some Gentlemens Seats along the Road from Charleston to Savanna) there is not within view of the whole road I travelled from Petersburgh to this place, a single house which has anyth^{g} of an elegant appearance — They are altogether of Wood & chiefly of logs — some ind^{d}. have brick chimneys but generally the chimneys are of Split sticks filled with dirt between them.

The accommodations on the whole Road (except in the Towns and even there, as I was informed, for I had no opportunity of Judging, lodgings having been provided for me in them at my own expence) we found extremely indifferent — the houses being small and badly provided, either for man or horse; though extra exertions when it was known I was coming, wch was generally the case, were made to receive me. — It is not easy to say on which road — the one I went or the one I came — the entertainment is most indifferent — but with truth it may be affirmed added, that both are bad. and to be accounted for from the kind of travellers which use them; which with a few exceptions only on the uppr Rd are no other than waggoners & families removing, who, generally, take their provisions along with them — The people however appear to have abundant means to live with the grounds where they are settled yielding grain in abundance and the natural herbage a multitude of meat with little or no labr to provide food for the support of their Stock — especially in Georgia where it is said the Cattle live through the winter without any support from the owners of them.

The manners of the people, as far as my observations, and means of information extended, were orderly and Civil. — and they appeared to be happy, contented and satisfied with the genl governmt under which they are placed. — Where the case was otherwise, it was not difficult to trace the cause to some demagogue, or speculating character. — In Georgia the dissatisfied part of them at the late treaty with the Ck Indians were evidently Land Jobbers, who, maugre every principle of Justice to the Indians & Policy to their Country would, for their own immediate emolument, strip the Indns of all their territory if they could obtain the least countenance to the measure. — but it is to be hoped the good sense of the State will set its face against such diabolical attemps. — and it is also to be wished — and by many it was said it might be expected — that the sales by that State to what are called the Yazoo Companies would fall through

The discontents which it was supposed the last Revenue Act (commonly known by the Excise Law) would create subside as fast as the law is explained — and little was said of the Banking Act.

Sunday — 5th

Left the old Town about 4 Oclock A. M.; & breakfasting at one Prides (after crossing Banister River 1½ Miles) abt 11 Miles from it, came to Staunton River about 12; where meeting

Col° Isaac Coles[1] (formerly a Member of Congress for this district &) who pressed me to it, I went to his house about one mile off to dine and to halt a day, for the refreshment of myself and horses; — leaving my Servants and them at one of the usually indifferent Taverns at the Ferry that they might give no trouble, or be inconvenient to a private family. —

Monday 6th

Finding my Horses fared badly at the ferry for want of Grass, & Col° Coles kindly pressing me to bring them to his Pasture, they were accordingly brought there to take the run of it till night. — dined at this Gentlemans today also. —

The Road from Hallifax old Ct H° or town to Staunton River passes for the most part over thin land a good deal mixed with Pine.

[1] Isaac Coles, son of John Coles, was born in Albemarle County, Virginia, March 2, 1747. He entered the class of 1768 at the College of William and Mary. He was a landholder and planter of great wealth, owning extensive lands in Halifax, Pittsylvania, and Brunswick Counties, and exercised a powerful influence in local politics. Some time before 1769 he was elected a member of the House of Burgesses. In the Revolutionary War he served in the State militia, being eventually promoted to the rank of colonel. For a time he was a member of the State Senate. In 1788 he was a delegate to the State Convention to consider the United States Constitution, in which his influence and vote were cast against its ratification. He was elected to the First Congress (March 4, 1789, to March 3, 1791); reëlected to the Third and Fourth Congresses (March 4, 1793, to March 3, 1797). He was an earnest supporter and friend of Thomas Jefferson and the politics he represented. He died June 2, 1813. (From *The Centennial of Washington's Inauguration*, edited by C. W. Bowen.)

When one of the ladies in the Coles family was asked, many years later, what had been said at her table by the august Washington, she replied that the only thing she could recall was that he *praised the pudding!* When Dr. Morgan Dix, rector of Trinity Church, New York, was visiting the Bruce estate in Virginia, he asked Lazarus, the colored butler, who had been in the Bruce family for sixty years, about this story. Lazarus, it must be understood, did not think much of any white folks but his master's. "Lazarus," said Dr. Dix, "I understand that General Washington once passed down Mr. Bruce's plantation road. Do you remember anything about it?" "General Washington? General Washington?" replied Lazarus. "I never heard of him, sah! He wa'n't none of our folks." — This story was told me by the Virginian historian, Dr. Philip Alexander Bruce.

Return to Mount Vernon

Tuesday — 7th.

Left Col^{o} Coles by day break, and breakfasted at Charlotte C^{t}. H^{o}. 15 Miles where I was detained sometime to get Shoes put on such horses as had lost them — proceeded afterwards to Prince Edward Court House 20 Miles further.

The Lands from Staunton to Charlotte C^{t}. H^{o}. are in gen^{l}. good; & pretty thickly settled; They are cultivated chiefly in Tob^{o}. Wheat & Corn, with Oats and flax. — The Houses (tho' none eleg^{t}.) are in gen^{l}. decent & bespeak good livers; being for the most part weatherboarded & shingled, with brick Chimnies — but from Charlotte C^{t}. H^{o}. to Prince Edward C^{t}. H^{o}. the lands are of an inferior quality with few inhabitants in sight of the Road. — it is said they are thick settled off it, the Roads by keeping the Ridge pass on the most indifferent ground.

Wednesday — 8th.

Left Prince Edward C^{t}. H^{o}. as soon as it was well light, & breakfasted at one Treadways 13 Miles off. — dined at Cumberland C^{t}. H^{o}. 14 Miles further — and lodged at Moores Tavern within 2 Miles from Carters ferry over James River —

The Road from Prince Edward Court H^{o}. to Treadways was very thickly settled, although the land appeared thin, and the growth in a great degree pine. & from Treadways to Cumberland C^{t}. H^{o}. they were equally well settled on better land, less mixed, and in places not mixed at all with pine — the buildings appear to be better. —

Thursday 9th

Set off very early from Moores but the proper ferry boat being hauled up, we were a tedious while crossing in one of the Boats used in the navigation of the River; being obliged to carry one carriage at a time without horses & crossways the Boat on planks. — Breakfasted at a Widow pains 17 Miles on the N^{o} side of the River, and lodged at a M^{rs}. Jordans a private house where we were kindly entertained and to which we were driven by necessity having Rode not less than 25 Miles from our breakfasting stage through very bad Roads in a very sultry day with[t] any refreshment & by missing the right road had got to it. —

From the River to the Widow Pains, & thence to Andersons bridge over the North Anna Branch of Pamunky, the Lands are not good nor thickly settled on the Road, but are a good deal mix[d] w. Pine; nor does the Soil & growth promise much (except in places) from thence for several miles further; but afterwards, throughout the County of Louisa, which is entered after passing the Bridge, the River over which it is made dividing it from Goochland they are much better & continued so with little exception quite to M[rs] Jordans

Friday — 10th

Left M[rs] Jordans early, & breakfasted at one Johnstons 7 Miles off reached Fredericksburgh after another (short) halt about 3 Oclock & dined and lodged at my Sister Lewis's

The Lands from M[rs] Jordans to Johnsons, and from thence for several miles further are good but not rich afterwards (as you approach nearer to Rappahannock River they appear to be of a thinner quality & more inclined to black Jacks

Saturday — 12th

About Sunrise we were off — breakfasted at Dumfries and arrived at M[t] V[n] to Dine. . . .

It is worthy of note that Washington, as evidenced by this tour, was revered and venerated as the true father of his country. In their address to Washington, the Masons of Prince George's Lodge, No. 16 (Modern), Georgetown, South Carolina, use the phrase: "At a time when all men are emulous to approach you to express the lively sensations you inspire as the Father of our country etc." The people of Georgetown, likewise, in their address to Washington, refer to him as "first Magistrate of the Federal Republic, that person, whom of all men we are most disposed to revere as our benefactor, and to love as the father

STUART PORTRAIT OF WASHINGTON
AT WASHINGTON AND LEE UNIVERSITY, LEXINGTON, VIRGINIA

of his country." And the City Council of Charleston in their address to Washington use the words: "When in the person of the Supreme Magistrate of the United States, they recognize the Father of the people etc." The idea of filial devotion to Washington as paternal guide and fatherly leader was uppermost in the minds and hearts of the people, and found voice in their addresses.

The gratification of the American people upon Washington's safe return to Mount Vernon was hearty and unaffected. It found voice in the public prints of the day, as in these lines from the "Columbian Centinel" of Boston:

> "Kind Heav'n, O send him safely back," we pray'd,
> Nor were the intercession urged in vain,
> The tour perform'd, and millions happy made,
> His VERNON hails in health its Lord again.

Nor was Philadelphia silent when the President finally reached the capital—his return being greeted by the ringing of bells, the firing of artillery, and general celebration. The Pennsylvania poet likewise found expression for his emotions over the happy event in this sentiment printed in the "Gazette of the United States":

> Not heroes in triumphant cars,
> Victorious in their country's wars,
> With captives, spoils, and glory crown'd
> Whose peans make the skies resound;
> Experience half the joys *they* know
> Who live to lessen human woe;
> The progress of whose godlike mind,
> *Is but a* TOUR *to bless mankind.*

Something of the contemporary deification of Washington

is exhibited in poems which call him the "Lord" of Mount Vernon and describe his mind as "godlike."

A study of the newspapers of the day likewise results in the discovery of essays on Washington, evoked by the tour and its attendant circumstances. "No year of the world," says an anonymous writer in the "Columbian Herald" of Charleston, South Carolina, "has ever been distinguished by any event perfectly similar to the ever memorable tour of the President of the United States, through a country of fourteen hundred miles extent, defended by the valour of his arms, and the intrepidity of that mind, which no combination of gloomy prospects could disturb or subvert. It is true, we read of no man in history, whose greatness of conception, or vastness of ambition had aspired to accomplish a revolution of equal magnitude, connected with equal virtue." After comparing — unfavorably to Washington — Louis XIV, Alexander the Great, Cæsar, Scipio Africanus, and Peter the Great, the writer launches forth upon an unmeasured eulogy of the "American General" — concluding with this highly pictorial tribute:

> If a stranger from some remote corner of the globe were to land in this city on Monday the 2nd instant, and observe the tumult and concourse of men, women and children, moving with the utmost expedition to the harbour; impatience and earnestness as evident in their countenances as their motion, would it not be natural for him earnestly to enquire what was the motive to all this scene, having to him the appearance of some confusion? but if it could be explained to him, that a hundred thousand persons were collected to receive and confer every applause in their power on a great man, whom they

hourly expected, who defended freedom, the equal rights of men, and laid the foundation of a mighty empire, governed by laws of the people's own enaction, and all this against the strongest fleet in the world, aided by a martial army, and supplied by the wealth of nations, — this man surely would not wonder to see the first characters in the state for eminence of wisdom and fortune, the three learned professions, the corporate body of the city, the merchants, the citizens, an immense concourse of strangers, a numerous appearance of ladies, who presented the splendid scene of beauty, gaiety and brilliant attire, all crowding to pay the homage of the heart to the deliverer of America. His appearance was peculiarly marked with dignity, and the serenity as well as the satisfaction which sat on his countenance, made every pulse in every frame responsive; which brought to our memory the following beautiful compliment to an eminent poet — would to God we had now such a poet for a subject more transcendantly bright and interesting to future generations.

voltus ubis tuus
affulsit populo, gratior it dies
Et soles melius nitent. *Hor.*

Whene'er thy countenance divine,
The attendant people cheers;
The genial suns more radiant shine
The day more glad appears.

In a more restrained tone, also from a Charleston paper, is "An Essay towards the Character of the President of the United States," which was approvingly copied in many gazettes of the day throughout the country. Speaking of Washington as military commander, the anonymous author pertinently observes: "Indefatigably laborious and active, coolly intrepid in action, he discerns, as by intuition, seizes with rapidity, and improves with skill, the short, favourable and often defective moments of battle."

A biographer of to-day might have written these lines descriptive of Washington: "Resolute and undejected in misfortune, he has risen superior to distresses and struggled with difficulties, which no courage or constancy, but his own, could have resisted or surmounted." A most significant feature of this tribute is this sentiment: "Arriving at a situation far more dignified than a king, you yet find him a citizen and a patriot." And genuine insight is exhibited in the concluding observation of the essay: "Many a private man might make a great president; but will there ever be a president who will make so great a private man as WASHINGTON?"

Better proof of the advantage which Washington himself reaped from this tour could not be found than the President's own observations, recorded in his diary, upon the people, the country, and the general conditions of thinking and living. Not the least significant testimony to the remarkable change in the agricultural stress in the South is found in Washington's omission of cotton from the list he gave of the "principal exports" from Charleston. "No mention yet of cotton among the staple products of the South," comments Edward Everett writing in 1860. "As late as 1794, it was not known to Chief Justice Jay, when he negotiated his treaty with England, that it was likely to be an article of United States Commerce. So recently has this great element of trade and of the wealth of nations made its appearance on this side of the ocean!" [1]

[1] *The Mount Vernon Papers.* (D. Appleton & Co., New York, 1860.)

Return to Mount Vernon

In a characteristic letter to the Marquis de la Fayette, for whom he felt a deep and genuine attachment, Washington once wrote: "Nothing but harmony, honesty, industry, and frugality are necessary to make us a great and happy people. Happily the present posture of affairs and the prevailing disposition of my countrymen, promise to co-operate in establishing those four great and essential pillars of public felicity." As if to assure the Frenchman, whom he regarded as an adopted American, that his expectations in these respects concerning a part of the United States, the South, had in great measure been fulfilled, Washington writes him from Philadelphia, July 28, 1791:

> On the 6 of this month I returned from a tour through the southern States, which had employed me for more than three months — In the course of this journey I have been highly gratified in observing the flourishing state of the Country, and the good disposition of the people — Industry and economy have become very fashionable in those parts . . . , and the labours of man are assisted by the blessings of Providence — The attachment of all Classes of citizens to the general Government seems to be a pleasing presage of their future happiness and respectability.

With an expression of confident belief that the establishment of public credit was "an immense point gained in our national concerns," Washington writes in similar strain to Gouverneur Morris (Philadelphia, July 28, 1791):

> In my late tour thro' the southern States I experienced great satisfaction in seing the good effects of the general Government in that part of the Union — The people at large

have felt the security which it gives and the equal justice which it administers to them. The Farmer — the Merchant — and the Mechanic have seen their several interests attended to, and from thence they unite in placing a confidence in their representatives, as well as in those in whose hands the execution of the laws is placed — Industry has there taken the place of idleness, and economy of dissipation — Two or three years of good crops, and a ready market for the produce of their lands has put every one in good humour — and, in some instances they even impute to the government what is due only to the goodness of Providence.

This shrewd and humorous observation may be said to announce the birth of political parties in American history.

A vivid and pleasant memento of the Southern tour is the exchange of letters between Washington and General Moultrie, given here in full:

CHARLESTON *July* 10.1791

DEAR & RESPECTED SIR

Permit me very sincerely to congratulate you on your safe return to Philadelphia and to hope that no more difficulties occurred to you on your return home than what happened on your journey through the lower part of this country while I had the honor to attend you; my earnest wish is, that your friendly visit to these Southern States will not be attended with any evil consequences to your constitution, but that the long journey and the very great change of climate may establish your health & lengthen your days in peace and happiness; the citizens of this country (especially the ladies) will ever have a gratefull sense of your visit — and be assured Sir (while I had the honor of being one of your family) I have set it down in the catalogue of my life among the very happy days which I have enjoyed, and have only to regret that my situation is such that I cannot have the honor of paying my respects to you more frequently; I will endeavour before my final close of life, to pay you my last farewell visit; In the meantime I must request you will do me the honor, to present my most respectfull compliments to M[rs] Washington.

I have the honor to be Dear Sir
with great respect & regard
Your most ob[t] & very hum[le] Serv[t]
WILL[m] MOULTRIE

THE PRESIDENT
(Endorsed): From
General Moultrie
July 10, 1791

PHILADELPHIA *August* 9, 1791

GENERAL MOULTRIE
Charleston

I have had the pleasure, my dear Sir, to receive your friendly letter of the 10th of last month — and I reply with affectionate regard to your congratulations and kind wishes — A slight indisposition, since my return, (occasioned by a tumor, not much unlike the one I had at N. York in 1789) of which I am now recovered, does not forbid the expectation that my health may be ultimately improved by my tour thro' the southern States — My happiness has certainly been promoted by the excursion, and no where in a greater degree than while resident among my fellow-citizens of South Carolina — To their attentions (yours in particular) I shall always confess myself much obliged, and particularly flattered by the regards of your fair Compatriots, to whom I wish, upon every occasion, to be remembered with grateful respect.

I shall realize your promise of a visit with sincere satisfaction — Till then, and always I beg you to believe me,
With the greatest regard and esteem,
My dear Sir,
Your &[ca]
G. WASHINGTON

The most detailed summary of Washington's impressions of the South as received on this tour, to be found preserved in his correspondence, is the letter to his former secretary and aide, David Humphreys. To this dear friend, now United States Minister to Portugal, stating that he has been "in the enjoyment of very good health" during his journey and has "rather gained flesh upon it," he gives this memorable epitome of the impressions made on him by the Southern Tour:

PHILADELPHIA *July* 20, 1791

DAVID HUMPHREYS ESQUIRE
Lisbon
MY DEAR SIR,

... In my last I mentioned my intention of visiting the southern States which I have since accomplished, and have the pleasure to inform you, that I performed the journey of 1887 miles without meeting with any interruption by sickness, bad weather, or any untoward accident — Indeed so highly were we favored that we arrived at each place, where I proposed to make a halt, on the very day I fixed upon before we set out — The same horses performed the whole tour, and, although much reduced in flesh, kept up their full spirits to the last day.

I am much pleased that I have taken this journey as it has enabled me to see with my own eyes the situation of the country thro' which we travelled, and to learn more accurately the disposition of the people than I could have done by any information.

The country appears to be in a very improving state, and industry and frugality are becoming much more fashionable than they have hitherto been there — Tranquillity reigns among the people, with that disposition towards the general government which is likely to preserve it — They begin to feel the good effects of equal laws and equal protection — The farmer finds a ready market for his produce, and the merchant calculates with more certainty on his payments — Manufactures have as yet made but little progress in that part of the country, and it will probably be a long time before they are brought to that state to which they have already arrived in the middle and eastern parts of the Union.

Each days experience of the Government of the United

States seems to confirm its establishment and to render it more popular. — A ready acquiescence in the laws made under it shews in a strong light the confidence which the people have in their representatives, and in the upright views of those who administer the government — At the time of passing a law imposing a duty on home made spirits, it was vehemently affirmed by many that such a law could never be executed in the southern States, particularly in Virginia and North Carolina. As this law came in force only on the first of this month little can be said of its effects from experience; but from the best information I could get on my journey respecting its operation on the minds of the people (and I took some pains to obtain information on this point) there remains no doubt but it will be carried into effect not only without opposition, but with very general approbation in those very parts where it was foretold that it would never be submitted to by anyone.

It is possible, however, and perhaps not improbable that some Demagogue may start up, and produce and get signed some resolutions declaratory of their disapprobation of the measure.

Our public credit stands on that ground which three years ago it would have been considered a species of madness to have foretold. The astonishing rapidity with which the newly instituted Bank was filled gives an unexampled proof (here) of the resources of our Countrymen and their confidence in public measures.

On the first day of opening the subscription the whole number of shares (20,000) were taken up in one hour, and application made for upwards of 4,000 shares more than were granted by the Institution, besides many others that were coming in from different quarters.

. . . .

Mrs. Washington desires her best wishes may be presented to you —

You are always assured, my dear Sir, of those of
Your sincere and affectionate friend
G. WASHINGTON

Washington's Southern Tour

In his "A Poem on the Death of General Washington," [1] Humphreys, the trusted friend and close associate, has bequeathed to posterity this faithful portrait of Washington, true Father of his Country, whose tours of the United States were prompted by paternal love for the American People, the children of his great heart:

When, nigh ador'd, too great to need parade,
He through the States his pleasing progress made;
What gratulations pure the patriot met!
What cheeks with tears of gratitude were wet!
While useful knowledge from each State he gain'd,
Prais'd their improvements and their bliss explain'd;
While bridges, roads, canals in every State,
And growing fabrics owned his influence great;
Such goodness mark'd each act, in every place
He left impressions time can ne'er efface.
Then rose the favour'd States beneath his smile,
Adorn'd, enrich'd, and strengthen'd by his toil;
Then millions felt what happiness ensued,
And hail'd their country's father great and good.

[1] *The Miscellaneous Works of David Humphreys.* (T. and J. Swords, New York, 1804.) See footnote, Chapter I.

THE END

Henderson, Archibald,
1877-1963.
Washington's southern
tour, 1791,

...on.
...ngton's southern tour.